GAMBLING FOR PROFIT

Lotteries, Gaming Machines, and Casinos
in Cross-national Focus

KERRY G. E. CHAMBERS

Gambling for Profit

Lotteries, Gaming Machines, and Casinos in Cross-national Focus

UNIVERSITY OF TORONTO PRESS
Toronto Buffalo London

$60.00

© University of Toronto Press 2011
Toronto Buffalo London
www.utppublishing.com
Printed in Canada

ISBN 978-1-4426-4189-1 (cloth)

Printed on acid-free, 100% post-consumer recycled paper with
vegetable-based inks.

Library and Archives Canada Cataloguing in Publication

Chambers, Kerry, 1958–
Gambling for profit : lotteries, gaming machines, and casinos in
cross-national focus / Kerry G.E. Chambers.

Includes bibliographical references and index.
ISBN 978-1-4426-4189-1

1. Gambling – Cross-cultural studies.   2. Gambling – Social aspects.
3. Gambling – Government policy.   4. Gambling – Economic aspects.
I. Title.

HV6710.C53 2011   306.4'82   C2011-904214-2

University of Toronto Press acknowledges the financial assistance to its
publishing program of the Canada Council for the Arts and the Ontario
Arts Council.

 Canada Council   Conseil des Arts
for the Arts   du Canada    ONTARIO ARTS COUNCIL
CONSEIL DES ARTS DE L'ONTARIO

University of Toronto Press acknowledges the financial support of the
Government of Canada through the Canada Book Fund for its publishing
activities.

Jody: how I wish you were here.

Contents

Figures and Tables

Preface

In this book, I explore the emergence of gambling for profit in cross-national focus. States can benefit from gambling for profit through direct or indirect involvement and/or through taxation of commercial or non-profit organizations. Throughout the book, I use a comparative historical approach to account for variations in the introduction and participation in lotteries, gaming machines outside casinos (GMOCs), and casinos across Australia, Canada, and the United States, although I also spend a brief amount of space examining these forms of gambling across 23 western countries.

Gambling as an object of study provides a unique opportunity to explore societies in past and present contexts. The same conditions that shape patterns of gambling activities underlie other aspects of daily life. Explaining differences in gambling practices by investigating the dynamic interaction of political, economic, social, and cultural features of a society opens a window through which we can observe the state of affairs in a specific setting. The wagering of 'life, limb, and personal freedom' among the ancient Germans (Bolen & Boyd, 1968, p. 619) says as much about their society as 'responsible gambling' does about ours. It also suggests that the social and cultural context strongly influences people's perceptions of, and participation in, gambling practices. While political and economic impetus can lead to the liberalization of gambling, citizens must first either be willing to accept the political and social change that accompanies such a move or be unable to stop it. Australians and Americans embraced *legal* gambling earlier than Canadians; yet, most American states outlawed gambling for nearly a century and Australia clearly has a more vibrant gambling culture today. In 2005, the per capita ratio of gaming machines outside casinos in

Australia was approximately eight times that of Canada and four times that of the United States. The pattern of lottery and commercial urban casino adoption in the twentieth century also differed in Australia. This divergence did not arise solely from political-economic crises nor did it occur directly out of distinct sociocultural features: a necessary convergence of political, economic, social, and cultural factors conducive to the legalization of gambling coalesced earlier in some regions than others.

The central theme in this book is that we should reject any explanations of the emergence of gambling for profit that are applied universally and/or ignore the dynamic intersection of political economic and sociocultural features of a given society. If we are fully to understand changes to gambling – from prohibition to adoption to (de)regulation – we must first recognize that historical contingencies produce a region's current political, economic, social, and cultural conditions. These institutional factors come together at specific points in time to enable or constrain some groups from imposing their perceptions and definitions of gambling on others. As illustration, a common explanation for the rapid growth of gambling for profit over the past four decades is that states turn to gambling when faced with fiscal or economic crises and are unable to raise revenue through other means. This book demonstrates that it is not that simple, and I offer an alternative interpretation using a new analytical framework that emphasizes that unique historical events cause different historical outcomes. The development of gambling for profit constitutes a process that begins and ends in the political realm, the outcome of efforts among groups to force their worldviews on others. Governments cannot rule without legitimacy and proponents of legal gambling must, at minimum, obtain voluntary compliance among other groups – including politicians – if adoption is to be perceived as legitimate (see Weber, 1968, p. 212). Pre-existing sociocultural contexts shaped by historical conjunctures play a crucial role in the struggle to define gambling. Individuals decide the legitimacy of *any* activity based on their beliefs. Nevertheless, their capacity to introduce or prevent legalized gambling depends on the types and amount of resources they can muster and their ability to enter into the political arena. Accordingly, political-economic impetus is necessary but insufficient for the legalization of any form of gambling. Pre-existing social and cultural conditions must be conducive to building legitimacy. Even then, however, political barriers such as the state's structural political features can restrict the success of proponents (or opponents). This explains why some states have legalized gambling for profit earlier and some have not moved at all: political crises emerged out of world economic recessions across western countries, but conditions have been more welcoming in some regions than others, and a combination that enabled or constrained mobilization influenced the likelihood of adoption. I unpack these arguments throughout the book using lotteries, GMOCs, and casinos in cross-national focus.

I am grateful to Virgil Duff at the University of Toronto Press for his patience and concern for scholarly publication in Canada. I would also like to convey my sincere thanks to the anonymous reviewers for their thoughtful critique and suggestions and to Robyn Gallimore for helping me polish the final copy.

It would take several pages to acknowledge the countless people who offered advice and encouragement while I was researching materials and writing this book. However, two in particular were instrumental in completing my task. My mentor, Richard Apostle, introduced me to comparative historical research and advised me to apply it to gambling studies. I would neither have started nor finished this book without Richard's conviction it would make a valuable contribution and was worthy of publication. His unwavering confidence in me has been humbling. I also cannot find the words to express my love and indebtedness to my wife and best friend Evelyn. She shared the good times and bad, always with warmth, affection, and a smile. She has assured me that she will no longer hold it against me.

Abbreviations

ACT	Australian Capital Territory
ALB	Alberta
ALC	Atlantic Lottery Corporation
AUD	Australian Dollars
AWP	amusement with prize machine
BC	British Columbia
CAD	Canadian dollars
COO	corporate owner-operator
EGM	electronic gaming machine
GMOC	gaming machine outside of casinos
HCALG	Hawaiian Coalition against Legal Gambling
IRS	Internal Revenue Service
MAN	Manitoba
MGCC	Manitoba Gaming Control Commission
NB	New Brunswick
NCALG	National Coalition against Legalized Gambling
NDP	New Democratic Party
NE	North East
NFLD	Newfoundland and Labrador
NPOO	non-profit owner-operator
NS	Nova Scotia
NSW	New South Wales
OIC	Order in Council
PEI	Prince Edward Island
RSL	Returning Servicemen League
SA	South Australia
SASK	Saskatchewan

SGLA	Saskatchewan Gaming and Liquor Authority
SHOO	state hybrid owner-operator
SOO	state owner-operator
U.S.	United States
USC 1976	US Commission on the Review of the National Policy toward Gambling
USD	United States dollars
VLT	video lottery terminal
VOO	vendor owner-operator
WA	Western Australia

GAMBLING FOR PROFIT

1 The Emergence of Gambling within a Historically Contingent Framework

This book examines one aspect of the evolution of legal gambling in late modernity.[1] Gambling for profit has waxed and waned since antiquity. What has changed over the past four decades is the corporatization of legal gambling and ever increasing stimulation of gambling markets by states, capital, and charitable organizations.[2] Historically, these processes have developed unevenly across time and space. Indeed, western countries have legalized gambling for profit at different times with varying structural configurations. As shown at table 1.1, most western countries had legal lotteries before 1970, eight countries permitted casinos, and nine had legal gaming machines outside casinos (GMOCs). Table 1.1 also reveals the rise of gambling for profit after 1970: eleven countries adopted casinos, nine legalized GMOCs, and Canada introduced and the United Kingdom re-established lotteries. Gambling for profit also developed unevenly within subnational units in federal states.

How do we account for these differences across and within nation states? In this book, I introduce an analytical framework to help answer this and other questions. In the next three chapters, I explore the political, economic, social, and cultural spheres that have shaped gambling for profit in late modernity. I begin by briefly looking at 23 western states to describe differences among welfare regimes and to set up Australia, Canada, and the United States as case studies for the main arguments. These neo-liberal Anglo states are quite similar (Feather, 1998; Jackson & Penrose, 1994; O'Connor, Orloff, & Shaver, 1999), yet the timing of adoption, structural arrangements, and participation in gambling for profit vary among and within them, in some cases considerably.[3] Despite the rapid expansion of gambling for profit, few

Table 1.1   Introduction of Lotteries, Casinos and Gaming Machines outside Casinos (GMOCs) pre–1969 and 1970–2005

Country	pre–1969 Lotteries	Casinos	GMOCs	1970–2005 Lotteries	Casinos	GMOCs
United States	■●	●	●			
Canada				●	●	●
Australia	●		●		●	
New Zealand	●				●	●
United Kingdom	■	●	●	●		
Ireland	●		●		Prohibited	
Iceland	●				Prohibited	●
Switzerland*	●				●	■
Japan	●		●		Prohibited	
Netherlands	●				●	●
Spain	●				●	●
Italy	■●	●				●
Greece*	●	●				■
Germany	■●	●	●			
Belgium	■●				●	●
Luxembourg	●				●	Prohibited
Austria	■●	●	●			
France	■●	●				Prohibited
Portugal	●	●			●	Prohibited
Denmark	●				●	●
Finland	●		●		●	
Sweden	■●				●	●
Norway	●		●		Prohibited	

Sources: State Gaming Agencies & Personal Contacts
● Legal
■ Legalized then prohibited
* Year of introduction of gaming machines unavailable

scholars have examined its nature and scope comparatively across and within nation states (Brian, 2009; McMillen, 1988a, 1993, 1996a; Morton, 2003; Pryor, 2008; Sallaz, 2006; Selby, 1996). Most explanations have emphasized political and economic similarities, paying little attention to the social and cultural factors involved (Cosgrave & Klassen, 2001; McMillen, 1993, 1996a).[4] Analyses of the expansion of legal gambling have additionally glossed over the establishment of GMOCs (McKenna, 2008).

I begin to address these limitations here using a comparative historical analysis to outline four propositions. First, historical narrative and conjunctures create regional variations in economies, political and social institutions, and cultural beliefs and practices. Second, these preconditions are dynamic and lead to a combination of enabling and constraining factors that generate different contexts for the potential development of gambling for profit. Third, a region's social and cultural milieu affects collective attitudes about gambling, and opposition can dramatically influence adoption. Finally, politicians avoid attempts to legalize gambling for profit when a sizeable majority of the people contest it and have the power to mobilize in opposition. However, they do try to minimize resistance through efforts to legitimize the activities.[5] At the same time, their rivals struggle to delegitimize the process.

In short, we cannot explain the jagged development of gambling for profit in late modernity without investigating both political-economic and sociocultural preconditions (McMillen, 1993, 1996a). Combinations of these determinants – that are contingent on historical events that shape the institutions and cultures of a region – produce variations in legal gambling. We should therefore reject any universal explanations of gambling for profit since different historical paths influence their development. We instead need to specify the enabling and constraining conditions that alter the production of legal gambling; we can then develop contingent theories about the probable outcomes from each pattern. In the remainder of this chapter, I outline my proposed analytical framework, main arguments, methodology, and a brief overview of the empirical arguments in the following chapters.

Enabling and Constraining Factors that Influence Adoption

Historical narrative refers to causal events that act like a fork in the road leading actors to choose one path over another (Paige, 1999; see also Weber, [1930] 1976); conjunctures may be defined as events that occur at one time and place with differing consequences (Paige, 1999; Thelen, 1999). Historical narrative and conjuncture alter regional economies, political and social institutions, and group world views or weltanschauung.[6] These, in turn, generate differences in gambling activities (McMillen, 1996a, 1996b).

Some will maintain these arguments are simplistic and obvious: they will argue that distinct social histories *should* generate different gambling practices. Such a stance overlooks the purpose of comparative historical research and the complexities of the legalization of gambling.

Comparative historians acknowledge that political, social, and cultural institutions vary across societies as an outcome of diverse historical trajectories. The question is why differences in gambling practices endure in one region compared with others and what factors have led to the proliferation of gambling in late modernity. My answer is that states only adopt gambling for profit when an appropriate combination of political-economic and sociocultural circumstances is present. Observing historical contingencies enhances our ability to detect these otherwise unobserved variations, which is why I have chosen to examine casinos, GMOCs, and lotteries cross-nationally.[7] While case studies of one type of gambling are appropriate for regions that share similar histories, exploring several forms provides a deeper understanding of the processes underlying adoption. It also helps answer the following questions: what prompts states to attempt to legalize gambling for profit, why does adoption succeed in different areas and at different times, and why do patterns of ownership, structural and spatial characteristics, and levels of participation vary across time and space?

Table 1.2 lists the enabling conditions relevant to my analysis[8] and Figure 1 graphically demonstrates the relationships.[9] Each factor is significant, but some are more powerful, and a few can nullify the others.[10] The list is provisional and will be refined with further studies. Therein lies the value of the framework; it allows for reflexive adjustment, it is dynamic, and it could be used to study other forms of gambling.

The Adoption Process

Gambling for profit may emerge when political-economic conditions, consumer demand, or a mixture of both create an impetus for adoption. All the same, the presence of appropriate sociocultural contexts is necessary, since a majority of the people must, at minimum, be indifferent, or opponents must be unable to thwart efforts to legalize. The degree of resistance, the access to and struggles within the polity, and the resources available to proponents and opponents are in part a direct outcome of the sociocultural environment, and they strongly influence the likelihood of adoption. This makes the legitimacy of gambling critical to its legalization and expansion.

IMPETUS FOR ADOPTION

In the late 1960s, technological change revolutionized production, reduced the costs of worldwide communication and transportation of

Table 1.2 Enabling Conditions for Gambling for Profit

Political	Status
Welfare state	Neo-liberal
Type of polity	Federal
Degree of centralization at state formation	Low
Constitutional/Criminal Code Amendment	No
Bordering state with gambling	Yes
Policy learning among states	High
Use of populist electoral practices	Low
Degree of organized resistance	Low
Access to polity by challengers	Low

Economic	Status
Impact of global economic recessions	Negative
Regional economic decline	High
Degree of devolution	High
State's ability to generate tax revenues	Low
Gaming industry resources available	High
Gambling provider competition	Low
Consumer demand	Medium +

Social	Status
Catholic / Liberal Protestant	Yes
Pre-existing favourable legal gambling	Yes
Organized crime involvement	Low
Gambling a traditional social institution	High

Cultural	Status
Perception of gambling as leisure	High
Gambling as a moral issue	Low
Traditional shared social values	Low
Self-expressive shared values	High
Political culture	Liberal

commodities, and intensified globalization. The collapse of the Bretton Woods Agreement freed financial capital, leading to widespread speculation on international money markets.[11] As capital moved factories to reduce labour costs, some cities became centres for finance and trade and business decisions (Sassen, 1999), whereas capacity to compete was reduced in many regions; economies were decimated, and inner cities were left in ruins (Harvey, 2000).

These rapid changes to capitalism created fiscal problems for national and regional governments. At the same time, citizens were demanding

Figure 1.1: Factors Influencing the Adoption of Gambling for Profit

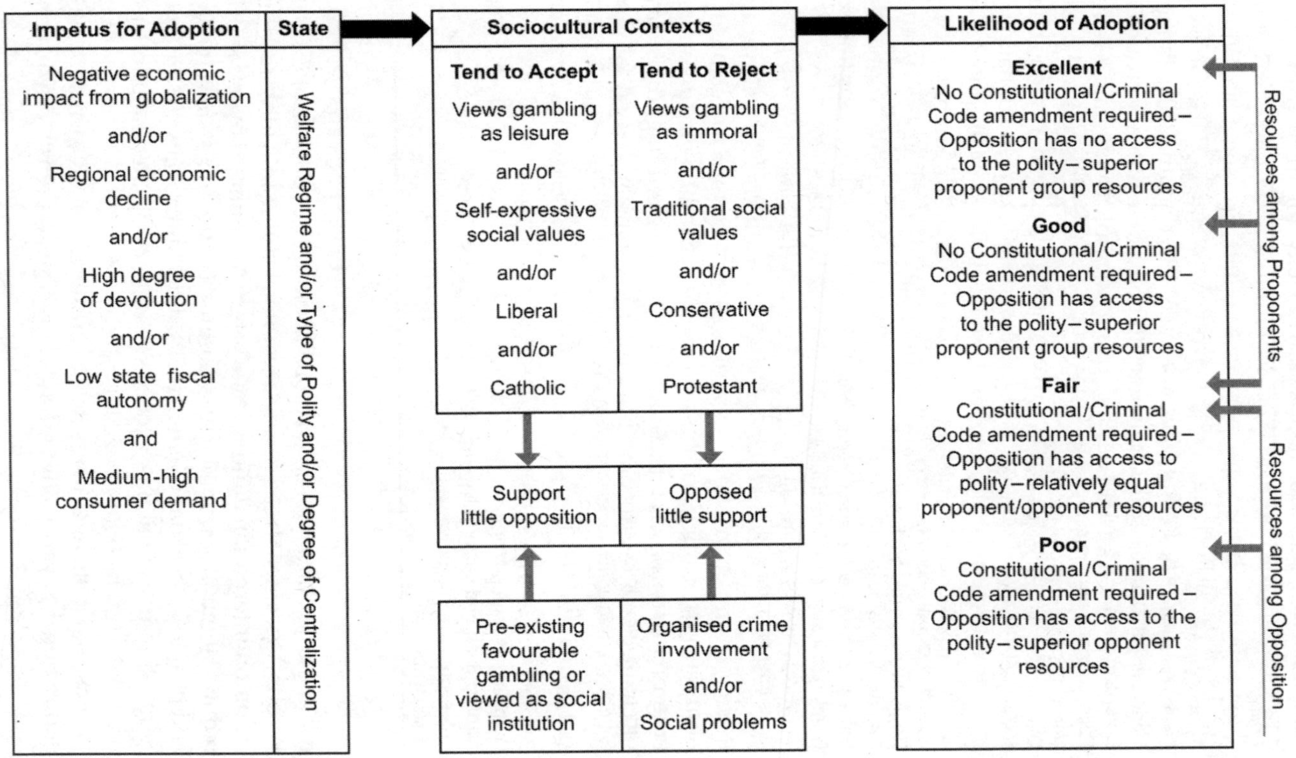

Resources among Proponents   Resources among Opposition

Impetus for Adoption

Negative economic impact from globalization

and/or

Regional economic decline

and/or

High degree of devolution

and/or

Low state fiscal autonomy

and

Medium–high consumer demand

State

Welfare Regime and/or Type of Polity and/or Degree of Centralization

Sociocultural Contexts

Tend to Accept	Tend to Reject
Views gambling as leisure	Views gambling as immoral
and/or	and/or
Self-expressive social values	Traditional social values
and/or	and/or
Liberal	Conservative
and/or	and/or
Catholic	Protestant

Support little opposition ← Pre-existing favourable gambling or viewed as social institution

Opposed little support ← Organised crime involvement and/or Social problems

Likelihood of Adoption

Excellent
No Constitutional/Criminal Code amendment required – Opposition has no access to the polity – superior proponent group resources

Good
No Constitutional/Criminal Code amendment required – Opposition has access to the polity – superior proponent group resources

Fair
Constitutional/Criminal Code amendment required – Opposition has access to polity – relatively equal proponent/opponent resources

Poor
Constitutional/Criminal Code amendment required – Opposition has access to the polity – superior opponent resources

more services yet were less willing to pay for them (Abt, Smith, & Christiansen, 1985; Alm, McKee, & Skidmore, 1993; Barker & Britz, 2000; Berry & Berry, 1990; Cosgrave & Klassen, 2001; Erekson, Platt, Whistler, & Ziegert, 1999; Furlong, 1998; Garrett & Wagner, 2004; Gross, 1998; Mikesell & Zorn, 1988; Miller & Pierce, 1997; Smith, 2000; Tannewald, 1998; Thompson, 1994). Challenges to political legitimacy ensued as the people witnessed urban decline, rising unemployment, and a reduction in services (McMillen, 1988a, 1993, 1996b). To relieve political pressures at the national level, many governments devolved responsibility by transferring some services and the associated costs to subnational and local governments. Politicians at these levels faced the unpopular choice of cutting services or raising taxes, and turned to gambling for profit instead (Abt et al., 1985; Barker & Britz, 2000; Cosgrave & Klassen, 2001; Gross, 1998; Thompson, 1994). The freeing up of liquid capital further facilitated the growth of transnational gaming corporations that sought to expand their operations (McMillen 1988a, 1993, 1996b).

Once states began legalizing and expanding gambling, policy diffusion followed (Boehmke & Witmer, 2004; Painter, 1991). Governments learned from other states' experiences and sought to establish gambling for profit, often with assistance from gambling corporations and entrepreneurs. When a jurisdiction legalizes gambling, the surrounding states face lost income but bear the financial and social burdens of excessive gambling. As a result, politicians in areas with high interstate competition often seek to pre-empt bordering states by establishing gambling operations first (Alm et al., 1993; Berry & Berry, 1990; Boehmke & Witmer, 2004; Eadington, 1999; Furlong, 1998; Hansen, 2004; Jensen, 2003; Kingma, 1996; McMillen, 1993; Mason & Nelson, 2001; Miers, 1996; Painter, 1991; von Herrmann, 2002).

The expansion of Indian gaming provided another impetus for gambling for profit in the United States. In the 1980s, Native Americans asserted their right to operate high-stakes bingo halls and casinos. This led to a Supreme Court ruling that tribes could operate specific types of gaming provided a state had previously legalized them. Following the ruling, Congress passed the *Indian and Gaming Regulatory Act* (IGRA), and tribal gaming spread rapidly, at times creating jurisdictional conflicts between states and Indian tribes (Eadington, 1996; McCulloch, 1994; Mooney, 2000). IGRA also permitted state governments to negotiate with tribes, and some states agreed in return for a share of the profits. Australia and Canada have different relations with the indigenous peoples, the result of divergent historical developments in each country.[12]

Consumer demand may also stimulate the legalization of gambling for profit; however, politicians can ignore citizens' wishes. Progressively more Australian state governments legalized gambling opportunities because of the 'social enthusiasm' for gambling in that country (Australian Institute for Gambling Research, 1999, p. 11). On the other hand, 63% of Virginians approved abolition of a constitutional ban on lotteries in 1969, but successive state governors blocked lottery proposals until 1987 (Bobbitt, 2007, p. 41). Overall, however, governments and corporate interests have stimulated demand through the legalization and liberalization of gambling.

Explanations for the proliferation of gambling are well documented, but have typically been limited to one form of gambling or a single liberal state, usually an English speaking country like the United States.[13] Questions have rarely been raised about how welfare-state regimes, type of polity, or degree of centralization within states affects the production of gambling (McMillen, 1988a, 1993, 1996b).

STATE INFLUENCES ON ADOPTION

Among the 23 industrialized states, welfare expenditures are lowest in the Anglo countries, increase among western European countries, and are highest in the southern European and Scandinavian countries (Castles, 2003). Given the trend of gambling adoption, we would expect states with the highest levels of welfare expenditure to aggressively pursue gambling to provide services. As shown in Chapter 2, the type of welfare state has impacted the timing of adoption, form of gambling for profit, and level of intervention in the gambling market.

Type of polity has also affected the production of gambling for profit. Unitary polities hold greater control over regional political-economic arrangements and can unilaterally decide whether or not to legalize gambling. Subnational units – states, provinces, länder, or cantons – have frequently introduced gambling without appeal to national governments. Indeed, many attempted to introduce gambling for profit earlier in late modernity because they faced increased global economic pressures, devolution of federal fiscal responsibilities, and regional competition; the latter has often involved cross-border outflow to early adopters.

Finally, decentralization of governance is a major characteristic of western societies. In some federal states, subnational units developed separate constitutions and legal processes, ensconcing gambling law; others retained legal powers over gambling at the national level: both legal structures have at times constrained adoption of gambling for profit. In addition, unitary and federal states – where the national government retained powers over gambling – do not have subnational competition that might lead to the spread of gambling since the central governments control gambling policies.

SOCIOCULTURAL CONTEXTS OF ADOPTION

Legitimacy is vital to legalization and participation in gambling activities (Cosgrave, 2009; Cosgrave & Klassen, 2001; Jensen, 2003). Politicians can and do act without consulting constituents but rarely introduce legislation they view pejoratively or as a threat to their political ambitions. Groups also reject behaviours they consider immoral or inappropriate. Nevertheless, gambling has no intrinsic meaning (Abt et al., 1985; Cosgrave & Klassen, 2001; McMillen, 1996a) and its symbolic values are inculcated through socialization and habitus.[14] Consequently, regional variations in the legitimacy of gambling practices are bound in tradition, social norms, emotion and faith, perceived inevitability, law, or a combination thereof (Weber, 1968; Horne, 2009).

Within traditional legitimacy, groups accept gambling when it is historically part of their culture and associated with customs and symbols that produce shared identities; these should be stronger when contained within a social institution like a club. Social-norm legitimacy occurs when persons exert pressures on others within their social relations to support a political decision or institution (Horne, 2009). In highly individualistic societies, people could help establish legitimacy for gambling for profit through assertions of the individual's right to choose (Cosgrave, 2009). Emotion and faith also play a role. Emotion is an affective state of consciousness that encompasses both pleasure and disapproval; to have faith is to believe unconditionally in religion, political action, and so forth. Historically, the working classes, upper classes, and Catholics enjoyed gambling as leisure and participated heavily in related activities (Morton, 2003; O'Hara, 1988; Rosecrance, 1988). Conversely, the Protestant middle class viewed gambling as a moral weakness that destroyed families and ruined the social fabric of communities, and they rejected any traditional gambling culture. Gambling over the past century has moved from sin to vice to entertainment: ongoing secularization of faith and emotions changed gambling from sin to vice, and the perceived inevitability and legal legitimacy altered its status to entertainment (Campbell & Smith, 2003). Nonetheless, faith and emotion can still impede adoption as demonstrated in efforts to legalize lotteries in the Bible Belt of the United States (Bobbitt 2007).

Sociocultural circumstances, whether material or symbolic, change with time. Middle-class moral indignation declined in late modernity as secularization, increasing use of creditization, hypercommodification, uncertainty over the future, and technological changes in work and leisure created a culture of risk. By the 1980s, citizens in western societies began to exhibit narcissistic desires for immediate gratification within hypercommodified consumption (Lasch, 1979; Lash & Urry, 1994). When combined with the constant flux of daily life, a culture of 'riskaphobia' changed to 'riskophelia' (Reiner, Livingstone, & Allen, 2001) and middle-class attitudes toward gambling shifted. Legal legitimacy followed in many regions as governments introduced or expanded gambling (Cosgrave & Klassen, 2001).[15]

When trying to establish gambling for profit, political and economic elites have often been forced to appeal to tradition, emotion, inevitability, and legal legitimacy, while downplaying faith and moral arguments. They have proposed GMOCs at racetracks to save the 'historic' horse race industry (tradition); they have advocated establishing lotteries, GMOCs, casinos, or all three, to reduce taxes and provide funds for good causes (emotional); they have maintained that gambling in bordering states will eventually make legalization necessary to counteract the loss of cross-border revenue (inevitability); and they have argued that gambling must be legalized to control organized crime and fraud (emotional, inevitability, legal). The outcomes of these proposals have been contingent on resistance and the ability of opponents to stop legalization. Variations in social-group pressures to organize (social-norm legitimacy) would have influenced the degree of collective action. Put differently, the sociocultural contexts are inexorably linked with the political-economic realm and different configurations determine when and where gambling for profit is legalized.

THE LIKELIHOOD OF ADOPTION AND PARTICIPATION

The adoption of gambling for profit depends on collective attitudes among politicians, business interests, and the people,[16] access to the polity and, where struggles erupt, the ability of both sides to marshal sufficient resources for the fight. If gambling is criminalized it will remain so until those in power have an impetus to act and believe legalization is a morally and economically appropriate course of action. Once politicians are prepared to legalize gambling, the issue becomes whether they can persuade business interests, social elites, and constituents that adoption will generate economic and communal benefits, or whether they have the power to impose their decision on these groups. The dynamics can also be reversed, but the point is that sociocultural environments manufacture support, opposition, or indifference. When struggles do erupt, the capacity of proponents and opponents to influence the polity through the mobilization of resources usually determines the outcome. However, the ability to legitimize or delegitimize the process can affect openings to the polity and efforts to mobilize resources.

Polity refers to the government or other realms where groups and individuals influence political-economic decisions. Members are typically politicians, legal, business, and social elites. Challengers gain easiest access in jurisdictions with legally binding populist practices. Entry is more difficult where a small group of elected officials and bureaucrats decide government policy which may arise from lobbying by powerful business interests. Resources involved in collective struggles include money and labour, shared goals, organizational structures, personal contributions, and experience in prior collective action (McCarthy & Zald, 1977; Edwards & McCarthy, 2004). Proponents usually have more resources than opponents, as a result of corporate funding and previous expertise in legalization campaigns.

Proposals for gambling for profit usually come from within the polity. Variations in political structure and constitutional arrangements, the requirement for amendments to legalize, and differential access by challengers produce different gambling arrangements. The likelihood of adoption is highest when members block entrance to opposing groups, when proponents hold superior resources, and when the ruling party can override resistance among members who are opposed.[17] All the same, strong opposition or support can open up a polity normally closed to outsiders. Politicians may find it politically necessary to hold a referendum or plebiscite if a group has enough resources to force the issue, or if it becomes politically contentious through other means.[18] Challengers might also enter through the legal system. On the flip side, adoption occurs less frequently or is delayed when legislative amendments are required, when citizens have access to the polity through populist politics, and when opponents can muster more resources than supporters.

Both opposition and support for legal gambling depend on a configuration of individual motive and expectation that contributions will provide some measure of success. Each person will have a mixture of motives that push and pull them toward opposition or support, and each will contribute if they perceive some possibility of success. Those most opposed will feel morally compelled to act, and perceptions of illegitimacy based in faith (religion) and emotion (perceptions of or experience with problems associated with gambling) should produce the staunchest opponents. Historically, Protestant evangelicals, traditionalists, and social conservatives have condemned gambling as immoral and attempted to exert social-norm pressures on others.[19] Catholics, liberals, and those who share self-expressive social values or are immersed in a strong gambling culture are more likely to tolerate change and view gambling as a legitimate leisure activity.[20] To mobilize and gain resources, opponents will try to delegitimize gambling activities through arguments based on morality or the potential for social disorder. Proponents will attempt to undermine these arguments by adding legitimacy through proposed selective or collective incentives, such as tax cuts, increased funding for public education, and strategies for social control.

Regardless of opposition or support, the issue is how far people are willing to go to defend their positions. Resistance to gambling for profit can range from casting a ballot to major protests. When enough individuals refuse to participate it calls into question the economic viability of gambling operations, and when a sufficient number openly challenge the state it can also create a legitimation crisis (Habermas, 1975; Klassen & Cosgrave, 2009). Individual resistance is one thing as it might affect business; the development of collective action is another as it could threaten the polity.[21] Resistance alone, however, may be insufficient to prevent adoption. Politicians who can restrict entrance to the polity may choose to ignore the issue, perhaps at the beginning of a political term, hoping to build legitimacy and co-opt the opposition. Indeed, when a state legalizes gambling for profit, it begins a process of legal legitimization that could demoralize many in the opposition leading to demobilization and a reduction of their resources.

In short, when it comes to the legalization of gambling for profit, ruling elites need and seek legitimacy and gambling providers need and seek customers. Neither will be forthcoming in a sociocultural environment where gambling is viewed as an illegitimate activity, and opponents have access to the polity and can mobilize sufficient resources to mount a challenge. Accordingly, adoption will occur less frequently, or not at all, where opposition is based in faith, emotion, or both, and it encompasses citizens, politicians, and competing business interests;

that is, when the opposition can successfully mobilize and prevent proponents from establishing widespread legitimacy for a particular form of gambling.[22] Nevertheless, the start-up costs of collective action for opponents would be higher in states with closed polities, and mobilization could be more difficult in regions with a history of legal gambling, since traditional, social-norm, and legal legitimacy would be firmly established, unless a perception exists that the proposed form of gambling will cause unacceptable levels of social problems.

To summarize, this book introduces an analytical framework to study the adoption and participation in gambling for profit. The main point is that historical contingencies create variations in political, economic, social, and cultural conditions that lead to differences in legal gambling across and within regions. These are general propositions, but the crux of the issue is that we should reject any universal explanation of macro-level changes to gambling. We instead need to create contingent theories by peeling away both the historical and contemporary contexts, asking what configuration of determinants led to particular paths and deviations in political-economic and sociocultural conditions, which in turn produced different gambling practices. Western societies have been completely transformed over the past four decades, creating conditions conducive to the introduction and expansion of legal gambling and, yet, the timing of legalization has been geographically inconsistent, with diverse policy directions, and varying levels of participation.

Gambling for profit can only emerge when sanctioned by the ruling elite who hold the power to push it forward. The legalization of gambling has historically involved moral politics (Eadington, 1996; Furlong, 1998; Mooney, 2000; Pierce & Miller, 1999), and in many cases still does.[23] It has been authorized in the past to fund wars, capital projects, and public benefits; to placate the political and economic elite; and to control gambling passions, crime, and fraud among the lower classes (see Kingma, 2004). These ventures lasted as long as the elite and the people tolerated them. With few exceptions, gambling was criminalized when the practices threatened elite interests or widespread protests developed. This began to change in the 1970s when a series of political-economic pressures impelled politicians to look to gambling for sources of revenue and economic development.

Governments can manufacture demand through the introduction of legal gambling (Cosgrave, 2009; Cosgrave & Klassen, 2001; Kingma, 2004), but the venture will be less effectual if the people perceive the gambling activity as immoral or unjust. Accordingly, proponents will try to establish legitimacy and undermine opposition by altering individual motives through symbolic and material incentives. Success will depend on the configuration of political, economic, and sociocultural circumstances based in the historical narrative and conjuncture of a particular region. Failure to legalize is most likely to occur in areas where the opposition is strong, where opponents hold resources that are easily mobilized, and where the polity is open to challengers. Alternatively, attempts to legalize gambling for profit will succeed, first and foremost, when the polity is closed to challengers, since this will reduce opponent's expectancy of success and affect their resource mobilization. These processes are dynamic, particular to each region, and shaped by a combination of diverse political, economic, and sociocultural factors. Nevertheless, documenting the differences and comparing them across cases will allow us to develop contextual explanations of why and how gambling for profit emerges, along with variations in policies and participation. On a final note, political economy has been central to most explanations of the expansion of gambling for profit, but focusing solely on these factors obscures our ability to see the impact culture has on processes leading to legal forms of gambling. In fact, when we hold political economy constant, culture emerges as a strong determinant in the differential production of gambling for profit across and within nation states.

Methodology: The Comparative Historical Approach

Classical sociologists often used comparative methods to describe structural and cultural features that affected change at the level of individual actors (see Weber, [1930] 1976). While this tradition waned with the development of positivist methodologies, Moore (1966), Wallerstein (1974), Tilly (1984), Skocpol (1979), and others recovered comparative methods during the 'seventies-generation revival' (Paige, 1999, p. 783). Underlying the revised approach was an epistemology that sociological explanation can subsume historical events within a general, universal, and teleological framework (p. 795). Many comparative researchers have since challenged these assumptions, arguing that contingencies negate universal explanations. They instead seek to construct conditional theories based on historical narrative and conjuncture using complex and contextual explanations to understand the conditions under which specific hypotheses are valid (p. 791). Some critics of comparative approaches – Mill's method in particular – object to the causal assumptions underpinning these methods (Lieberson, 1991), but other scholars have shown that Mill's method is both warranted and valid when the research objective is to establish conditional, as opposed to universal, causal propositions (Paige, 1999).

Comparative analysts generally examine either similarities or differences across cases, but not both. In this book, I employ a contingent comparative historical method and seek out cross-national divergences in political, economic, and sociocultural factors that have affected the legalization of gambling. I focus on the differences across regions for several reasons. First, I am interested in the uneven development within the system; that is, how specific factors led to different policies and forms of gambling across time and space. This information would be inaccessible without observing variations between nation states and subnational units (see Kohn, 1987). Second, most studies have explored the political-economic realm, limiting sociocultural analysis in the process. Indeed, Ragin (1994) stresses that observing divergence across cases is especially useful for interpreting cultural dynamics that lead to change. Looking for similarities in cross-national contexts is less productive than comparing differences, especially when countries share political-economic structures but have diverse social and cultural conditions. Finally, my analytical framework is intended to explore the enabling and constraining conditions on the expansion of gambling for profit.

Where possible, I consulted primary sources, such as government documents, industry reports, and personal contacts. For the most part, however, I gathered an eclectic mix of secondary sources and empirical evidence from existing gambling studies. Using data amassed by others is not novel. Quantitative researchers routinely do it and there is precedent within comparative historical research (see Mann, 2004). In fact, comparative historians often use *no* primary sources at all. Skocpol explains:

> Because wide-ranging comparisons are so often crucial for analytic historical sociologists, they are more likely to use secondary sources of evidence than those who apply models to, or develop interpretations of, single cases. Secondary sources are simply published books and articles by historians or by scholars specializing in the study of one geocultural area of the world. Some people believe that such publications are automatically inferior to primary sources, the original residues of the past that most historians use as their basic evidence about given times, places, and

issues. From the point of view of historical sociology, however, a dogmatic instance on redoing research for every investigation would be disastrous; it would rule out most comparative-historical research. If a topic is too big for purely primary research – *and* if excellent studies by specialists are already available in some profusion – secondary sources are appropriate as the basic source of evidence of a given study. Using them is not different from survey analysts reworking the results of previous surveys rather than asking all questions anew, or students of comparative ethnography synthesizing results from many different published field studies. (1984, p. 382; emphasis original)

Producing a cross-national study of this magnitude would be impossible without relying heavily on secondary sources. I therefore used the evidence and conclusions gleaned from previous research to build on and reinforce my analysis. Nevertheless, some sources are from what Griffiths and Wood (n.d.) refer to as 'grey literature' or non-peer reviewed or academically scrutinized information. My sources also included non-English websites, and I employed a variety of internet translators to convert the documents. Information gathered from these sites is solely comprised of dates of events, such as the introduction of lotteries.

Comparative research has limitations. First, differences might be methodological artefacts if the concepts compared across units are unequal in value (Kohn, 1987). Second, a shortage of resources can make the accuracy and reliability of some sources open to challenge, a problem noted above. Third, measurement error can have a stronger impact on studies with a small number of cases (Lieberson, 1991). Fourth, untangling the political, economic, and sociocultural spheres can be tricky (Kohn, 1987). Fifth, some argue that a limited knowledge of the cases can hinder analysis and interpretation (Ragin, 1987; Tilly, 1984). Finally, anomalies found in comparative historical research are often treated as more suspect than in other forms of analysis; for example, a scatter plot with a small number of cases. The principal concern should be with the pattern and not the anomaly; that is, all empirical analysis has idiosyncrasies that run contrary to the analysis. The question should be whether the deviations cancel out the remaining evidence, not whether they occur at all. Dismissing a complex framework as presented here based on atypical observations hinders theoretical development and our understanding of change.

Conclusions

I begin in Chapter 2 with a broad and descriptive analysis of the emergence of gambling for profit among 23 industrial nations. My goals in this chapter are to demonstrate that differences in welfare regime and type of polity have influenced adoption and structural features of gambling, and to provide empirical evidence to support my choice of Australia, Canada, and the United States for the comparative case studies. Nevertheless, this chapter could stand alone, since I do not include my proposed analytical framework or concepts taken up in the remainder of the book.

In Chapter 3, I examine the political-economic impetus and social features that enabled and constrained adoption of commercial casinos in Australia, Canada, and the United States. These three countries faced similar economic conditions from the 1970s to 1990s. Nevertheless, the *trend* was for Australia to adopt urban commercial casinos before Canada and the United States (see Eadington, 1998; McMillen, 1988b; Rychlak, 1995).[24] Furthermore, the introduction of commercial – non-tribal – casinos in the United States has been limited to a few geographical areas. A central question in this chapter is why differences exist among the three countries. An analysis of the political-economic impetus, social features, and factors involved in adoption show that the Australian states faced stronger fiscal pressures, and, to a lesser degree, the social conditions were more conducive than in Canada and the United States. I also introduce two theoretical paradigms from the social-movement literature to theorize why people support or oppose legalization and the ways their collective action could influence the outcome of legalization campaigns; this should help account for variations in the likelihood of adoption.

In Chapter 4, I examine lotteries and GMOCs from a cultural perspective. Cultural and social values regarding gambling differ across groups and regions. Although the political elite decides whether to legalize gambling for profit or not, its decisions are embedded in personal cultural beliefs and social values which may differ from the majority's. Illegal gambling will occur when a strong gambling culture exists among the masses, but the elite refuses to accept it. Conversely, proponents will be forced to legitimize proposals for new forms of gambling if they face strong organized resistance. In Chapter 4, I show that culture specifies when gambling for profit is adopted, the level of participation in it, or both. Indeed, this is most apparent with cross-national comparisons as demonstrated among Australia, Canada, and the United States where cultural variation specified the temporal adoption of lotteries, and to a lesser extent GMOCs. Participation in machine gambling is also markedly different across the three countries. Focusing on the cultural realm emphasizes the importance of political-economic variables. Legitimacy is necessary for legalization and participation, and struggles to construct and deconstruct legitimacy take place within the polity.

In Chapter 5, I provide broad conclusions by comparing the findings for Australia, Canada, and the United States in the contexts of the theorized analytical model.

To conclude, the main goal in this book is to uncover the factors that explain temporal, spatial, and structural differences in the development of legal gambling generally, and in Australia, Canada, and the United States specifically. My assertion is that historical junctures produce regional variation in political-economic and social institutions and cultures, which strongly influence future struggles to define gambling. Governments have historically legalized gambling when it has served elite interests and prohibited gambling when it has threatened them. This has always taken place through a dynamic process of collective action embedded in political-economic and sociocultural contexts (McMillen, 1993, 1996b). Those with the most resources are generally more successful in altering the legal status of gambling through legitimation.

Governments have dramatically altered their stances toward gambling over the past several decades endeavouring to manufacture consent for gambling for profit in the process. Where some have succeeded, others have not, and I intend to show that different configurations of political, economic, social, and cultural conditions can tell us why. The scope of the enquiry has necessarily led to analysis conducted in broad strokes, and while it may seem too ambitious, many questions would go unanswered if we did not extend beyond our reach. Still, as Moore (1985) cautions, such an approach can raise more questions than answers, which is typical of inquiries that explore unfamiliar terrain.

Gambling for Profit in the
Welfare Regimes

In this chapter, I explore the emergence of casinos, gaming machines outside of casinos (GMOCs), and lotteries among 23 western industrial countries. I want to demonstrate that welfare regime type has influenced the emergence of gambling for profit in late modernity, and that federal neo-liberal states have tended to legalize and organize gambling differently than the other regimes. For this reason, I chose Australia, Canada, and the United States as case studies to lay out my central arguments. Accordingly, this chapter offers a broad glimpse of gambling among the welfare regimes, and I provide a detailed analysis of federal states that have moved furthest into a risk model of gambling governmentality in Chapters 3 and 4 (see Kingma, 2004).

McMillen (1996b) has stressed that globalization strongly influenced the expansion of state-operated and commercial casinos but that structural and cultural factors led to uneven growth. I extend McMillen's analysis here by showing that similar patterns exist for GMOCs. The chapter also examines the ways that polities and decentralization within federal states alter adoption, policies, and participation in legal gambling. Finally, I use Kingma's (2004) 'alibi to risk' model to demonstrate that Anglo countries have moved more aggressively in liberalizing gambling.

Welfare Regimes in Late Modernity

Industrial nations vary in market regulations, familialism, and the forms and extent of social protection the state offers its citizens.[1] Esping-Andersen (1990, 1999) created a typology of different welfare regimes by measuring the level of liberalism, socialism, conservatism, degree of labour market regulation, and familialism found in each advanced industrial state.

Under Esping-Andersen's schema liberal states are characterized as providing residual social guarantees with minimal state intervention in the market. Australia, Britain, Canada, New Zealand, and the United States fall within this form of governance. All display low levels of labour market regulation, marginal familialism, and limited eligibility and scope for social assistance. High levels of prudentialism and individualization of risk are also common in these states.

The Nordic and Scandinavian countries are the polar opposite. Although social democratic countries have limited familialism, they stand in marked contrast in universalism, egalitarianism, and state involvement in the market. The other welfare regimes may have universal social policies, but social democratic states tend to suppress market provision of social services and offer wider and more generous coverage of social benefits.

Conservative (corporatist) regimes fall between liberal and social democratic states and comprise the bulk of the European countries. Governments in these countries stress corporatism, statism, and welfare-state familialization through strong labour market regulation and corporatist social protection guarantees. As in liberal states, welfare is residual but is reserved for male heads of households and distributed through corporatist channels. Such regimes rely on family units as caregivers, and state assistance is based on needs, not institutionalized rights.

These are the welfare-state institutions as outlined by Esping-Andersen (1990, 1999). To analyse the emergence of gambling across nations, I combined Esping-Andersen's (1990) rankings of liberalism, socialism, and conservatism with his grouping of countries by labour market regulation, familialism, and provision of welfare services (Esping-Andersen, 1999). Esping-Andersen did not include Iceland, Greece, or Luxembourg in his typologies, which left me to categorize them. Table 2.1 displays four welfare regimes. Ireland could go in the liberal category, and Switzerland, Japan, and The Netherlands in the corporatist; Iceland is a special case, having adopted many liberal policies in the early 1990s.[2] However, policies within these countries did not correspond with one regime type, which meant a fourth was necessary. Nevertheless, there are no quantitative points, and two countries could vary widely despite their similar position on the continuum.

As shown in Figure 2.1, all welfare regimes experienced major swings in economic growth between 1971 and 2005.[3] Without exception, countries that established casinos after 1970 did so during economic downturns. Australia, Canada, The Netherlands, Luxembourg,

Table 2.1   Welfare State Regimes from Most Liberal
to Most Social Democratic

Liberal	Corporatist
United States	Spain
Canada	Italy
Australia	Greece
New Zealand	Germany
United Kingdom	Belgium
	Luxembourg
	Austria
	France
	Portugal
Liberal – Corporatist	Social Democratic
Ireland	Denmark
Iceland	Finland
Switzerland	Sweden
Japan	Norway
Netherlands	

and the United States introduced casinos during economic downturns
in the mid-1970s. Denmark, Finland, and New Zealand adopted in
the early 1990s, and Switzerland and Sweden legalized casinos during the economic slump of 2001–3. Similar patterns exist for GMOCs.
Thus, while recessionary periods influenced adoption of casinos and
GMOCs, the type of welfare regime, in part, specified when it occurred
in each state.

Casinos in the Welfare Regimes

The forerunner to the modern-day casino was a small gambling house
used to generate profits as early as 1378 (Kelly, Marfels, & Nevries,
1999, p. 371). By the eighteenth century, casinos had spread to health
spas and resorts throughout Europe, with states authorizing casinos
at some points and proscribing them at others. For example, Napoleon
failed to suppress casinos in France and controlled them through licensing and taxation, eventually restricting them to French spas. Although
the French King banned gambling in 1836, officials enforced the laws
weakly, since they considered casinos necessary for their resorts' survival (Vercher & Thompson, 1999, p. 360). Ongoing resistance led to a
reversal of gambling policies in 1907 and the French National Assembly
legalized casinos that year (p. 360). The German states also permitted

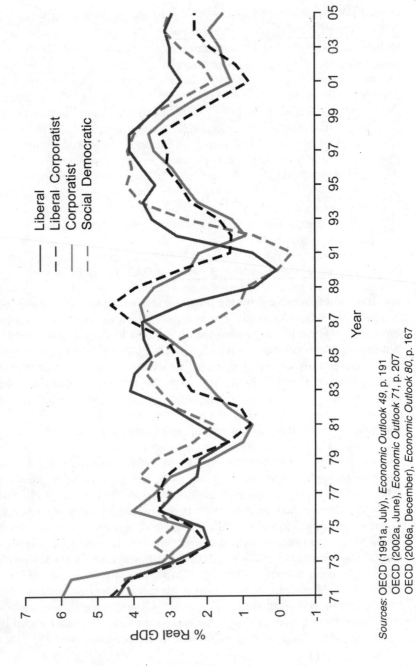

Figure 2.1: Economic Growth in the Welfare Regimes 1971–2005

Liberal
Liberal Corporatist
Corporatist
Social Democratic

% Real GDP

Year

Sources: OECD (1991a, July), Economic Outlook 49, p. 191
OECD (2002a, June), Economic Outlook 71, p. 207
OECD (2006a, December), Economic Outlook 80, p. 167

state-owned casinos at health spas to generate profit and support the resorts. Germany was the gambling hub of Europe by the early nine-teenth century offering large casinos organized alongside luxurious theatres, concert halls, and other amenities. In 1848, the Frankfurt assembly banned casinos and, despite a short period of revival, the state prohibited them once more in 1871 (Kelly et al., 1999, p. 371). Casinos did not reopen in Germany until 1933 when the National Socialists real-ized they could help finance their fascist agenda (p. 371). While casi-nos were closing throughout Europe, Charles III of Monaco looked to casino gambling to avoid state bankruptcy and annexation to France. In the early 1860s, Monaco established the famous Casino de Monte Carlo using the German tradition of state ownership and opened gambling halls next to lavish hotels and spas (Thompson, 1999, p. 441). Monaco's success led other southern European countries to reconsider casinos early in the twentieth century.

As these examples show, casino gambling existed throughout parts of Europe for several centuries with periods of development and decline. States legalized casinos for economic reasons and tried to limit social problems by restricting entry to local elites and rich tourists. The northern European states and Anglo countries (excluding Nevada in the United States) prohibited casinos until the late 1960s, the result of dif-ferent politics and cultures. This started to change in the 1970s as global forces created pressures favourable to casino expansion (McMillen, 1996b). The shift also corresponded with the social and cultural trans-formation of societies in late modernity. Nevertheless, differences in welfare regimes, polities, and degree of centralization within each have all contributed to the legalization of casinos and the form adopted in each country. However, before unpacking these arguments, it is nec-essary to distinguish between American and European ideal types, keeping in mind that all casinos comprise a mix of these characteristics; Thompson (1998) provides an excellent overview of both.

Casinos of the American ideal type comprise large facilities, post-modern in substance and appearance.[4] They are concentrated in urban areas providing high volume traffic that allows convenient and unlim-ited access to locals and tourists. Gambling is encouraged through pro-motions and open credit policies; few measures are in place to restrict or control problem gamblers. Large corporations own the casinos, and they compete for profit in a deregulated market. States impose mini-mal taxation and benefit through job creation and increased tourism. Community involvement is low or mixed (Thompson, 1998).

In contrast, casinos in the European ideal type are small and elitist. Governments restrict them to resorts, towns, or regions that attract tourists. In some cases, the state prohibits local citizens from attendance and commonly attempts to identify and control problem gamblers. Hours of operation are limited and access is restricted through entrance fees, dress codes, and identification checks. The state owns the casinos or allows private monopolies and maintains strict regulations on the game mix, promotions, and availability of credit and alcohol. Profit is allocated to the public sector or highly taxed, from 40% of net revenue in Portugal to 70% in Germany (Thompson, 1998; Swiss Institute of Comparative Law, 2006, p. 977).

As shown at Table 2.2, although global economic and social change drove the liberalization of casinos in the late twentieth century, the type of welfare regime influenced when each country implemented casinos and what model they adopted (McMillen, 1996b). Looking at Table 2.2, corporatist countries with a tradition of casino gambling tended to re-establish casinos before nation states where they did not previously exist. Casinos were a social institution for elites in these countries and changing political conditions in the eighteenth and nineteenth centuries led to their closure. Table 2.2 also reveals that some liberal states legalized casinos ahead of social democratic states; all had done so by the mid-1990s. Notwithstanding these differences, with the exception of the United Kingdom, liberal states chose the American casino model while corporatist and social democratic countries have favoured variations of the European ideal type.[5]

Liberal governments intervene less in citizens' lives and the markets, subscribing to variations of the classical liberal tradition where state involvement in these spheres constitutes a violation of economic and personal freedom. Consequently, liberal governments – to varying degrees – take on a less paternalistic role than corporatist or social democratic nations when weighing the economic benefit of casinos against the individual and social cost. Liberal governments also expect citizens to act more prudently by gambling responsibly and within their means. We can see indicators of the different approaches in Table 2.3.

State ownership and prohibition of casinos are more predominant outside liberal countries. Gross gambling revenue (GGR) is also higher in liberal states.[6] The median GGR is $81 USD (per capita) in the liberal regimes, compared with $52 USD in liberal-corporatist, $13 USD in corporatist, and $10 USD in social democratic countries.[7] The higher GGR in liberal countries makes sense; casinos unimpeded by the state

Table 2.2   Introduction of Casinos by Welfare Regime and Period

Country	Pre –1900	1900–1909	1910–1919	1920–1929	1930–1939	1940–1949	1950–1959	1960–1969	1970–1979	1980–1989	1990–1999	2000–2005
United States					●							
Canada									●			
Australia									●			
New Zealand											●	
United Kingdom								●				
Ireland					Prohibited							
Iceland					Prohibited							
Switzerland	■											●
Japan					Prohibited							
Netherlands									●			
Spain	■								●			
Italy	■			●								
Greece							●					
Germany	■				●							
Belgium	■											●
Luxembourg								●				
Austria	■					●						
France	■	●										
Portugal		■			●							
Denmark											●	
Finland											●	
Sweden											●	
Norway					Prohibited							

Sources: State Gaming Agencies & Personal Contacts
● Legal
■ Legalized then prohibited

should generate a higher profit. We would expect these findings, given the political, economic, and sociocultural differences found among the welfare regime types. Population size could be a factor, but nations with relatively small populations, like Australia, Canada, and New Zealand, are among the highest GGR producers. Social democratic systems also turned to casino gambling once they had fallen on 'hard times' (Esping-Andersen, 1999, p. 80) (Figure 2.1) and had to make choices between reducing welfare benefits or using casinos to maintain services through increased tourism and taxation. Unlike liberal regimes, these countries either reserve the proceeds for public sector benefits (Finland and Sweden) or contribute considerably higher proportions of taxes for

Table 2.3   Type of Casino and Gross Revenues by Welfare Regime and Year

Country	Charitable	Privately Owned	State Owned	Year End	Estimated Gross Revenues (USD)†	Estimated Per Capita (USD)††
United States		449(a,c)		FY2005	42,100(e)	144
Canada	16(b)	2(b)	41(b)	FY2003	2,592(b)	80
Australia		13(c)		2004–2005	1,979(c)	99
New Zealand		6(d)		2004	313(d)	81
United Kingdom		135(e)		2003	1,553(e)	26
Ireland					Prohibited	
Iceland					Prohibited	
Switzerland		21(f)		2003	418(f)	56
Japan					Prohibited	
Netherlands		12(e)		2004	771(e)	47
Spain		27(e)	5(e)	2004	450(e)	11
Italy			4(e)	2003	697(e)	12
Greece	17 in total – ownership unclear(f)			2003	100(e)	9
Germany		40(e)	44(e)	2004	1,085(e)	13
Belgium		8(e)		2004	51(e)	5
Luxembourg		1(e)		2003	78(e)	191
Austria		12(e)		2004	232(e)	28
France		180(e)		2004	2,958(e)	49
Portugal		8(e)		2004	339(e)	32
Denmark		10(e)		2004	52(e)	10
Finland			1(e)	2004	28(e)	5
Sweden			4(e)	2004	155(e)	17
Norway					Prohibited	

Sources:
(a) American Gaming Association (n.d.) & Australia Gaming Council (2007);
(b) Canadian Partnership for Responsible Gambling (2005): Gambling Digest 2004–2005;
(c) Australian Gaming Council (2007);
(d) New Zealand Department of Internal Affairs (n.d);
(e) Swiss Institute of Comparative Law (2006);
(f) Commission fédérale des maisons de jeu (2003) *Rapport Annuel*
†   Gross revenues in millions converted using yearly average of country currency to USD at OANDA Historical Exchange Rates: http://www.oanda.com/currency/historical-rates
†† Author's Calculations: estimate based on population 15 years and above from *CIA World Factbook*

social provisions (Swiss Institute of Comparative Law, 2006, p. 977). Moreover, they did not simply re-establish casinos as in most corpo- ratist states. Historically, the predominance of conservative Protestant religious sects in the Nordic countries produced a world view disap- proving of such affairs. Cabot, Thompson, Tottenham, and Braunlich (1999) note that parties with socialist leanings opposed casinos, viewing them as elitist institutions that exploited the working classes. Finland and Norway authorized GMOCs in the 1920s and 1930s but directed the proceeds to charitable causes.

As demonstrated in Table 2.2, once the liberalization of casino gam- bling began in the 1970s, the welfare regime in each state influenced if and when a state adopted casinos along with the model chosen. Liberal states relaxed restrictions against casinos and social democratic nations followed. In addition, social democratic and, to a lesser extent, corporatist states continued to resist attempts by transnational gam- ing corporations to establish American-style casinos in those countries (McMillen, 1996b). Notwithstanding the welfare regime, however, the type of polity and degree of centralization in each provides further nuance in the way casino gambling developed in western countries over the past 40 years.

Breton and Fraschini (2003) distinguish between federal and unitary political systems. They maintain that both types of polity are decen- tralized because both have several layers of elected government. What distinguishes the unitary state from a federal one is the 'ownership of powers' (2003, p. 58). Central governments in unitary states can devolve powers to lower levels of government and later reclaim them. Constitutional and legal arrangements in federal systems make it dif- ficult for a province, state, länder, or canton to unilaterally (re)possess a power except through secession (p. 58). The type of polity and level of decentralization can influence the governmentality of gambling in several ways.

Unitary states can prevent a region from establishing gambling inde- pendently, and central governments can alter gambling policies without reclaiming powers from lower legislative units. In contrast, when federal governments relinquish authority over gambling law, they leave policy development to subnational governments. When this occurs, federal states adopt gambling policies without a central and well-coordinated strategy; policy changes often arise through individual circumstance and competitive thinking. For example, the United Kingdom permitted casino gambling shortly before Australia and Canada but disallowed

American-style casinos in spite of regional interests and strong lobby-ing from the casino industry (McMillen, 1996b). New Zealand also had a unitary polity and permitted American-style casinos, but later placed a moratorium on further casino development.

The degree of decentralization can also influence changes in gam-bling policies. Decentralization within a nation state is contingent on the strength of the central government when states are formed and current political-economic asymmetries in the federation (Congleton, Kyriacou, & Bacaria, 2003). This is partly why federal liberal states have had similar yet distinctive experiences with casino gambling.

In summary, Tables 2.2 and 2.3 show that a country's political econ-omy has influenced the availability and form of casino gambling. We can also connect these variations to historical conjuncture and choices within each state that reflect sociocultural difference. Postmodern American casinos emerged during globalization in late modernity and transnational capital has transported them to several western countries. Nevertheless, the degree of penetration of the American model has so far depended on the type of welfare regime, polity, and culture of the country where capital has attempted to transplant them.

Gaming Machines outside Casinos in the Welfare Regimes

The introduction of gaming machines is emblematic of mechanized commodification invading the cultural sphere under monopoly capi-talism. The appearance of gaming machines in late nineteenth-century Australia, the United States, Britain, and Europe launched a new era in the production of gambling. Inventors of the earliest machines based them on casino games – roulette, dice, and poker. The early poker machines had a series of levers that displayed the cards, and players with winning hands received free drinks, cigars, or cash prizes. These machines became very popular and were initially widespread in bars, saloons, and tobacco shops. However, public disapproval of mechanized gambling increased as Protestant reform movements spread across western countries.

During this period, phonographs, kinetoscopes, and specialty foods also became available for mass consumption through coin-operated machines in penny arcades. Gaming-machine operators wanted access to this market but negative perceptions and legal issues forced them to change the machines to dispense chewing gum, mints, and other small prizes, in lieu of cash. Many had spinning reels of fruit symbols, and any combination would pay out small prizes; these subsequently became known as 'fruit' or 'mint' machines. Machine designs in Britain and Europe also incorporated elements of skill into the games, quite possibly for the same reasons. Two types of machines emerged from these developments. The slot machine paid out cash and, although illegal, continued to flourish in parts of Australia, Canada, the United States, and some European countries. The United Kingdom and a few other western countries tolerated fruit machines if the games involved skill or dispensed small non-cash prizes. Some of these distinctions exist to this day.

Gaming machines, and the markets for them, underwent radical changes during the 1970s, providing further evidence of the impact of globalization and information technologies on gambling. As deregulation began, transnational manufacturers emerged to take advantage of the new and growing markets. More importantly, producers slowly began integrating computer technologies into their designs. Over time, electronic gaming machines with a spectacle of lights, sounds, and parodies of pop culture icons replaced the mechanized slot machine that was symbolic of gambling in modernity.

Given the timing and extent of change, I anticipated that type of welfare regime and polity would have the same influence on the liberalization of gaming machines as did casinos. Table 2.4 shows the year each country legalized gaming machines and, although the patterns are not as evident as for casinos, they are consistent with the findings above. We can draw a distinction between 'low-intensity' amusement with prize machines (AWPs) and 'high-intensity' electronic gaming machines (EGMs), video lottery terminals (VLTs), and slot machines (Slots) (Productivity Commission, 1999, N. 20). AWPs are similar to other gaming machines, but differ by rate of play, maximum stakes, and size of cash prizes. The machines are slower, accept smaller wagers, and pay out small cash prizes or token amusements. Compared with AWPs, the speed of play on EGMs, VLTs, and slots can be considerably faster. The latter normally permit higher wagers and accept banknotes, bank cards, and credit cards. The cash prizes or vouchers redeemable for cash can also be substantial.

Psychologists have concluded that gaming machines are highly addictive as the play is repetitive with intermittent awards. Moreover, rapid play and high maximum wagers increase the potential for harm; faster machines with larger stakes reduce the gambler's finances more quickly (Ladouceur & Sévigny, 2006; see also Productivity Commission,

Table 2.4 Introduction of Gaming Machines outside Casinos by Welfare Regime and Period

Country	Pre-1900	1900-9	1910-19	1920-9	1930-9	1940-9	1950-9	1960-9	1970-9	1980-9	1990-9	2000-5
United States		⊙										
Canada											⊙	
Australia											⊙	
New Zealand												
United Kingdom											⊙	
Ireland							●					
Iceland								●			Prohibited	
Switzerland*											○	
Japan						◉						
Netherlands										●		
Spain												
Italy							●					●
Greece*									●		Prohibited	
Germany					●							
Belgium										●		
Luxembourg				Prohibited								
Austria							●					
France				Prohibited								
Portugal				Prohibited								
Denmark							●					
Finland				○						●		
Sweden											⊙	
Norway					●						⊙	

Sources: State Gaming Agencies and Personal Contacts

⊙ Electronic gaming machines (EGMs) / Video lottery terminals (VLTs) / Slot machines
● Amusement with prizes (AWPs)
◉ Pachinko: non-cash payout & Payazzo: cash payout (Skillbased gaming machines)
○ Pachislo – Japanese slot machine: non-cash payout
* Date of introduction unavailable

1999). Governments decide the types and numbers of GMOCs, the maximum stake and payout percentages, and the social environment where the machines will be located. These can affect problem gambling rates and the levels of distress experienced by the individual problem gambler.

The different types and spatial and structural characteristics of gaming machines across countries make comparisons difficult. Nevertheless, focusing on low-intensity versus high-intensity machines, the numbers of machines, and per capita revenue, the liberal states are more inclined than European countries to place their citizens at increased risk.

Table 2.4 requires further description due to graphic limitations. High-intensity machines are found in most Australian states, all Canadian provinces, New Zealand, and a number of American states. Overall, adoption of GMOCs has been more difficult in the United States, the result of moral issues, the possibility of crime and corruption, and populist electoral practices. The per capita number of machines and GGR would, arguably, be higher had more state governments been successful in introducing GMOCs.[8] The United Kingdom is the only liberal country that prohibits high-intensity machines outside casinos and, until recently, had conservative gambling policies. Overall, the liberal-corporatist and corporatist states prohibit GMOCs or solely permit AWPs. Iceland is an exception and was the first European country to legalize high-payout VLTs during a period when the government was taking up neo-liberal economic policies. Sweden established VLTs in 1995 – also while adopting neo-liberal policies – but the government permits only a small number of machines in community settings (Table 2.5). Sweden's per capita number of machines and GGR is among the lowest of all the western countries. Until 2007, Norway had the most liberal slot machine laws in Europe (Martin, 2003). Slots became legal in Norway through gaps in the legislation in the 1990s whereas the other governments with high-intensity machines introduced them more directly.

Many countries with GMOCs have reduced the number of machines, restricted their locations, and introduced or plan to integrate responsible gambling technology with gaming machines. But the types of policies and technology will impact levels of problem gambling. For example, in 2007, Norway banned slot machines and bill acceptors from public spaces. The government reintroduced new machines in 2008, placing them under a state monopoly and in age-restricted premises. Players can gamble for an hour followed by a 10-minute break with an approximate maximum loss of $400 (USD) per month (Bakken, Øren, & Götestam, n.d.; Hansen & Rossow, 2010; Revheim & Buvik, 2009). Compare this to the current situation in Australia where continuous play can lead to losses of approximately $1,100 (USD) *per hour* (Australian Government Productivity Commission, 2009, p. xxviii). Table 2.5 provides the numbers and GGR for GMOCs across the welfare regimes. Median gross revenue was $105 USD (per capita) for liberal countries, $69 USD for liberal-corporatist, $32 USD for corporatist, and $88 USD for social democratic states.[9] Australia, New Zealand, Norway, Finland, and Canada are the five highest GGR producers. The other neo-liberal states, the United Kingdom, and the United States ranked ninth and last respectively. GMOCs are illegal in most jurisdictions in the United States and, as noted above, the low revenue is more a reflection of religion and populist electoral practices than liberal govermentality. Finland and Norway had the third and fourth highest GMOC revenue but Finland had a low GGR for casinos and Norway's gaming-machine GGR has dropped considerably with new restrictions on GMOCs.

Ownership and operation of gaming machines are further distinguishing features of GMOC gambling across the welfare regimes. Social democratic countries are predisposed to state monopoly or charitable ownership funnelling profit to good causes. For example, Finland ranks fifth in GMOC GGR but also directs the highest percentage of taxes to public goods (Swiss Institute of Comparative Law, 2006, p. 1062). Denmark and Sweden fall closely behind (p. 1062). Corporatist and liberal regimes are more likely to permit commercial ownership or a mixture of commercial/charitable ownership and operation.

Compared with casinos, more variation exists in the concentration of capital with GMOCs. Whereas large corporations operate casino chains across several continents, gaming-machine operators run the gamut from charities to owners of local arcades, pubs, restaurants, transnational hotel chains, and governments. Wide diversion of operators leads to a weaker lobbying position. As a result national and transnational machine operator associations have appeared that attempt to influence states on their member's behalf. This does not mean that global capital is not involved in gaming-machine gambling. Transnational gaming-machine manufacturers and industry associations comprise a formidable force in the industry's development.

In terms of governance, evidence showing that polity and degree of centralization shape gaming-machine policies is not as clear as with casinos. Nevertheless, Australia and the United States, the two federal

Table 2.5   Gaming Machines outside Casinos: Numbers and Gross Revenues by Welfare Regime 2003–2005

Country	EGMs Slots VLTs	AWPs	Total	# per 10,000††	Estimated Gross Revenues (USD)†	Estimated Per Capita (USD)††
United States	107,590(a)♦		107,590	34	3,934(b)♦	13
Canada	48,901(c)♦		48,901	16	4,448(c)▲	105
Australia	187,896(d)▲		187,896	136	7,442(d)▲	374
New Zealand	21,343(e)▲		21,343	77	682(d)▲	171
United Kingdom		211,000(f)*	211,000	47	3,407(f)*	57
Ireland	12,951(f)*	8,806(f)*	21,757	54	274(f)*	69
Iceland	Unavailable					
Switzerland	Prohibited					
Japan	Unavailable					
Netherlands		25,489(g)*	25,489	18	639(f)*	39
Spain		251,482(f)*	251,482	72	2,881(f)*	72
Italy		200,000(h)▲	200,000	73	2,340(h)▲	36
Greece	Prohibited					
Germany		196,000(f)*	196,000	27	2,640(f)*	32
Belgium	Unavailable				155(f)*	15
Luxembourg	Prohibited					
Austria	Unavailable					
France	Prohibited					
Portugal	Prohibited					
Denmark		19,500(f)▲	19,500	43	284(f)▲	53
Finland		16,700(i)▲	16,700	38	645(f)*	124
Sweden	7,132(f)*		7,132	9	266(f)*	30
Norway		18,000(j)♦	18,000	48	7(j)♦	155

* = 2003 ♦ = 2004 ▲ = 2005

Sources:
(a) United States State Gaming Commissions; McQueen (2004);
(b) Christiansen Capital Advisors (2003);
(c) Canadian Partnership for Responsible Gambling (2005): *Gambling Digest* 2004–2005;
(d) Australian Gaming Council (2007);
(e) New Zealand Department of Internal Affairs (2005);
(f) Swiss Institute of Comparative Law (2006);
(g) Van Speelautomaten (2007);
(h) Sezioni Appparecchi Per Pubbliche Attrazioni Ricreative (S.A.P.A.R)(n.d.);
(i) Raha-automaattiyhdistys (2006);
(j) Norsk Tipping årsrapport (2006);
† Gross revenues in millions converted to USD using yearly average of country currency at OANDA historical exchange rates: http://www.oanda.com/currency/historical-rates
†† Author's calculations: estimate based on population 15 years and above from *CIA World Factbook*

liberal countries most decentralized upon formation, permitted rapid-play and high-payout machines outside of casinos earlier than other liberal states. Furthermore, all federal states have authorized gaming machines in community settings while unitary states such as France, Greece, Luxembourg, and Portugal prohibit them. Greece provides an interesting example of a unitary state reversing policy; allowing AWPs, but abolishing all electronic games from public spaces until 2010 (Koutantou, 2011, January 26).

In summary, the findings further demonstrate that the welfare state and, to a lesser extent, type of polity, have influenced choices about gambling in western countries. In addition to these factors, social dynamics and technology also played a role. Gaming machines emerged during a period of industrialization when capital was increasingly entering the realm of leisure through mechanization. Although the games achieved some levels of acceptance, particularly in frontier locales, public perceptions changed when social disorder became associated with the machines, and when Protestant reform groups began campaigning against gambling. Yet, the machines did not disappear, in part, because the public tolerated them as amusement devices. Over time, some western countries authorized gaming machines to provide funds for good causes and to combat illegal gambling. Nevertheless, most jurisdictions prohibited the games and attempted to enforce the laws with varying levels of success.

By the 1970s, gaming machines, illegal and marginalized, were in a process of revival. Technological developments brought the machines more in line with regulatory issues (McMillen, 1997) and American-style casinos were increasing the amount of floor space for slot machines. During this same period, states began considering machine gambling outside of casinos as possible sources of income for the state and charitable causes.

As with casino gambling, the political-economy and culture of a state influenced whether or not governments legalized GMOCs, the number and type of machines, and the strength of regulations. All of the liberal countries permit high-speed and high-payout machines that could reduce a gambler's resources (and increase the state and operator's coffers) more quickly than GMOCs found in most European states. Additionally, several countries, like Iceland and Sweden, shifted to neo-liberal policies and adopted high-intensity machines in the process. These policies are congruent with the individualism and notions of personal responsibility found in liberal countries. Nevertheless, most

European states derive higher taxation, direct the profit to charities or public good, and intervene more frequently and directly in attempts to protect their citizens from problems associated with GMOCs.

Lotteries in the Welfare Regimes

This section examines the role of the welfare state and governance in the production of lotteries, one of the earliest recorded forms of organized gambling; their use for revenue generation dates back to antiquity. As with casinos and gaming machines, the lotteries that developed in the mid-sixteenth century reflect a particular period of capitalism (see Reith, 1999).

In the early 1500s, merchants in German and Italian cities began to promote their wares in what were the 'predecessors of today's commercial sweepstakes' (Willman, 1999, p. 5). In seventeenth-century Genoa, state officials annually chose governments by lot and individuals frequently made bets on who would be successful (Bellhouse, 1991, p.146). When the city sanctioned the bets, it gave rise to one of Europe's earliest state-endorsed lotteries (p. 146.). A numbers lottery involving cash prizes followed in Florence in 1530, and many consider this the forerunner to the modern game of lotto (Blanche, 1950, p. 71).

Over the next few centuries, monarchs and politicians used lotteries to fund wars, capital projects, cultural venues, and benevolent causes. Private ventures also garnered considerable sums through lottery schemes while commerce evolved into mercantile capitalism altering attitudes toward chance and risk (Reith, 1999). State-operated and private lotteries burgeoned from the sixteenth to the nineteenth centuries; so too did corruption, fraud, and associated social disorder. As a result, many states outlawed lotteries altogether, others permitted solely state-run lotteries. As shown in Table 2.6, almost half of western countries established and then prohibited state lotteries by the mid-twentieth century. The pattern in Table 2.6 does not invalidate my contention that type of welfare regime and polity has affected the availability and organization of gambling across western states. It *specifies* the forms – casinos and GMOCs – most affected by these factors.

Table 2.6 shows that Canada, the United Kingdom, and the United States established lotteries last. The United Kingdom and the United States established and then prohibited lotteries only to re-establish them much later. Conversely, the Protestant Nordic countries, where we would expect anti-gambling sentiments, legalized lotteries and

Table 2.6   Introduction of State-Operated Lotteries by Welfare Regime and Period

Country	Pre-1900	1900–1909	1910–1919	1920–1929	1930–1939	1940–1949	1950–1959	1960–1969	1970–1979	1980–1989	1990–1999	2000–2005
United States	■							●				
Canada									●			
Australia	●											
New Zealand					●							
United Kingdom	■										●	
Ireland					●							
Iceland					●							
Switzerland				●								
Japan					●							
Netherlands	●											
Spain	●											
Italy	■				●							
Greece					●							
Germany	■				●							
Belgium	■				●							
Luxembourg						●						
Austria	■		●									
France	■				●							
Portugal	●											
Denmark						●						
Finland						●						
Sweden	■				●							
Norway						●						

Sources: State Gaming Agencies and Personal Contacts
● Legal
■ Legalized then prohibited

pools between 1930 and 1950. Thus, historical contingencies *prevented* three liberal states from adopting lotteries during periods of increasing welfare expenditures; they established lotteries later while retracting social spending. Changing economic conditions after the 1970s *compelled* social democratic states to alter their course, introducing casinos, gaming machines, and increasing use of lotteries to maintain welfare-state provisions. We can see this by examining the allocation of state lottery revenue.

Several liberal countries, and a majority of corporatist and social democratic states, established lotteries for the expressed purpose of raising funds for the public purse. Corporatist and social democratic states also instituted lotteries for charitable purposes, sports, cultural activities, and to channel gambling passions into forms considered less prone to addiction. Moreover, Sweden and Norway permitted lotteries to limit the potential for private operations.

The distinction between generating revenue for public funds and augmenting financial support for good causes is an important one. Many have described lotteries as a regressive tax. Those with less disposable income spend a disproportionate amount on lottery tickets (Clotfelter & Cook, 1987; Brown, Kaldenburg, & Browne, 1992; Kitchen & Powells, 1991; Oster, 2004; Pirog-Good & Mikesell, 1995; Price & Novak, 1999; Rubenstein & Scafidi, 2002; Scott & Garen, 1994). All western politicians have looked to this regressive tax to provide state funding. As shown in Table 2.7, individuals in social democratic countries spend more on lotteries than do some corporatist and all liberal countries. The median GGR was similar across liberal, liberal-corporatist, and corporatist states: $61 USD (per capita), $58 USD, and $54 USD respectively, compared with $98 USD in social democratic countries.[10] Nevertheless, despite the disparity of GGR in revenue by welfare state, with few exceptions, liberal states allocate lottery profits to general revenue, infrastructure, or activities typically funded by the state. Thus, while the lower classes give up a disproportionate percentage of their disposable income to lotteries, politicians acting within a liberal ideology use lottery profits to provide tax relief and benefits to the middle classes. On the other hand, many corporatist and social democratic states direct lottery proceeds to charitable and community organizations, thereby redistributing the profits more equitably.

With regard to polity type and level of centralization, federal states established lotteries at the same time as the unitary states. The United States and Canada are exceptions, but political-economic and sociocultural barriers prevented these states from moving with the rest. Nonetheless, differences do exist between the two polity types. Apart from Switzerland, many subnational units in the federal states established lotteries to prevent cross-border revenue outflow, whereas only a few unitary states introduced lotteries in response to competition from other states.

The degree of centralization when the state was formed has also been a factor in the creation of lotteries in two federal liberal states. Gambling in Austria, Germany, Iceland, Switzerland, and Canada is under federal law, whereas in Australia and the United States it remains within state jurisdiction. This, in part, explains why these countries established

Table 2.7   Gross Lottery Revenues by Welfare Regime 2003–5

Country	Year	Total Sales (USD)†	Estimated Per Capita (USD)††
United States	2003	17,400(a)	59
Canada	2003–4	2,193(b)	67
Australia	2004–5	1,220(c)	61
New Zealand	2003	159(d)	40
United Kingdom	2003	3,837(e)	64
Ireland	2003	300(e)	76
Iceland	unavailable		
Switzerland	2003	229(f)	31
Japan	unavailable		
Netherlands	2003	887(e)	54
Spain	2003	1,275(e)	32
Italy	2003	5,097(e)	88
Greece	2003	537(e)	50
Germany	2003	5,650(e)	69
Belgium	2003	550(e)	53
Luxembourg	2002	21(e)	46
Austria	2003	674(e)	82
France	2003	3,493(e)	58
Portugal	2003	908(e)	86
Denmark	2003	486(e)	90
Finland	2003	549(e)	105
Sweden	2003	752(e)	84
Norway	2003	66(f)	145

Sources:
(a) Christiansen Capital Advisors (2003);
(b) Canadian Partnership for Responsible Gambling (2005): *Gambling Digest* 2004–5;
(c) Australian Gaming Council (2007);
(d) New Zealand Department of Internal Affairs (2005);
(e) Swiss Institute of Comparative Law (2006);
(f) Société de la Loterie de la Suisse Romande *Rapport d'Activité* (2003);
(g) Norsk Tipping årsrapport (2006)
† Gross revenues in millions converted to USD using yearly average of country currency at OANDA Historical Exchange Rates: http://www.oanda.com/currency/historical-rates
†† Author's calculations: estimate based on population 15 years and above from CIA World Factbook

lotteries at different times. Federal governments that retained jurisdiction over gambling could decide when lotteries were appropriate for the country as a whole.

Finally, it would be a mistake to think that capital did not play a role in establishing lotteries in decentralized states. Braidfoot (1988) maintains that a forceful and committed group of lottery-industry businesses have been instrumental in the legalization of lotteries in the United States. Thirty-one of 42 American states that legalized lotteries did so through referenda or an initiative process, which opened the door for the lottery industry to attempt to win over the voting public through election tactics (Pierce & Miller, 1999). The degree to which capital is involved in other nation states is less clear.

In short, lotteries have existed for at least two millennia. The lottery that emerged in the sixteenth century reflected a mercantile mode of production, and the merchants of the day would have continued to operate lotteries had the state not recognized the potential for revenue and fraud. During the seventeenth and eighteenth centuries, many countries introduced lotteries to replenish their treasuries during times of war and capital campaigns. Some chose, or were forced to forego, the prospective revenue from lottery schemes when stock market bubbles, financial manias, and corrupt lotteries produced social disorder. States turned to lotteries again in the twentieth century when faced with escalating expenses associated with the welfare state.

As with other forms of gambling, welfare regime, polity type, and degree of centralization have affected the timing and governance of lotteries in each country. These factors were not the sole influences in the legalization of lotteries in western countries. Social and cultural forces have also played a role; each country faced different situations when attempting to liberalize gambling, and each has done so within unique political-economies, social institutions, and cultures.

Governmentality: From Protection to Risk

Gambling practices in western countries developed unevenly, the result of historically conditioned institutional differences. Type of welfare state influenced the legalization of gambling and the spatial and structural arrangements of each form. When economic pressures increased in late modernity, the neo-liberal anglo countries liberalized their gambling policies earlier, or more aggressively, than did the European countries. For example, excluding the United Kingdom, the liberal states garner more from casinos and gaming machines than the European countries, and the social democratic states tend to get most gambling proceeds from lotteries.[11] Finland is the exception with higher GMOC revenue. The liberal states also adopted regulatory structures that fall further within risk governance. This becomes clear when we consider the above findings in the context of Kingma's (2004) 'alibi' and 'risk' types of governmentality.

Within the alibi mode of governmentality, the state takes the position that gambling is morally questionable and intervenes to protect populations from undesirable outcomes arising from the activities. Governments legitimize the legalization of gambling as a method of reducing crime and redirecting revenue from illegal operations to good causes. States organize and oversee legal gambling within small tightly controlled monopolies.

Within the risk mode, the state legitimates its actions by signifying gambling as commercial entertainment that holds the potential to stimulate economic development and provide revenue for the state. This reshaping of the image of gambling reduces opposition and increases participation, which in turn leads to additional opportunities for liberalization and new risk assessments (Kingma, 2004; Cosgrave & Klassen, 2001). Eventually, governments intervene, primarily to protect state and business interests, by managing the unintended consequences of gambling. They accomplish this with stricter regulatory controls than for other economic activities. At the same time, the industry redirects responsibility for gambling-related harm on to individuals. All western countries have adopted risk-styled gambling policies. Yet, liberal states have moved further into the risk form of governmentality. Policies in liberal countries are less restrictive and by and large aimed at reducing the unintended consequences of gambling after the fact.[12] Corporatist and social democratic regimes also attempt to minimize social problems and crime, but lean toward an interventionist approach to protect the public in advance.

These differences are within Hood, Rothstein, Baldwin, Rees, and Spackman's concept of the 'risk regulation regime' (1999, p. 4). Some states tolerate risk more than others, and how a state manages risk arises out of different configurations of three essential components: 'director,' 'detector,' and 'effector' (1999, p. 5). *Director* comprises the means of setting goals and targets to manage risks, *detector* corresponds to ways states monitor the management systems, and *effector* constitutes actions taken to change the state of a system (p. 5).

Table 2.8   Alibi and Risk Governmentality Ideal Types

ALIBI	RISK
Corporatist political approach – direct government intervention and external control with numerous restrictions to contain gambling or ensure revenues goes to social interests; policy focus is on demand *and* supply:	Liberal political approach – indirect government intervention to manage negative outcomes arising from liberalisation and the free market, increasing state and capital involvement to exploit revenues, deregulation, policy focus is on demand *not* supply:
• Rigid gambling policies – used to shield the population in advance from gambling as an 'undesirable' activity • Minimal bureaucracy for administering gambling policy and organising games	• Flexible gambling policies – used to control unintended outcomes of gambling after the fact • Large scale bureaucracies for administering gambling policy and organising games
• Gambling is legitimised as a way to reduce crime and illegal gambling and to provide funds for 'good causes' within the welfare state • Little – if any – expansion in gambling products or gambling markets • No market stimulation. Control of gambling is to restrict supply and eliminate crime, both demand and supply are considered – government monopolies offered as legal alternative to illegal markets	• Gambling is legitimised as a government revenue generator, a form of commercial entertainment, economic development, boon to tourism and so forth • Widespread expansion of gambling products and markets • Stimulation and channelling of markets toward gambling products that hold minimal harmful impacts. Control of gambling markets is to deal with (reduce) addiction and crime. Legal gambling within a free market approach (often public – private mix) is solely offered as a legal alternative to illegal markets
• Gambling holds little economic importance outside of funds allocated toward 'good causes' – welfare state principles drive policy • *Commercial interests lobby governments to legalise and deregulate gambling* • *Little or no formal (ie. scientific) assessment of potential impacts that could follow the introduction or liberalisation of gambling*	• Gambling markets hold considerable economic importance and profits drive policy with gambling addiction the main, and often only, reason for restrictions • Commercial associations provide internal regulation within a potentially hostile environment in attempts to ensure smooth operations with increased profits • Increased importance of (scientific) measurement and reporting to buttress arguments for/against gambling and (even) for consumption practices

(Continued)

Table 2.8   (*Continued*)

• Inconsistent risk assessment of generalised social problems such as family breakdown and crime associated with gambling	• Consistent and ongoing risk assessment that arises out of political pressures and self-interest – focus on effects on the gambler (individualistic), competition between gambling providers, and profits
• Gamblers are marginal in policy decisions – interest is in management of demand and elimination of illegal gambling	• Gamblers are central in policy decisions – most interest is attached to characteristics of gambling addicts but this focus also allows for methods to increase consumption of gambling products
• *Social problems associated with gambling are linked to criminal activities (illegal gambling)*	• State transfers responsibility for social problems caused by gambling (where it can) to gambling providers and individual gamblers;
• *Little or no state involvement in dealing with gambling related social problems.*	

Note: Italicized items *have not been* taken from Kingma, *Gambling and the Risk Society: The Liberalisation and Legitimation Crisis of Gambling in the Netherlands* (2004).

Liberal states exhibit detector-effector risk regime policies by monitoring gambling activities and dealing with problems after they arise. The European states lean toward a director-effector regulatory approach through policies and intervention to control problems before they occur. Furthermore, the detector-effector course fits with the 'risk' side of these ideal types and the director-effector approach is congruent with alibi governance.

Comparing combined median GGR among the three types of gambling provides a further indicator of risk regulation regime: liberal and liberal-corporatist countries generate higher revenue from gambling than corporatist and social democratic states ($216 USD versus $131 USD).[13] The former states also obtain more revenue from casinos and GMOCs; both pose higher risk for their citizens ($80 USD versus $28 USD).[14] This makes sense, since most corporatist and social democratic countries either prohibit or restrict access to casinos and, in some instances, GMOCs.

Welfare regimes have attempted to increase gambling for political, economic, and social reasons. Liberal states have done so within a liberal ideology managing gambling in a way that elevates the potential risks and places the onus on individuals to control their actions through responsible gambling. Social democratic and corporatist regimes also invoke responsible gambling through self-regulated behaviour. However, they lean toward interventionist approaches to control the actions of their citizens and mitigate the problems in advance.[15]

Conclusions

This chapter demonstrates that historical conjuncture and narrative have influenced current gambling practices and policies in 23 industrialized states. Welfare regime, polity type, and degree of centralization during state formation have specified the temporal, spatial, and structural characteristics of legal gambling in the late twentieth century.

Western countries have responded to challenges arising from postindustrialization, globalization, and shifting social and cultural dynamics. Changing macroeconomic and sociocultural conditions forced governments to transfer costs from the welfare state directly on to citizens, an unpopular political move. They instead offset the shortfall indirectly through gambling. As government participation in these activities increased, it provided a new legitimacy that fit well with changing attitudes. Transnational gambling conglomerates also emerged during this time and attempted to sway states into adopting policies that would open up markets or deregulate existing ones. However, success or failure has been a function of the governmentality, social institutions, and culture of each state. Each government has constructed its overall orientation and approach to gambling through different ideologies and institutional structures, all created through historical narrative and conjuncture.

Within this context, the Anglo states have been more likely than the European countries to have legalized, within competitive deregulated markets, American-style casinos, high-paced/high-payout gaming machines, and lotteries, for the purpose of allocating general revenue to state coffers. Liberal federations that were highly decentralized when formed displayed the strongest tendencies in this regard. On the other hand, corporatist and social democratic states have leaned toward an interventionist approach with stronger regulatory bodies; many also direct gambling revenue to social and cultural causes.

These characteristic features of gambling in each welfare regime were predictable given the historical conditions and philosophies underlying the style of governance in each country. Many European countries have long histories with gambling. If these countries had adopted a liberal, as opposed to corporatist or social democratic, political orientation and culture, it is plausible that transnational casino corporations would have been more successful in establishing American-style casinos. When American postmodern casinos did emerge, the combination of historical/cultural traditions and a corporatist/social democratic orientation intervened and most European states did not allow them, although this is now changing (McMillen, 1996b). These two factors were absent in liberal states. They did not have a long standing history of legal gambling, nor did they incorporate strong corporatist or social democratic principles into their governance.

Thus, globalization has been a driving force in the expansion of casinos, but we must also account for regional factors that intervened (so far) to prevent transnational casino corporations from pushing their agenda (McMillen, 1996b). We can make a similar case for gaming machines and lotteries. In short, variations in gambling are due to the complexities of a state's political-economy, social institutions, and culture.

3 Casinos in Australia, Canada, and the United States[1]

In this chapter, I examine the pattern of commercial casino adoption that began in the 1970s in context of the analytical framework presented in Chapter 1. The main argument is that gambling for profit emerges through a dynamic and fluid process that encompasses political, economic, social, and cultural conditions bound in historical contingency. The impetus is most often economic, but the decision to attempt adoption and the success of the endeavour will lay in individual motives, combined with the extent to which actors can be mobilized to support or oppose legal gambling activities. This means that the sociocultural environment and degree of resources available to proponents and opponents, including access to the political sphere of influence (polity), will determine whether gambling for profit is adopted. I use the emergence of casinos in Australia, Canada, and the United States to develop these themes.

Casino gambling is a global multi-billion dollar industry. In 2007–8, casinos in the United States yielded $32.5 billion (USD) and added $5.7 billion (USD) to state coffers, while employing more than 357,000 people (American Gaming Association, 2009, p. 2). Australian casinos generated over $4 billion (AUD), paid $1.2 billion (AUD) in taxes to the Commonwealth and state governments, and employed over 20,000 people (Allen Consulting Group, 2009, p. 363). Casinos in Canada produced gross revenue of $5.6 billion (CAD) with $2.2 billion going to provincial treasuries (Canadian Partnership for Responsible Gambling, 2009, pp. 6, 11). We should also not underestimate the popularity of casino gambling: more people went to a casino in Indiana in 1998 than attended Disney World (The Wager, 1999, January 26). About 49% of Australians (Allen Consulting Group, 2009, p. 9), 25% of Americans (American

Table 3.1   Period of Introduction of Casinos in Australia as of 2005

State	To 1970	1970–5	1976–80	1981–5	1986–90	1991–5	1996–2000	2001–5
Australian Capital Territory						1		
Christmas Island					1		Closed	
New South Wales						1		
Northern Territory			1					
Queensland				1				
South Australia				1				
Tasmania		1						
Victoria						1		
Western Australia				1				

Sources: McMillen 1993; Australian Institute for Gambling Research 1999
1 – Commercial   2 – Public   3 – Public / Private   4 – Charitable   5 – Tribal

Gaming Association, 2009, p. 33), and 18% of Canadians (Canadian Partnership for Responsible Gambling, 2009, p. 18) visited casinos in 2008 and 2002 respectively.[2]

Tables 3.1 to 3.3 show that this remarkable growth of casino gambling occurred unevenly across time and space. Comparing the geographic and temporal configuration of adoption, the *trend* was for Australia to establish commercial casinos ahead of Canada and the United States.[3] Indeed, McMillen observed in 1988: 'one of the most obvious differences between Australian casino developments and the United States, where there are many more casinos but confined to Nevada and New Jersey, is that casinos have been legalised in almost every Australian state, operating under government-guaranteed regional monopolies' (1988b, p. 153). In her landmark study of casino development in Australia, McMillen (1993) describes the emergence of Australian casinos as appearing in three waves (Table 3.1). Tasmania and the Northern Territory adopted during the first wave. Christmas Island, Queensland, South Australia, and Western Australia followed in the second, and the Australian Capital Territory, New South Wales, and Victoria completed the transition during the third wave.[4]

Comparing Tables 3.1, 3.2, and 3.3 also shows that ownership and capacity to operate casinos varies across the three countries. Private

Table 3.2   Period of Introduction of Casinos in Canada as of 2005

Province	To 1970	1970–5	1976–80	1981–85	1986–90	1991–5	1996–2000	2001–5
Alberta	4							5
British Columbia			4				3	
Manitoba	4				2			5
New Brunswick								
Newfoundland								
Nova Scotia						1		
Ontario						3	4, 5	
Prince Edward Island								
Québec						2		
Saskatchewan			4				2, 5	

Sources: Provincial Gaming Agencies
1 – Commercial   2 – Public   3 – Public/Private   4 – Charitable   5 – Tribal

companies own and operate casinos under monopoly conditions in the Australian states. Unlike Canada and the United States, casinos do not exist on aboriginal lands. As shown in Table 3.2, casinos in Canada first emerged in the western provinces as small temporary charitable facilities. Manitoba led the country in 1989 by establishing the first permanent commercial casino, and Québec, Ontario, and Nova Scotia followed between 1993 and 1995; Saskatchewan and British Columbia legalized commercial casinos in 1996 and 1999. Compared with Australia and the United States, the Canadian provinces chose different forms of ownership and operations: public ownership; public or charitable ownership and private operations; and, private ownership and operations. Several provinces negotiated with First Nations bands and permit on-reserve casinos to assist with economic development. However, the *Criminal Code* and a Supreme Court of Canada decision constrained the First Nations from solely benefiting from casino profits on their lands.

Nevada legalized casinos in 1931, but crime and corruption associated with them constrained other states – indeed other countries – from entertaining thoughts of similar venues for more than four decades (Table 3.3). In 1976, after failing in its first attempt, New Jersey gained voter approval for privately owned casinos confined to Atlantic City. Proponents appealed to emotional legitimacy by promising urban renewal and allocating the revenue for seniors and people with disabilities. New Jersey's success prompted numerous other campaigns, but 13 years passed before Iowa and South Dakota succeeded. By 2005, 11 states had legalized commercial casinos and 22 had Class III tribal gaming, a result of the Indian Gaming Regulatory Act.[5, 6] My interest here is with the *pattern* of commercial casino expansion that started in the late 1960s. The earliest American-style casinos emerged in Nevada, but I consider the early Nevadan casinos an anomaly to the normalization of commercial casino gambling and expansion in the three countries. In essence, the Nevadan casinos were an 'experiment,' an 'off limits' preserve where well-heeled Americans could gamble (King, 1969, pp. 119–20, 129). The distance between Nevada and major urban centres meant that legal casino gambling was out of reach for the majority of average Americans (Skolnick, 1978). Casinos also lacked legitimacy. President Truman called Nevada 'the only black spot on the United States continent' (Starkey Jr., 1964), and even Las Vegans tried to alter that city's image as a gambling mecca run by criminals.[7] At times, illegal casinos were tolerated in other areas and proponents unsuccessfully advocated legalization as early as 1964.[8] When casinos opened in New Jersey many incorrectly predicted a flood elsewhere (Dombrink & Thompson, 1990, pp. 90–4). In fact, casino campaigns failed in 10 states between 1978 and 1984 (p. 186), leading Thompson to proclaim that 'the casino movement [in the United States] is dead' and would not be revived soon (1984, p. 64). The movement regained momentum in the late 1980s. By this time, five of nine Australian jurisdictions had adopted casinos.

American-style casinos first opened in the Nevadan desert, and Las Vegas is unrivalled as a global gambling attraction. Nevertheless, a majority of Australian states legalized *urban commercial casinos* earlier than most American states and Canadian provinces (Eadington, 1998; McMillen, 1988b). Some might object to this assertion, but while many Australian and American states looked to casinos for economic development and public funds between 1970 and 1985 (see Dombrink & Thompson 1990; McMillen, 1993), the Australian states had more success. The timing of adoption is also significant. All three countries were entering a recessionary period with increasing unemployment in the early 1970s, but Australia's economy outperformed the United States during this period (Figures 3.1 and 3.2). The global recessions of the 1970s through 1990s were central to the expansion of gambling for profit in late modernity (McMillen, 1996b). As regions faced economic decline, politicians and businesses collaborated to introduce gambling as a means of economic revitalization (Australian Institute

Table 3.3 Period of Introduction of Casinos in the United States as of 2005

State	To 1970	1970–5	1976–80	1981–5	1986–90	1991–5	1996–2000	2001–5
NORTHEAST								
Connecticut						5		
Maine								
Massachusetts								
New Hampshire								
New Jersey			1					
New York						5		
Pennsylvania								
Rhode Island								
Vermont								
SOUTHEAST								
Alabama								
Arkansas								
Delaware								
Florida								
Georgia								
Kentucky								
Maryland								
Mississippi						1,5		
Louisiana						1,5		
Oklahoma						5		
North Carolina						5		
South Carolina								
Tennessee								
Texas								
Virginia								
West Virginia								
MIDWEST								
Illinois						1		
Indiana						1		
Iowa						1,5		
Kansas						5		
Michigan						5	1	
Minnesota						5		
Missouri						1		
Nebraska								
North Dakota						5		
Ohio								
South Dakota					1	5		
Wisconsin						5		

(*Continued*)

Table 3.3 (*Continued*)

State	To 1970	1970–5	1976–80	1981–5	1986–90	1991–5	1996–2000	2001–5
WEST								
Alaska								
Arizona						5		
California						5		
Colorado						1,5		
Hawaii								
Idaho						5		
Montana						5		
New Mexico						5		
Nevada	1					5		
Oregon						5		
Utah								
Wyoming								
Washington						5		

Sources: State Gaming Agencies, National Indian Gaming Association
1 – Commercial   2 – Public   3 – Public/Private   4 – Charitable   5 – Tribal

For Gambling Research, 1999; Blevins & Jensen, 1998; Campbell, 1994; Doughney, 2002; Eadington, 1996; Furlong, 1998; McMillen, 1988a, 1993, 1996b; Moran, 1997). McMillen's (1993) intricate analysis of casinos in Australia shows that the Australian states with weak economies introduced casinos first; others adopted after experiencing increased economic pressures, cross-border losses in gambling revenue, and competition for tourist dollars. Numerous jurisdictions in North America faced similar circumstances; many American states unsuccessfully attempted to introduce casinos, and the Canadian provinces turned to commercial casinos only well after the deep economic recession of the early 1970s (Figure 3.1).

Figure 3.2 provides further evidence of the structural differences and casino adoption among the three countries. Unemployment often raises questions about a group's ability to govern creating a legitimacy crisis (see Habermas, 1975; McMillen, 1988a, 1993, 1996b) and can generate strong inducements to legalize casinos (McMillen, 1993; Brian, 2009). As shown in Figure 3.2, Australia had the lowest rates of unemployment between the mid-1960s and mid-1980s and the highest numbers of casino adoption. In theory, the American states and

Figure 3.1: Introduction of Casinos by Real GDP 1970–2005

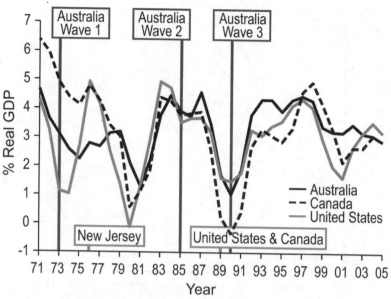

Sources: OECD (1991a, July), Economic Outlook 49, p. 191; OECD (1999a, June), Economic Outlook 65, p. 227; OECD (2002a, June), Economic Outlook 71, p. 207; OECD (2006a, December), Economic Outlook 80, p. 167

Canadian provinces should have introduced casinos earlier than they did. Numerous American states floated proposals while the Australian casino development was gathering steam, but they failed to secure political or voter approval. Four Canadian provinces also legalized small charitable casinos; however, the economic impact would be considerably lower than with large-scale commercial casinos. The provinces moved long after experiencing the highest unemployment in decades and adoption was uneven. The foregoing presents the challenge of determining why cross-national and regional differences exist in the timing of adoption and geographic dispersal of commercial casinos among Australia, Canada, and the United States. I begin to explore this question here by drawing on the concepts introduced in Chapter 1. I start with the impetus for adoption: the macro-level processes that created political-economic conditions conducive for a political and business elite to introduce casino proposals. I then turn to two sociocultural influences – religion and organized crime – that influence acceptance or opposition to casinos. I next examine the determinants that affect the

Figure 3.2: Introduction of Casinos by Unemployment 1970–2005

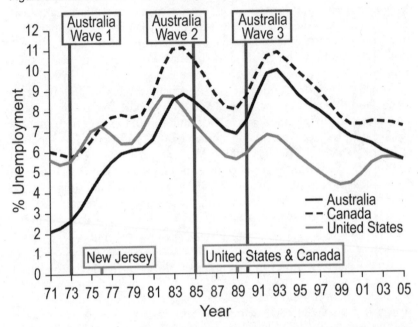

Sources: OECD (1991b, July), *Economic Outlook 49*, p. 208; OECD (1999b, June), *Economic Outlook 65*, p. 248; OECD (2002b, June), *Economic Outlook 71*, p. 221; OECD (2006b, December), *Economic Outlook 80*, p. 180

likelihood of adoption. Social and cultural factors feed into political-economic mechanisms that enable or constrain mobilization; this is where motivations, and the ability to mobilize resources, coalesce with governance – including populist practices, elite support, and access to the polity – causing variations in patterns of adoption. In the final section, I briefly outline the introduction of commercial casinos in each country and among aboriginal groups. I conclude by discussing the historically contingent developments among the three countries that set the stage for casino adoption.

Impetus for Casino Adoption

Global Factors

A shift in global capitalism following the Second World War directly shaped casino development in the liberal systems (McMillen, 1993, 1996b). Dramatic changes in global finance, technology, and production transformed the nature of capital, triggering deindustrialization, regional economic decline, and increased unemployment. As welfare-state costs climbed and revenue fell, Anglo western states shifted to neo-liberalism and politicians sought innovative ways to reverse the trend. Many looked to gambling for profit and others followed when their economies faltered. Nevertheless, globalization is but one chapter in the story; regional political-economic differences specified where the global challenges had the most impact and casino adoption occurred.

Changes to global capitalism in the latter part of the twentieth century unleashed processes that were a strong impetus for the introduction of casinos (McMillen, 1988a, 1993, 1996b). Prior to the 1970s, financial institutions were tightly connected to industry with the principal goal of maintaining long-term profit (Thrift, 1992). The abandonment of the Bretton Woods system of currency regulation decoupled finance capital from industrial production, which led to widespread speculation in the international money markets and freed up liquid capital for the development of service industries, including casinos. As the global economy moved to 'casino capitalism' (Strange, 1986), finance capital took larger risks for short-term profit (Thrift, 1992) and industrial capital reorganized production. Before the collapse of Bretton Woods, industry was structured under Fordist principles and aligned with nation states. Fordist production needed a stable workforce and ever-increasing consumption. Capital provided workers with higher wages while the state intervened to regulate the supply of labour. But Fordism waned in the 1970s with technological advances; more international market forces, deindustrialization, and the growth of service economies ensued. Outcomes from these global processes were important for the emergence of casinos in Australia, Canada, and the United States.

First, deindustrialization and the flight of capital to the third world devastated regional economies and drove up unemployment. Demands on the welfare state mounted while state economies and revenues were shrinking. This threatened the legitimacy of the political order and necessitated a response that came in the form of varying degrees of neo-liberal ideologies and economic reform.

Second, national and regional governments started exercising fiscal constraint, reducing social spending, and enacting flexible labour policies to appease wandering capitalists. Deregulation and devolution followed. Some view deregulation as the principle component in the growth of legalized gambling generally (Atkinson, Nichols, & Oleson, 2000; Cosgrave & Klassen, 2001) and the emergence of casinos specifically (Eadington, 1999; Furlong, 1998; Huebusch, 1997; Mason & Nelson,

2001).[9] Devolution, or 'fend for yourself federalism' (Tannewald, 1998, p. 61), has also been cited as central to the spread of legalized gambling in the United States (Mason & Nelson, 2001). As federal and state governments transferred fiscal and economic responsibilities to lower-level polities, economically vulnerable regions experienced additional burdens, which forced politicians to seek alternative forms of economic development, and casinos fit the bill.

Third, the shift to neo-liberalism altered the state's function, from arbitrator between labour and capital, to facilitator of economic growth. Heightened unemployment allowed capital to demand incentives stimulating interregional competition. Consequently, politicians encouraged strategies to provide competitive advantages over other regions and countries (Broomhill, 2001) and the 'entrepreneurial city' was central to the plan (McIntosh & Hayward, 2000, p. 3). Key cities were identified that would stabilize regional economies and attract investment, and casinos were meant as anchors for these sites.

Fourth, global change marked the development of the service economy with consumption as its economic engine. Nevertheless, deindustrialization and concomitant unemployment threatened citizens' ability to consume. Moreover, attitudes were focused on thrift and saving. Capital and the state responded by encouraging household spending through the introduction of consumer credit and microeconomic reforms that altered attitudes towards money[10] (Ritzer, 1995), increased female labour force participation, and both encouraged consumption.[11] As states recognized the importance of consumer spending in the economy, some considered tourism and casinos to address economic deficiencies while simultaneously facilitating the accumulation of wealth among capital (Campbell, 1994; Comaroff & Comaroff, 2000; McMillen, 1993).

National and Subnational Impetus

McMillen's (1993) study of casinos in Australia conclusively links global recessions with the introduction of casinos in that country. Figure 3.2 demonstrates that the Australian states introduced casinos during or immediately after a recession. Yet, despite McMillen's convincing analysis for Australia, Figures 3.1 and 3.2 still lead to the question of why Canada and the United States lagged behind. Clearly, global economic processes cannot fully explain regional variation in casino proposals. Differences in regional fiscal autonomy, fiscal imbalance, and geography further intervened to specify those regions where international economic pressures were most conducive to attempts to legalize casinos (McMillen, 1996b).

States have proposed casinos primarily to revitalize economies. A secondary reason has been to shore up finances needed for service delivery and infrastructure that could attract investment. Of the three countries, the Australian states have the least fiscal autonomy and the Canadian provinces the most (Broadway & Watts, 2004), which partly explains differences in casino development.

From federation forward, the Australian Commonwealth government has continuously centralized tax structures and usurped the states' monetary sources forcing them to develop gambling as a source of income (McMillen & Eadington, 1986). The most significant development occurred during the Second World War when the federal government assumed powers to collect personal income tax (Dollery, 2002), leaving the states to rely on intergovernmental transfers, land, payroll, estate, and gambling taxes (Australian Bureau of Statistics, 2001a; Reinhardt & Steel, 2006). Indeed, gambling provided 3.5% of state revenue before the war and jumped to 12.9% following it (Australian Bureau of Statistics, 2001a). Land and payroll taxes began to fall in the early 1960s and the states abolished estate taxes out of interstate competition (Australian Bureau of Statistics, 2001a). Gambling could have made up the short-fall, but racing and lottery revenue were flat (Smith, 2000). In fact, as a percentage of state finance, gambling taxes declined to 4.3% by 1958–9 (Australian Bureau of Statistics, 2001a). This drop in income exacerbated the states' fiscal difficulties and created significant inducements to consider casinos (McMillen, 1993, 2009; Smith, 2000) for economic development and as a method of invisible taxation (McMillen, 1990).[12] For example, Tasmania, the first state to legalize casinos, had a low fiscal capacity and one of the highest levels of expenditure (Bernd, Spahn, & Shah, 1995). Tasmania introduced casinos to revive the economy and strengthen that state's finances (Australian Institute for Gambling Research, 1999; McMillen, 1993).

Given the interstate competition over taxation and reliance on gambling monies it makes sense that the states would protect their tax base, and Smith claims that 'defending revenues from legalized gambling in other States contributed to the spread of casino and gaming-machine operations in a number of Australian states' (2000, p. 125). She further argues that these same pressures were behind expansion of gambling for profit in Canada and the United States (p. 122). However, the Canadian provinces did not face the same fiscal issues until the mid-1980s and no interstate competition for casino or gaming-machine profits until the early 1990s. Moreover, Manitoba was the first Canadian province to legalize commercial casinos and did so after four years of high unemployment and a substantial drop in real GDP (Statistics Canada – A, n.d.). In fact, Manitoba had the weakest provincial economy between 1981 and 1991 (Statistics Canada – A, n.d.). Provinces that adopted later did so out of economic pressures and fiscal issues, not interstate competition.[13] Most American states and Canadian provinces had fiscal options unavailable to the Australian states. When these became politically risky, the state and provincial governments looked to other means, such as casinos.

The difference in fiscal power also produced a higher vertical fiscal imbalance (VFI) in Australia necessitating higher transfer equalization payments to the states.[14] The VFI in Australia dropped substantially in the mid-1970s and a lower VFI can exacerbate regional disparities leading to increased competition between subnational units (Bird & Tarasov, 2002).[15] It is significant that most Australian states *proposed* casinos by 1980 as interstate competition for tourists and gambling taxes grew (see Australia Institute for Gambling Research, 1999; Smith, 2000). Norrie and Wilson (2000) suggest there is no VFI in Canada since both levels of government have access to the same major sources of revenue. The VFI increased marginally in the United States between 1982 and 1995 (Bird & Tarasov, 2002). A requirement for constitutional amendment, and a lack of provincial autonomy, further served to constrain casino adoption.

Geography is another differentiating factor that influences casino development. Economic crises and the ability to respond to them have progressively become a function of 'place' through regional disparity. Winning regions have the appropriate infrastructure to attract investment capital and sustain their success; losing regions decline as capital and labour are drawn to the more economically successful areas (Zukin, 1991). Accordingly, regions with weak or deteriorating economies were first to consider commercial casinos as an economic strategy, which is what we find in Tables 3.1 through 3.3: states and provinces with underdeveloped (Tasmania, Northern Territory, Manitoba, South Dakota) or deteriorating economies (New Jersey and the midwestern United States) introduced casinos earlier. Even Ontario and Québec, historically economic strongholds, looked to casinos when deindustrialization and the liberalization of trade policies with the United States ravaged their manufacturing sectors.[16]

A second aspect of place is its appeal to tourists. During the 1980s, tourism increased dramatically in Australia almost doubling other countries' rates. All the same, Australia is a 'long haul' destination, and the majority of tourism is internal (Australian Bureau of Statistics, 2001b, p. 785–6). Once Tasmania and the Northern Territory made casinos politically palatable, politicians in the remaining states saw both the promise and potential loss of international and internal tourism (McMillen, 1993). Zimmerman (2004) notes that politicians attempt to increase state funds by 'exporting taxation' through fees and taxes paid by non-residents and businesses. One method is to entice non-residents to cross the border to gamble. Brian (2009) found a strong positive relationship between tourism and casino legalization: a 5% increase in the importance of tourism resulted in a 45.4% increase in casino adoption. The competition for tourists and increased gambling taxes provided a strong incentive for the Australian states to launch casinos (McMillen, 1993). However, the evidence appears mixed in Canada and the United States. Bilateral tourism depends heavily on cross-border visitation.[17] Manitoba was the first province to adopt casinos in Canada but it is the eighth most visited destination in Canada (Statistics Canada – B, n.d.). Moreover, Grand Forks, North Dakota, which would be the closest plausible external market for Manitoba's first casino is approximately 150 miles away. On the other hand, Ontario placed its first casino next to Detroit, which was a clear effort to draw American day trippers across the border. Tourism was and is extremely important to Atlantic City, but New Jersey still ranked 10th as an international and domestic destination (United States Census Bureau – B, n.d.).

Place holds further importance for processes of policy diffusion, a significant factor in the expansion of gambling for profit and the establishment of casinos (Furlong, 1998; Painter, 1991; McMillen, 1993; Mason & Nelson, 2001). States close to each other trade policies more readily than those further apart, and political elites tend to be motivated to adopt gambling for profit after witnessing positive or negative developments in other jurisdictions (Mason & Nelson, 2001), losing income to bordering jurisdictions, or both. Politicians in states unthreatened by bordering casinos should accordingly proactively establish casinos, while those in states experiencing revenue slippage and social problems from a bordering state's adoption should move reactively.

Summing up, globalization, regional economic decline, devolution, and the reduced ability to raise taxes created differential impetus for casino development across and within Australia, Canada, and the United

States. Australia initially outperformed Canada and the United States in economic growth and unemployment, both key predictors of casino adoption. Yet the Australian states were more successful in establishing casinos earlier on. How do we account for these differences? Although the Australian states faced similar economic and fiscal crises, they were constrained by the commonwealth government and had a higher VFI that dropped suddenly in the 1970s. Both created additional economic burdens and forced them to rely more heavily on gambling. Moreover, the Australian states were in competition for tourism and gambling profit, which, at the time, was less an issue for the American states or Canadian provinces. While important, this political-economic impetus is inadequate to explain variations in timing and adoption of casinos in Australia, Canada, and the United States. Sociocultural factors intervene to influence people's motivations to accept or reject proposals for gambling for profit. Whether or not a state adopts casinos is partly contingent on the strength of individual motives and the mobilization of resources in support or opposition.

Intervening Social Factors Affecting Casino Adoption

We must move beyond political-economic impetus and examine intervening circumstances that generate support, opposition, or indifference, each of which could affect the likelihood of adoption. What is most important is whether political elites and the people accept or oppose gambling for profit, the measures they are willing to take to achieve their goals, and their power to affect decisions concerning legalization. Social and cultural environments produce individual habitus and both influence perceptions of gambling and potential for resistance. Opposition should be strongest when individuals view gambling as illegitimate and hold perceptions that it will debase community morals or increase social disorder. Religion and fear of social disorder have historically been good predictors of whether people accept or reject gambling. Conservative religious groups and those who view gambling as disruptive have been most likely to oppose gambling on moral or pragmatic grounds.

Religion

The strongest opposition to gambling for profit arises out of religious beliefs. Religious affiliation is a good indicator of where resistance might emerge. The Catholic Catechism is less condemnatory of gambling than Protestant theologies;[18] however, both conservative Catholics and Protestants have been linked to austere attitudes and opposition to gambling (Ellison & Nybroten, 1999).[19] Conservative religious concerns over the legitimacy of gambling are based more in faith (morality) than emotion (pragmatism), and a person's faith is difficult – if not impossible – to challenge which means stronger resistance based in moral obligations.[20] Conversely, casino proponents can build emotional legitimacy by pointing to objective circumstances and cost/benefit arguments. As we move from conservative fundamentalists to the liberal Christian and Catholic churches, views of gambling shift from a faith perspective to an emotional world view. Gambling is illegitimate for conservative religious groups because it violates scripture *and* harms individuals and communities; liberal Christians tend to view the latter as problematic. Religious commitment specifies support – stronger religiosity leads to stronger opposition (Economopoulos, 2006; Brian, 2009). Still, Arano and Blair (2008, p. 2050) found Protestants in Mississippi were significantly more likely to attend church regularly than Catholics and four times more likely to attend than 'non-denominational' groups. Additionally, highly religious, conservative Christians would still question gambling on faith beyond those with strong liberal, religious beliefs.

Comparing religious affiliation cross-nationally helps clarify variations in casino adoption found in Tables 3.1 through 3.3. In the mid-1960s, Australia had a similar proportion of Protestants as had the United States, while Canada had the lowest.[21] But, the Australian Protestant churches' influence waned early in the twentieth century (O'Hara, 1988) and, excepting Tasmania, the churches did not obtain enough support to generate widespread opposition to casinos in the other states (Street, 1991).[22] There are also fewer evangelical Christians in Australia;[23] the percentage of evangelical denominations is highest in the United States where opposition has been strongest.[24] Protestant elites also dominated the political agenda in Canada until the late 1960s, significant in preventing the legalization of gambling (Morton, 2003).

Religious affiliation also offers a partial explanation for differences in casino adoption in Canada and the United States. To minimize opposition, Ontario built its first casino in the predominantly Catholic city of Windsor, where there was high unemployment (Klassen & Cosgrave, 2009). The Atlantic provinces had the highest percentages of evangelical Protestants in 2001, although Catholics made up approximately 50% of the population in New Brunswick and Prince Edward Island

(Statistics Canada, 2003). Nova Scotia established a casino in that region despite opposition from a majority of the population (Nova Scotia Lottery Commission, 1993). Evidence from the United States is also revealing. Data from the *American Religious Identification Survey* (Kosmin, Mayer, & Keysar, 2001) shows evangelical Protestants negatively correlated (– .353 p<.05) and Catholics positively associated (.334 p<.05) with casino adoption and tribal compacts.[25] Including Baptists, those reporting conservative church affiliation are considerably higher in the southern United States where resistance to gambling has been most pronounced.[26] Other studies support this finding.[27]

Crime, Corruption, and Social Problems

A second influence differentiating the legalization of casinos has been the real or perceived threat of crime, corruption, and social disorder. Illegal gambling and the corruption associated with it have flourished in all three countries. However, differences in immigration, settlement patterns, and choice of political structures created situations more amenable to the institutionalization of organized crime in the United States. Crime and social problems were inexorably linked to illegal gambling in America by the 1930s, and ongoing publicity over the next five decades reinforced these perceptions (Thrower, 1971). Consequently, the real or perceived threat of criminal involvement in commercial gambling has been a major impediment to casino expansion in the United States (Dombrink & Thompson, 1990).

American organized crime also gained easy access to Canada because of its proximity to the United States and traditional organized crime (i.e., Italian based crime syndicates) established operations in Montreal, Toronto, and Vancouver (Criminal Intelligence Service Association, n.d.). By the 1960s, authorities on both sides of the border had demonstrated a close link between American and Canadian crime syndicates, which heightened public fears, and framed the Canadian response. Municipalities and federal-provincial conferences further strengthened public perception of organized crime in Canada, and the 1977 *Fight against Organized Crime in Québec* provided clear evidence of its existence and its associated problems (Beare & Naylor, 1999). The extent to which the Canadian provinces were constrained from opening casinos due to the threat of organized crime is unclear. It is noteworthy, however, that charitable casinos did not open in regions where organized crime was strongest (Ontario and Québec). Indeed, Campbell and Ponting (1984) observed that organized crime and corruption would be a major impediment to the growth of charitable casinos in Alberta, suggesting it was a serious concern.

Australia has a long history of corruption associated with gambling, and American organized crime was linked to gaming-machine suppliers in New South Wales in the 1960s (see O'Hara, 1988; Wilcox, 1983; Wood, 1997). Fear of social problems and organized crime associated with Nevadan casinos also produced resistance to casinos in Tasmania (Australian Institute for Gambling Research, 1999). Nevertheless, debate exists about the extent of organized crime in Australia. Morrison (2002, p. 4) asserts that 'it seems reasonable to surmise that Australia's first hand experiences of organised crime have been fortuitously limited . . . in comparison with many previously colonised countries' and she further claims that 'earlier published work found little evidence of extensive or pervasive organised crime in Australia.'[28]

The *Parliamentary Joint Commission on the Australian Crime Commission* (2009) presents a different and conflicting view concluding Australia has a long history of organized crime that included Italian crime families. Pinto and Wilson (1990) also claim strong links between illegal gambling and organized crime in Australia, and McMillen's (1993) analysis of casinos in Australia demonstrates that crime and corruption were rampant in New South Wales. Although its presence across the Australian states is unclear, criminal involvement in illegal gambling, corruption, and the associated social disorder created controversy, public debate, and political sensitivity that hindered casino development in several Australian states (Australian Institute for Gambling Research, 1999; McMillen, 1988b, 1993).[29] However, by the third wave, the experiences of the other states demonstrated that stringent controls could minimize the prospect of criminal involvement and corruption. Thus, concerns over crime gave way to interstate competition and the potential economic benefits of casinos (Street, 1991; McMillen, 1993).

A full account of casino development must include social conditions like religion and crime. Yet, these factors, by themselves, are insufficient to explain variation in casino adoption. The legalization of gambling for profit is the outcome of the dynamic interaction between sociocultural and political-economic conditions. Local conditions generate attitudes and beliefs toward gambling, which, in turn, influence motivation to act. Strong support or opposition and the ability to successfully mobilize will decide if a form of gambling is legalized and the manner in which it is organized.

Likelihood of Adoption

For casino adoption to occur, the elite and the population must agree or, at a minimum, be ambivalent. Strong public demand for gambling might exist, but legislators can refuse to legalize out of personal opposition, perceived or real threats to the social order, or lobbying by a powerful group within society. However, successful proposals in support of gambling also depend on configurations of individual motives, a group's ability to mobilize resources, and the governance and politics involved. Gambling for profit in a society develops from struggles among individuals and groups with competing beliefs and interests (McMillen, 1993, 1996a). The route to adoption is fluid and contingent on the relationship between motives, resource mobilization, and governance. The perceived legitimacy of gambling depends on individual habitus and sociocultural circumstances. These shape personal motivation to accept or reject gambling, which in turn drives interest in adoption and social-norm pressure. Strong motives should stimulate larger contributions for collective action, which can help produce more effective mobilization, influencing adoption. A successful campaign can increase legal legitimacy and may demobilize those opponents who see the situation as futile. Accordingly, styles of governance are important because the state can facilitate or impede access to the polity, thereby altering motives, contributions to the cause, and mobilization.

Motivation and the Likelihood of Adoption

Groups engaged in collective action often face people refusing to contribute their resources to obtain a public good even though they will benefit from it. Olson (1965) argues this is because rational and self-interested actors will 'ride for free' if they can do so at the expense of others. Under Olson's free-rider dilemma, contributing to either side of a casino campaign would constitute an irrational act because the casino would produce a public good for proponents and a collective 'bad' for opponents. Why would rational individuals support or oppose a casino campaign when they could let others do the work and ride for free? In addition, are people who feel morally compelled to act knowing that others will not, acting irrationally? Pinard's motivation theory of collective action helps sort out these issues.

Pinard (1983a, 1983b) and Pinard and Hamilton (1986) assert that three separate and interrelated determinants are necessary before an individual will commit resources toward a collective goal:[30] internal motives, external motives, and some expectation that the group's actions will be successful.

Internal motives include individual aspirations, deprivations, and/ or moral obligations. People with aspirations, such as the ability to gamble legally, might contribute toward a casino campaign. They will also view casinos as legally legitimate. Moral obligations will arise from religious or social convictions, and deprivations will be rooted in perceived individual losses such as a decline in property values. A combination of the three motives drives opposition. However, a sense of moral obligation should generate more passionate involvement than either deprivation or aspiration, and religious beliefs will produce the strongest moral commitment to act because it raises questions of faith legitimacy as opposed to emotional legitimacy.

External motives comprise either selective incentives for individuals, collective incentives for the group, or a combination of the two.[31] Selective material incentives should overcome all other considerations when actors are completely self-interested; examples include increased personal capital or employment opportunities. Collective incentives produce public goods, such as funding for education. Notice, however, that there would be collective disincentives leading to opposition; for example, a perceived breakdown of morality or collective harm.

Particular configurations of motives should invoke issues of traditional, emotional, and social-norm legitimacy. A region's previous experience with gambling and the strength of the gambling culture will determine the legitimacy for casinos based in past traditions.[32] Aspirations, moral obligations, and deprivation should all appeal to emotional legitimacy; simple aspirations should increase it, and a sense of duty and/or deprivation should decrease it. Those who feel strongly about the proposed casino may also feel compelled by social-norm legitimacy and attempt to force their normative views on others. Proponents often refer to utilitarian values such as an individual's right to choose, and opponents frequently turn to deontological moral codes which might include the premise that casinos always cause crime.

Even with sufficient internal and external motives, individuals will only contribute resources if they hold a reasonable expectation the collective action will succeed. Therefore, anything that adds to perceptions of success or failure will affect mobilization through changes to morale, increased knowledge of effective strategies, and gains or losses of resources that can be used (Jenkins, 1983).

Pinard's motivation model provides insight into what moves people to engage in casino campaigns and underscores the tactics used by casino proponents and opponents; both try to alter individual motivations to legitimize or delegitimize a particular gambling activity by increasing support and undermining resistance or by stimulating opposition. Proponents attempt to shift deprivation to aspiration by highlighting economic and social benefits while downplaying perceived or real problems associated with casino gambling. Opponents emphasize the social and/or moral costs, questioning the economic rewards, hoping to persuade others of the impending harm to, or weakening of, community moral standards. Both sides mobilize their resources generating differences in perceived success, and casino proponents hold the advantage since the political and economic elite are more likely to support casino proposals and typically hold more resources.

Pinard's model would also be useful for explaining variations in casino adoption by linking structural components to motives that generate or limit mobilization, particularly among those opposed. Public opinion measures are necessary to untangle why some people contribute to the cause while others do not; nevertheless, we can still derive some provisional inferences.

Regions that were economically underdeveloped or experiencing fiscal stress introduced casinos earlier. Politicians in these regions promoted casinos by promising economic development through capital investment, increased tourism, and employment. Many governments also invited corporations to outline the economic and social benefits produced by casino developments elsewhere. These strategies should have raised individual aspirations and anticipation of collective good, and generated expectations that the casino would appear – with or without the people's approval.

However, if it was this simple, why did adoption vary among different regions experiencing urban decline? Why have some states and provinces failed or not even attempted to introduce casinos? Part of the answer is the sociocultural context in which casinos are proposed and individual circumstances generate diverse combinations of motives that intervene between the political-economic factors. People are more sensitive to casino developments when moral obligation and/or the perceived cost outweigh the anticipated individual and collective benefit. This could be why many casino campaigns failed in the United States: religion, threats of organized crime, or both would have lowered traditional legitimacy, undermined emotional legitimacy, and removed the potential for legal legitimacy. Conservative evangelicals would also be more effective at invoking social-norm legitimacy, which, if successful, would be helpful in soliciting support. A similar, although less pronounced, situation existed in areas of Canada, and the criminalization of gambling prevented gambling for profit for some time.

The circumstances in Australia were different. While there was little demand for casinos, Australians do not view gambling with the same moral opprobrium as do North Americans. For example, 32% of Americans (Angus Reid, 2007, June 5) and 28% of Canadians (Angus Reid, 2007, December 25) consider gambling as 'morally wrong,' whereas Australians are more likely to consider gambling from a social not a moral perspective (Australian Institute for Gambling Research, 1999). Nonetheless, when the Tasmanian government first proposed a casino the people opposed it on moral grounds and out of fears it would produce the crime and social problems associated with Nevadan casinos (McMillen, 1993). The Tasmanian government chose to hold a referendum and supporters prevailed 53% to 47% (Tasmania Parliamentary Library, n.d.). With the exception of Victoria, resistance to casino developments shifted primarily to social issues following legalization of the Tasmanian casino (Australian Institute for Gambling Research, 1999). This should have moved the focus to individual and collective deprivations, which would have dropped as more states introduced casinos without serious public issues. Consequently, emotional legitimacy and legal legitimacy would have risen, making it easier for other states to introduce casinos.

Lastly, the configuration of motives may function differently than predicted when individual aspirations outweigh all other considerations. For example, Mississippi has one of the highest levels of conservative religious affiliation in the United States, but when the state adopted casinos, it gave people in local areas a choice to reject them. Casinos were accepted in the poorest regions of the state, suggesting that when forced to choose between ideology and material deprivations, people may opt for the latter.

Mobilization and the Likelihood of Adoption

The likelihood of casino adoption depends on the power of individuals or groups to impose their will on others (Dombrink & Thompson, 1990, p. 172). The outcome rests, in part, on individual passions and willingness to get involved. A strong movement attracts new members, lowers competitors' hope for success, and affects their mobilization efforts. The larger the movement, the more politicians are forced to acknowledge the issue and deal with it. On the other hand, adherents drop out as resources dwindle or the movement encounters obstacles that diminish its opportunities for success. The ensuing demobilization limits the group's impact on the political process (McCarthy & Zald, 1977). Nevertheless, the type and amount of resources held, the composition and unity of the organization, and facilitation of a group's actions dramatically influence the success or failure of collective action (see Tilly, 1978).

Groups engaged in collective action attempt to marshal both tangible (financial support, facilities, and means of communication) and intangible resources (human and symbolic: leadership, paid staff, and volunteers; previous experience in collective action and capacity to share knowledge; and the reputation, credibility, and image of the leaders and the movement) (Jenkins 1983; see also Dombrink & Thompson, 1990). Gambling corporations frequently underwrite casino campaigns giving proponents a stronger financial base to pay for facilities, media promotions, staff, and lobbying. However, competing interests, media outlets, and politicians occasionally unite with the opposition bringing their resources with them. Moreover, grassroots organization and assistance from national organizations could assist in mobilizing opponents.

Success in establishing or stopping a casino development requires quick and uncomplicated mobilization. Organizations that respond most effectively to opportunities and threats are communally segmented with members who hold similar identities and values and have pre-existing well-organized structures (Oberschall, 1973). This is one reason that many religious groups in the southern United States have successfully opposed legalization of gambling for profit.[33] Conversely, groups with weak social attachments, few networks, and strong external ties have more difficulty in recruiting and rallying their members (Jenkins, 1983).

A group's resources and organizational structure will only take it so far. Facilitation or domination by the state and other groups are crucial to a movement's success, and this primarily involves access to and control of the polity. Access increases in local regions and states with decentralized governments and decreases as the political process becomes more centralized;[34] it is highest where populist electoral systems exist.[35] Barriers can constrain both casino proponents and opponents, but members of the polity – political, economic, and social elites – encounter fewer difficulties, because their unrestricted access lowers mobilization costs and raises their power within the political process (see Tilly, 1978, p. 52–5). However, sometimes *members* reject propositions based on their own beliefs and perceived incentives/disincentives. When this happens, the power differential among the members or different polities becomes a critical component. Adoption is less likely to occur where a politician can veto legislation or a federal government holds power over the subnational units. In short, casino proposals will fail more often when challengers gain access to the polity or when political mechanisms allow members of a polity to control the process.

Governance and the Likelihood of Adoption

Australia, Canada, and the United States formed their governments, jurisdictional powers, and electoral processes in a way that gave Australian politicians more powers to legalize gambling for profit in the twentieth century and affected mobilization in each country. Unlike the Canadian provinces, gambling falls within each state's jurisdiction in Australia, and unlike many American states, there were no legal reforms or referenda required for the Australian states to introduce casino gambling.

When the three former British colonies became countries, Australian and American legislators chose a more decentralized system of governance than did Canada, and the jurisdictional powers for gambling remained at the state level. This affected the likelihood of casino adoption in two ways. First, it created differences in the level of the polity where members make decisions about legalizing gambling. Moving from local to federal polities increases barriers to admission for small businesses, churches, and citizen groups, which means higher mobilization costs for non-members for or against casinos. Federal politicians are also responsible for larger geographic areas and must appease a more heterogeneous electorate. For example, the province of Québec might have legalized gambling earlier than the other provinces, but provincial politicians were not always welcomed into the federal polity. Even if the Canadian government was willing, a *Criminal Code* amendment requiring assent in the House of Commons was required, and it would have alienated many voters in the other provinces. Furthermore, the Canadian government restricted the types of gambling that provinces could operate; gaming machines only became legal in 1985, which constrained the potential for American-style casinos. On the other hand, politicians in the Australian and American states could pursue gambling policies with little interference from their federal government, but it would also reduce barriers to the polity, facilitating easier mobilization among supporters and opponents.[36] The Australian states were not constrained, and many American states could have used gambling as a source of income earlier had legal and electoral processes not acted as constraints.

The Australian and American states also established their own constitutions, whereas the Canadian provincial powers were limited within the *British North America* and *Constitution Acts*. Most American states enshrined prohibition of lotteries and slot machines in their constitution, forcing casino proponents to obtain approval through legal amendments, populist electoral practices, or both. Initiatives and referenda open the polity to challengers and the American states routinely use these electoral practices to decide political questions. Indeed, the American states' inability to introduce casinos since 1976 has largely been the result of failed referendum campaigns (Dombrink & Thompson, 1990; Mason & Nelson, 2001).

It is significant that, in Tasmania, church leaders and members of the upper house (i.e. challengers and members of the polity) united to force open the polity through a referendum, and that it was almost defeated. Most of the remaining Australian states and the Canadian provinces that introduced casinos were careful to control polity access, in some instances through commissions of inquiry: these can provide the illusion of open access to government while limiting the number and types of submissions from challengers. Some Canadian municipalities opposed to casinos and electronic gambling pressured their provincial government to allow plebiscites over gambling in their communities, and the people frequently rejected the proposals.

Lastly, differences in governance provide variations of control over the polity. Governors in the United States, arguably, have a more dominant position than their counterparts in Australia or Canada, since they can veto legislation. There are many cases where an Australian or Canadian premier has stopped a casino proposal from moving forward. However, the ruling party could vote against them, as could the state legislators in the United States; either case may call the political order into question.

Summary

Elite groups attempt to introduce gambling for profit when they personally consider it legitimate, politically expedient, and believe it will not threaten their interests. There are numerous inducements to legalize gambling for profit, and I have broadly considered several that pushed politicians in Australia, Canada, and the United States to consider casinos as a solution to political-economic problems. Regardless of the impetus, politicians and other groups will fail in casino campaigns if the people put up enough resistance to call political legitimacy into question. Moreover, the degree of individual and collective grievances/aspirations will drive resource contributions for mobilization; we would expect faith and emotionally based grievances to outweigh simple aspirations, although material deprivations could prevail. Those with strong moral beliefs should also be less likely to 'ride for free,' thereby facilitating mobilization. Thus, casino campaigns in regions with high proportions of religious adherents, *and* perceptions that casinos will bring crime and corruption, should fail more often because of difficulty in building faith and emotional legitimacy.

Nevertheless, individuals will only contribute to mobilization efforts if they hold a reasonable expectation of success. The types and amount of resources, previous outcomes, coalitions, and access to the polity affect these perceptions. In Tasmania, a coalition of churches, political elites, and other groups mobilized the electorate along moral and social lines, and a referendum opened the polity to these challengers. The remaining Australian states did not hold referenda but some saw barriers to the polity reduced through alliances between members and challengers, or conscience votes; casino adoption, in these cases, was more difficult to attain. Accordingly, mobilization is complex, and holding superior resources does not necessarily ensure a group's success.

In the next section, I turn to mesolevel differences and examine the adoption of casinos in each country and among Aboriginal groups. The evidence suggests that the configuration of enabling conditions is varied and complex. Furthermore, the story in Canada and the United States is less clear than that of Australia's, since scholars have yet to compile extensive comprehensive studies of casinos for Canada and the United States, as McMillen (1993) has done for Australia.[37]

Casinos in Australia, Canada, and the United States

Australia

McMillen's (1993) landmark study of casinos in Australia provides meticulous detail of casino developments in that country and, unless otherwise noted, I have drawn on her materials for this section.

As McMillen (1988b) points out, despite a vibrant liberal gambling culture, the Australian states strictly prohibited casinos from the colonial period forward. In addition, there was little demand for casinos since they did not fit with the predominant working-class views on gambling (O'Hara, 1988). Thus, the introduction of casino gambling was a major departure from Australian policy (McMillen, 1990). The immediate impetus for casinos in Australia was a need for economic renewal and fiscal recovery following global recessions and the withdrawal of Commonwealth state funding. The strength of each state's economy, and ability to respond to these pressures, were the most decisive factors in the establishment of Australian casinos in each state. Nevertheless, increased public acceptance of further gambling opportunities and the growth of tourism facilitated the introduction of casinos in Australia (McMillen, 1988b). The likelihood of adoption depended, in large part, on mobilization within and outside of the polity. At times, members of the polity delayed adoption, at times, a coalition formed between members, anticasino groups, competing gambling interests, or a combination and, at times, community groups mobilized to pressure members to reconsider adoption.

The first states to legalize casinos had marginal economies and looked to casinos for economic renewal and infrastructure that would appeal to tourists. Tasmania and the Northern Territory had consistently poorer economic performance from 1861 through to 1992 (Neri, 1998). Resource extraction and agriculture were the traditional economic sectors of both states, and since neither could rely on an 'export minerals shield,' they were particularly vulnerable to the global recessions of the 1970s (p. 155).

In the late 1960s, Federal Hotels began lobbying the Tasmanian government to authorize construction of a casino at Wrest Point in Hobart. The government introduced legislation in 1968 that immediately sparked intense political and public debate, which culminated in a referendum driven by a coalition of church groups and conservative politicians. The main issue involved a perception that casinos would attract organized crime and the social problems associated with Nevadan casinos. Despite strong opposition, the electorate narrowly approved the referendum, and the casino legislation passed soon after. Thus, the Tasmanian government provided access to the polity through public forums and a referendum, but limited the opposition's opportunity to mobilize after the vote, an important factor when one considers the (narrow) margin of victory. In 1973, a small casino fashioned after British and European models opened in Wrest Point. The state authorized a second casino in the late 1970s after the Commonwealth government further reduced revenue transfers to the states (Australian Institute for Gambling Research, 1999).

Tasmania's successful use of casinos to stimulate its economy through tourism and to generate public revenue – and more importantly the notable absence of corruption, scandal, or social problems – was not lost on the Northern Territory. On 1 July 1978, the Commonwealth government granted the Northern Territory self governance. The new autonomy and loss of revenue from the federal government provided an additional incentive for the state to consider casinos. In 1977, the administration struck an inquiry chaired by the head of the Tasmanian Racing and Gaming Commission who recommended legalization of casinos. Once it had decided to proceed, the government limited debate by withholding opportunities for a public forum. The churches also had difficulty mobilizing opponents. The first casino opened in Darwin in 1979, and although similar in style to the Hobart model, it did not have machine gambling. The 1977 inquiry had recommended against it on the grounds it would cause social problems and crime. Pressures from the operator and the state's treasury department led to a policy reversal in 1981 (Australian Institute for Gambling Research, 1999).

By the end of the 1970s, several events had changed the potential for casino gambling in Australia. First, the developments in Tasmania and the Northern Territory demonstrated the value of casinos for boosting tourism and tax revenue and that stringent regulatory controls could prevent or control crime and social problems. Second, corporate investment in large transnational gaming corporations had sanitized the image of casinos for the public, and casino gambling was becoming more popular. Third, international tourism to Australia was growing at a spectacular rate, but the global economy and Commonwealth revenue transfers were further contracting. Fourth, Queensland, Western Australia, and South Australia had withstood the initial recession, but a drop in mineral prices and deindustrialization began to take their toll; developing the tourism industry was a move to revitalize their economies and increase revenue. Finally, the introduction of large American-style casinos furthered interstate competition for gambling and tourist dollars. However, it is significant that recommendations, proposals, and/ or attempts to legalize through legislation surfaced in most states after the Wrest Point facility opened, but political elites rejected casinos out of personal opposition, on economic and social grounds, and at times in response to public opinion.[38]

Queensland's economy was primarily based on mineral-resource extraction, although it also obtained rail tariffs and Commonwealth grants. As the recession persisted and the price of minerals dropped the state had to restructure its economy, and tourism became an integral part of diversification. Tourist operators had pressed the Queensland government for casinos from 1963 onward but coalition governments generally, and Premier Bjelke-Petersen specifically, rejected them based on moral grounds. Indeed, Bjelke-Petersen sided with anticasino groups in 1973 and opposed casinos despite majority approval from his cabinet. Bjelke-Petersen maintained he would allow casinos if a large majority of Queenslanders approved in a referendum, which was never held.

The motivation for change came in the late 1970s as the state experienced economic difficulties. Cabinet approved a casino in 1981 despite strong opposition from the premier and other conservative ministers. A series of committees followed, and while the government sought input from selected interest groups, it restricted community participation. Opposition mounted among church groups, conservative moral forces, and small registered clubs that sought to obtain poker machines, but the proponents won public support by promising economic benefits and regulatory mechanisms that would control crime and corruption. The *Casino Control Act* passed in 1982, although issues involving operator selection delayed the first casino opening until 1985. This started the second wave of casino development in Australia and the introduction of American-style 'grind' casinos.

Unlike Queensland, the state of Western Australia was not marked by 'institutionalized moralism' and took a laissez-faire approach to gambling (McMillen, 1993, p. 201). Not with casinos; the government used a Royal Commission in its first attempt at legalization. But despite a recommendation for approval, the coalition government refused to consider them since rural conservatives were opposed and the Liberal party was likely worried about an electoral backlash. A further modest attempt came with a backbench committee recommendation in 1981, which the party rejected.

By 1983, the ongoing recession led to a decline in mineral exports exacerbating the economic problems. Reductions in Commonwealth funding added further fiscal pressures. At this point, tourism became a central plank for economic reform, and both parties supported a proposal for casinos during the election campaign of 1983. The Australian Labor Party initiated a committee process to examine guidelines for operation and control of a large-scale American-style casino. The government sought submissions from the public, and the churches loudly protested the introduction of casinos. However, without cabinet support, the churches failed to mobilize the public despite the economic problems facing the state.

The *Casino Control Act 1984* was passed with a casino planned near Perth. The government subsequently set up a committee of inquiry to recommend regulatory options and ease concerns the casino would cannibalize existing forms of gambling. The inquiry denied public access and limited police input. The final report recommended against introducing poker machines into the state, effectively stifling opposition by assuring strict control over gambling policies. The casino opened in Burswood in 1985.

Casino legislation in South Australia was defeated three times between 1973 and 1983, primarily the result of the 'deep puritan antipathy to gambling' (McMillen, 1993, p. 219), a relatively strong economy, the perceived threat of corruption, and a small gambling industry that would have difficulty competing with casinos. In 1973, the Dunstan government consulted the public and allowed community and church groups to express concerns about a casino proposal; the primary concerns were crime and social problems. The government put forward legislation allowing members to vote their consciences, which allowed for additional influence from anticasino groups, and the legislation was defeated.

By 1981, South Australia's manufacturing sector had declined dramatically while the tourism industry had grown exponentially, well beyond that of the other states. Adelaide's tourist facilities and infrastructure needed overhauling to maintain tourism, and a casino complex would be beneficial while addressing other economic problems. A casino would act as an entertainment attraction, increase jobs and capital investment in the construction industry, and provide income to reduce government debt. The government put forward draft legislation in 1982 and struck a committee to seek input from the public, interest groups, and consult with administrators, the police, and other casino jurisdictions. Although the majority of submissions focused on negative impacts and public opinion ran contrary to it, the committee recommended a casino on the pretext that economic benefit outweighed possible costs. However, the bill was defeated in a conscience vote, which was less a response to public opposition than a political manoeuvre to win the next election.

When the Australian Labor Party took office in 1983, it reversed its position and a private member's bill saved the government the embarrassment of supporting legislation it had rejected months previously. It did not hurt that a Gallup poll showed that 52% of South Australians now favoured a casino (McMillen, 1993, p. 226). The *Casino Act 1983* passed by a slim margin but only after the government made two important concessions to provide legal and emotional legitimacy for the move: it prohibited poker machines in the casino and allocated a proportion of casino profit to a hospital fund and the South Australian Housing Trust (McMillen, 1993, p. 226). The Lotteries Commission would also oversee the casino license and would appoint an operator on the government's behalf. When the casino opened a private member immediately introduced a bill to permit poker machines. The government refused to consider the proposal but eventually granted approval in 1991 when market pressures threatened the casino's operations.

In 1987, the Commonwealth government accepted a Perth developer's proposal to turn Christmas Island into a casino resort to attract wealthy Asians. A referendum garnered 94% support from the local population (Australian Institute for Gambling Research, 1999, p. 139) and, when the casino opened in 1993, it immediately became one of the world's most profitable casinos. However, the Indonesian government prevented direct access among its citizens, and litigation problems along with the collapse of the Asian economy in 1997–8 led to its demise in 1998 (pp. 140–1).

The second wave of casino development might have continued in the Australian Capital Territory, New South Wales, and Victoria. However, different economic, social, and cultural circumstances prevented these state governments from seriously considering casinos until economic pressures compelled political elites to move toward legalization. New South Wales and Victoria had relatively strong industrial economies, and funding from the Commonwealth government shielded the Australian Capital Territory from the economic problems of the 1970s and early 1980s. Although ongoing recessions, combined with major reductions in federal transfer payments, created political and economic crises within each state, crime and corruption associated with illegal gambling, well organized opposition, or both prevented these states from successfully introducing casino legislation until the early 1990s.

The gambling environment in New South Wales was considerably different when the issue of legal casinos emerged in the mid-1970s. The state legalized poker machines in registered clubs in 1956, and illegal

European-style casinos, facilitated by widespread political and police corruption, operated openly in Sydney. In 1974, a Royal Commission found links between the gaming-machine industry and American crime syndicates, and Justice Moffitt, head of the Commission, advised that casinos could bring organized crime. Three other inquires conducted in Victoria also influenced debates over casinos in New South Wales. The Costigan Royal Commission in 1984 stepped outside its state boundaries and found evidence of 'official corruption,' and an inability and reluctance of the New South Wales government and police to deal with illegal gambling and associated crime (McMillen, 1993, pp. 270–1). The Wilcox and Connor Inquiries of 1983 further recommended against casinos in Victoria. Thus, government proposals for casinos in New South Wales were met with political and public resistance between 1976 and 1990, based on the findings that the government and police were unwilling, or unable, to control criminal activities associated with gambling. This reason, more than any other, prevented the state from introducing casino gambling despite five attempts by successive governments to do so.

In the early 1980s, New South Wales' economy was reeling from a decline in its industrial base, reduced Commonwealth protectionism for its exports, and cutbacks in funding. Unemployment grew along with cuts to social programs. In 1985, the government announced a state-run casino for Darling Harbour as part of a revitalization project. Before the government tabled the bill, and in an apparent attempt to secure emotional legitimacy, it changed the proposal to include a privately owned casino with the profit allocated for specific state welfare purposes, such as hospitals (McMillen, 1993, p. 275). The government proclaimed the *Darling Harbour Casino Act* in 1986. Following a series of scandals that led to the Australian Labor Party's defeat in 1988, a new Liberal government repealed the act, and the premier declared that the inevitable involvement of organized crime precluded any possibility of a casino (p. 282). He reversed his stance in 1990 after the Commonwealth government announced major cuts in transfer payments to the states. While New South Wales had traditionally relied on gambling taxes, gaming expenditures had not kept up with the casino states, and the government argued that casinos had been the most effective stimulus to the economy and tourist sector in the other states. At this point, anticasino groups lost their momentum in light of the economic problems facing the state. The government also attempted to gain legal legitimacy by: consulting with other casino jurisdictions and police agencies; setting up a public inquiry into the operations and socio-economic impacts of the proposed casino; establishing an oversight committee; and providing a forum for groups to express their concerns over the casino. After further political wrangling and delays, the Darling Harbour casino opened in September 1995.

Casino development in Victoria faced resistance from both the political elite and a morally charged electorate. Victoria had a long history as the most conservative Australian state and a reputation for strong moral standards, which were heavily influenced by churches and created a high degree of political conservatism. Victorians were also concerned about the social costs of gambling, and governments had previously legitimized existing gaming activities by directing the proceeds to welfare benefits. In addition, state politicians were aware of corruption and social problems associated with the poker machines in New South Wales. Although Victoria had less fiscal autonomy than New South Wales (McMillen, 1993, p. 292) and relied heavily on taxation of gambling, governments were unwilling to legalize gambling fearing that it would create social disorder.

In 1979, Federal Hotels proposed a multimillion dollar casino, entertainment, and convention centre complex. It received strong backing from the tourist sector and support in principal from the Victoria government. The Liberal Party passed the casino proposal with a slim majority despite widespread community concerns about the social and economic impacts. However, it abandoned the proposal after competing gambling interests used anticasino sentiments to lobby government members and they threatened to block the legislation. When the Liberal party fell in 1982, the new Labor government implemented Keynesian policies that increased spending, while the state faced increased economic problems and declining fiscal capacity. The government set out to raise revenue through various means including gambling taxes, but gambling returns were decreasing. In response, the new Labor government moved cautiously toward legalizing casinos and in 1982 initiated a public inquiry to recommend whether Victoria should establish casinos. Justice Xavier Connor, QC, conducted the inquiry in an open and participatory manner, allowing submissions from the public and interest groups. Churches and antigambling groups took advantage of the opportunity and mobilized other casino opponents. Connor presented his report in 1983 and advised against casinos; in his view the potential economic benefit did not outweigh the risks of social problems. Several months later, Justice Wilcox, the head of an inquiry into poker machines, also gave counsel to reject poker machines and casinos in Victoria. The government accepted these recommendations and shelved the casino proposal. It instead moved to obtain concessions from Tattersall's for an increased share of lottery profit. New South Wales' announcement of its casino increased the pressure, but the premier stood his ground with a majority of electorate backing.

In the late 1980s, Victoria's economy and federal revenue transfers were shrinking. The government had previously cut services and raised taxes, and these avenues were no longer an option. As unemployment grew, the government began to face a legitimacy crisis. When the premier resigned in 1990, the Labor Party reversed its stance and announced it would legalize casinos as part of a wider package aimed at economic recovery. The government anticipated anticasino mobilization and again appointed Justice Connor to examine policy options for casino development and operations, this time within a two-month time frame. Connor once more recommended against casinos even though it was not within his mandate. The government dismissed Connor's assessment as 'personal views' (McMillen 1993, p. 303) and proceeded to establish a casino using his policy recommendations. A temporary site opened in Melbourne in 1994, followed by a permanent casino in 1997.

As in several other Australian states, casino proponents in the Australian Capital Territory were unsuccessful in legitimizing casinos for some time. The proposals were based on the same objectives: stimulate the economy through tourism and provide funds for public administration, particularly as the Territory moved toward self-government. However, these suggestions met firm resistance from an anticasino coalition comprised initially of church, community, and welfare groups, followed later by existing gambling providers. The coalition also became better organized as time went on.

The first bid emerged in 1976 upon speculation of the transfer of powers from the Commonwealth government and claims a casino would help its economic prospects. Business interests lobbied hard but the anticasino coalition mobilized quickly with strong organizational and negotiation skills. The movement first used moral arguments and then switched to issues concerning the Territory capital's image, which garnered support from a former prime minister along with the incumbent. The Commonwealth government rejected the proposal.

A second attempt took place in 1979, and protestors again mobilized rapidly, this time with support from licensed clubs with poker machines, adding to their list of grievances the possibility that a casino would threaten the viability of existing gambling providers. The prime minister and cabinet were ambivalent, and the federal government again dropped the proposal.

In 1981, the federal government proposed a casino for the third time, and sought corporate interest. The House of Assembly also established a committee to review the situation. Once again, a highly professional and well-organized anticasino group mobilized, but despite their efforts the committee advised that the benefit would outweigh the cost. It also recommended rejecting poker machines in the casino as a concession to the club sector. The committee's response increased the intensity of opposition, and the government rejected the proposal, because they felt it disregarded community objections. Political fortunes changed with the election of a new Labor government and a prime minister who advocated for a Canberra casino. The reversal outraged casino opponents as the previous position was to allow local residents to decide. When the prime minister pressured the cabinet and Territory House of Assembly into supporting the proposal, the anticasino movement lobbied the Senate, which overturned the lower house's decision. The protestors demanded a referendum on the issue and the Prime Minister refused, putting the issue on hold for another five years.

The casino proponents' fortunes changed in 1987 with the move toward self-government and recognition that tourism would provide a substantial boost to the economy. Casino opponents stressed the negative social impacts found in the other casino states and the potential negative impact on the existing gambling providers. However, they also developed a new argument: a casino would damage the cultural significance of the Canberra landmarks. In an effort to soften opposition, the government commissioned a social-impact study and struck a committee to initiate a 'dialogue' with the community, to no avail. The government finally ignored the protests, announced a casino would be built, and passed the *Casino Control Ordinance*. Debate continued in the house, but concern for the state of the economy prevailed. Following establishment of a Casino Surveillance Authority, a temporary small European-style casino opened in Canberra in 1992. The casino does not have poker machines despite lobbying and claims that this gives other Australian casinos a competitive advantage (see Violante, 2009).

To summarize this section, the only impetus initially missing among the Australian states was consumer demand. Australians, for the most part, were disinterested in casino gambling until a few states introduced it. Furthermore, the states had the power to establish casinos without public participation. It is significant that most rejected casino proposals until they faced economic and/or fiscal crises. Thus, political-economic factors were crucial to adoption, but so too were intervening social and cultural dynamics, often within the polity, that prevented casino proposals from moving forward. People objected more on grounds of emotional legitimacy than faith and, even though Australia has a long history of legal gambling, traditional legitimacy did not arise, perhaps because casinos did not initially appeal to the working classes (O'Hara, 1988). Crime and corruption associated with casino gambling and/or poker machines – and sometimes moral convictions – prompted objections and mobilization in many states. In terms of the likelihood of adoption, members of the polity created the first hurdle, often because of their habitus. Once members were convinced casinos would benefit the state or themselves, they had to limit opposition, which tended to be less problematic because challengers had restricted or no access to the polity. Nevertheless, as demonstrated in the Australian Capital Territory, well organized groups can force their way into the polity, especially with help from members. In the end, the legalization of casino gambling in Australia involved a complex and dynamic series of political-economic and sociocultural factors, but most importantly, diverse configurations led to differences in the timing of adoption and form of casino chosen.

Canada

Like Australia, uneven economic burdens on the Canadian provinces increased enabling conditions for the emergence of casinos, but other factors facilitated adoption in some regions and constrained them in others.

Although the Canadian government prohibited gambling in 1892, a 1925 amendment to the *Criminal Code* allowed summer and agricultural fairs to offer modest games of chance. Charitable gambling grew out of this tradition and the first legal casino operations took place at the week-long Edmonton Klondike Days Festival in 1967 (Campbell, 1991). In 1975, a charitable group lobbied the Alberta government to permit a temporary casino license with the funds going to a children's summer camp (Smith & Hinch, 1996). This led to the development of small, temporary charitable casinos across the western provinces, possibly building some traditional legitimacy in that region.

It is no accident that Manitoba was the first province in Canada to establish a permanent commercial casino. Manitoba had the weakest provincial economy and the highest government growth throughout the 1980s (Statistics Canada – A, n.d.; Frontier Centre for Public Policy, 2002) and could not continue spending without additional revenue. Manitoba also had considerable experience with charitable gambling and developed government organizations geared to regulating and operating casinos. The province first permitted temporary charitable casinos at two seasonal festivals in the mid-1970s. In 1985, the government licensed the first permanent charitable casino in Canada and distributed the casino revenue to an umbrella group of charities (Manitoba Gaming Control Commission, n.d.; Manitoba Intercultural Council, 1985). When the province opened the commercial Crystal Casino in December 1989, funds were directed to health research, and later expanded to include education, community and social services, and economic development (Canadian Partnership for Responsible Gambling, 2007). The lack of visible organized crime/corruption, and contributions to public goods, built emotional and legal legitimacy, and it appears that faith-based legitimacy was not an issue: less than 9% of the population held conservative Protestant affiliation and almost a third claimed no religious affiliation whatsoever.

Winnipeg's first casino was intended to prevent Manitobans from going to bordering states to gamble on slot machines (Black, 2008) and to draw tourists from nearby jurisdictions. Nevertheless, there are very few urban centres close to Winnipeg in Canada or the United States (Statistics Canada – C, n.d.). The government also opened two additional gaming facilities, in 1993, in suburban areas unlikely to attract tourists. South Dakota established a casino in the same year; it is unclear how much policy diffusion took place between these two jurisdictions.[39]

Québec and Ontario followed Manitoba's example, almost certainly through a process of policy learning. Given the history of gambling in Québec, the large proportion of Catholics, and the permissive atmosphere found in Montreal, why did legal casinos not emerge first in that province? Québec's economy had historically been strong, but it faltered in 1976 when the Parti Québécois, committed to political separation from Canada, came to power. The economy continued to decline throughout the 1980s (Statistics Canada – A, n.d.; Frontier Centre for Public Policy, 2002), and cost overruns for the 1976 Montreal Olympic Games left that city badly in debt. Further structural constraints undermined both Québec and Ontario's economies in the late 1980s after Canada liberalized its trade policies with the United States. Yet, although Québec had more enabling conditions than Manitoba, one difference restricted casino development in Québec and played a role in Ontario as well: a stronger presence and higher visibility of organized crime. The ABSCAM affair in New Jersey confirmed that casino licensing processes could be compromised, but the Manitoba model of state-owned and operated casinos demonstrated that strict controls could reduce the threat.[40] Indeed, Québec followed Manitoba's example of government ownership and operation. In December 1992, the Québec cabinet issued an Order in Council authorizing construction of a casino in Montreal and one in Pointe-au-Pic.[41] Both casinos were large American-style facilities. At the same time, the government created the Société des casinos du Québec to oversee operations, and it further expanded near the Ontario border in Gatineau in 2006 and in Mont-Tremblant in 2009 (Société des casinos du Québec, n.d.).

Ontario also had few economic choices when it considered casinos (Statistics Canada – A, n.d.; Frontier Centre for Public Policy, 2002). Deindustrialization devastated Ontario's manufacturing-based economy and the bottom fell out when American firms moved south after the Canadian-American free trade agreement.[42] The Ontario government also obtained policy advice from polity members who helped introduce commercial casinos into Manitoba (Klassen & Cosgrave, 2009).

In 1993, the Ontario government passed the *Ontario Casino Corporation Act* to enhance economic development, generate public funds, and ensure gambling policy was for the public good (Ontario, 1993). To avoid opposition, the government selected Windsor as the first casino site, primarily because of its large Catholic population, high rate of unemployment, and geographic location across the river from Detroit where casino gambling was illegal (Klassen & Cosgrave, 2009). The government established the Ontario Casino Corporation in 1994 and negotiated with First Nations bands to operate casinos. The bands receive the revenue minus a win tax for economic development. In 1996, Ontario opened a second cross-border casino at Niagara Falls. The Windsor and Niagara Falls casinos were established to obtain revenue from Americans, and the bulk goes into the government's general fund (Canadian Partnership for Responsible Gambling, 2007). After facing fierce opposition toward the introduction of video lottery terminals (VLTs) in 'convenience' locations (see Chapter 4), the Ontario government placed charitable casinos in communities that would accept them and slot machines at racetracks. A proportion of the revenue is allocated to public good and communities that host the casinos.

By the early 1990s, other Canadian provinces were also considering their options to deal with economic problems. Among the Atlantic provinces, Newfoundland and Labrador and Nova Scotia fared the worst during the 1980s, and Nova Scotia emerged from a serious recession in 1988 with a large provincial deficit (Statistics Canada – A, n.d.; Frontier Centre for Public Policy, 2002). The Atlantic provinces had introduced video lotteries by 1991, and the associated social problems stirred up controversy and opposition. A casino that relied solely on locals would have cannibalized government revenue from VLTs. Moreover, the population base and proximity to feeder markets made casino gambling for the Atlantic provinces risky despite relatively strong tourist bases.

In 1993, the Liberal Party of Nova Scotia took office facing a large debt and with an ambitious reform platform that required additional revenue. In 1995, the government issued an Order in Council authorizing casinos under the existing *Gaming Control Act* (*Nova Scotia Royal Gazette*, 2002, Appendix A, n.d.).[43] Nova Scotia's casinos are privately owned and operated under monopoly conditions until 2020, after which time the province will assume ownership and operation. The Nova Scotia government made these arrangements to protect the province from any potential capital loss from developing its own casinos. Nova Scotia's casinos have performed poorly, which, until recently, likely dampened interest among the other Atlantic provinces.[44]

Saskatchewan had enabling conditions similar to those of Manitoba, both provinces having weak economies during the 1980s (Statistics Canada – A, n.d.; Frontier Centre for Public Policy, 2002) and few conservative Protestants. Still, the province has a smaller population and modest tourist base, and the cities of Regina and Saskatoon are considerably smaller than Winnipeg. Interestingly, Saskatchewan adopted casino gambling during a period of strong economic growth (Baldwin, Brown, Maynard, & Zietsma, 2004), which goes against trends found elsewhere. Nevertheless, the province was struggling with a large accumulated debt, had witnessed the success of Winnipeg's casinos, and was attempting to prevent the outflow of gambling dollars to neighbouring jurisdictions (Saskatchewan Legislative Assembly, April 5, 1994). In addition, First Nations were pushing hard for casinos to assist with their economic development. In fact, casinos came to the fore in Saskatchewan in 1993 when a First Nations tribe opened a casino on a Saskatchewan reserve. The government quickly shut down the casino, but the band sued and the courts suggested the two parties seek common ground to operate casinos. When Saskatchewan did legalize casinos, 25% of revenue was earmarked for Saskatchewan First Nations and 25% went to charitable causes. It is also interesting to note that the citizens of Saskatoon have twice managed to prevent the establishment of a large permanent casino in that city by forcing a plebiscite on the issue.

British Columbia introduced commercial casinos in 1998. The province holds the lowest proportion of conservative Protestants and highest percentage of those with no religious affiliation. It also has a longstanding tradition of charitable casinos dating back to the early 1980s (Campbell, 2000). With a large population base and strong tourism potential in the lower mainland region, the province experienced strong economic growth between 1984 and 1990 (Statistics Canada – A, n.d; Frontier Centre for Public Policy, 2002). The threat of organized crime, pressures from non-profit groups receiving revenue from charitable casinos (Campbell, 2000), and moral arguments, to some extent, constrained the government from adopting commercial casinos for some time. Indeed, gambling was widespread and operated by charitable groups that remained well-organized for mobilization until most were co-opted by the government (e.g., British Columbia Association for Charitable Gaming, n.d.; Campbell, 2000).

Between 1991 and 1994 British Columbia's economy contracted, and small businesses and corporations lobbied the government to introduce VLTs and an American-style casino along the Vancouver waterfront. In 1994, the government initiated a public inquiry that heard from a large number of charitable gaming organizations, and the committee recommended against American-style casinos out of concern for potential impact on charities and religious organizations, but advocated gaming machines outside of casinos (Campbell, 2000). This led to immediate opposition at the municipal level.

When a weak economy and deficits surfaced in the mid-1990s, the government ignored the opposition and proposed new gaming facilities, in part, as a response to cross-border competition from casinos in the state of Washington (British Columbia Legislative Assembly, 16 June 1999). Two models were planned under the draft legislation: charitable casinos would become commercial community casinos and destination-style casinos would be established with government approval (British Columbia Lottery Corporation, 2001). The decision to allow for-profit casinos was met by strong community resistance that included court challenges from charities and municipalities. The opponents successfully challenged the province to conduct further inquiries and forums that would permit local municipalities to decide the types and levels of gambling in their communities. This moved decisions to a lower-level polity, which increased accessibility for interest groups and shaped the number and location of casinos. We can view this process as similar to the referenda that have stalled numerous casino proposals in the United States. The net proceeds from casinos in British Columbia go to 'good causes' such as education, health care, non-profit organizations, and the local communities that agreed to host them.

New Brunswick was the latest province to adopt casinos using the same arguments as many other jurisdictions: revitalize the city of Moncton, increase tourism, and provide funding for public goods (CBC News Online, 8 November 2007). The province was, arguably, more interested in protecting gambling revenue than revitalizing the economy. New Brunswick was the first province in Canada to legalize VLTs and, although there was little political or public debate (see Chapter 4), the gaming machines quickly became a contentious issue. As a result, the conservative churches and anti-VLT opponents constrained political leaders from considering casinos. The strength of the economy during the 1980s also helped.

Much of New Brunswick is a thoroughfare for American and Canadian tourists going to and from Prince Edward Island and Nova Scotia. In 2001, local business lobbied the city of Moncton to consider situating a casino in the area to tap into the potentially lucrative tourist trade. The city convened a committee, but it concluded that the impact of a casino was unclear (Bourgeois, 2001). Nevertheless, they pointed out that New Brunswickers favoured gaming machines inside, as opposed to outside, casinos. This should have gained the provincial government's attention since a referendum to ban video lottery terminals had been narrowly defeated just a month prior to release of the report (see Chapter 4, p. 157). The committee recommended that the city establish a casino and, in 2002, Moncton contracted KPMG to conduct a cost-benefit analysis. KPMG concluded that Moncton was the best choice for a destination-style casino in New Brunswick. KPMG also reported that a Moncton casino would pull more than 200,000 visitors from Casino Nova Scotia, creating approximately $50 million (CAD) in profit, with a minor impact on current VLT revenue, and negligible crime and other social costs. It would also increase funding and resources for problem gambling (KPMG, 2002, pp. 4–6).

The province recognized the potential for community resistance and, in 2007, it released a new responsible-gambling strategy with a proposed destination-style casino embedded in it. To increase emotional legitimacy for the casino, the new strategy called for a 25% reduction of VLTs and relocation of the remaining machines into age-restricted premises with a moratorium on new VLT sites (New Brunswick Department of Finance, 2007, p. 6). It is noteworthy that 20% of VLTs from community settings were slated for the casino; in other words, the province could plausibly reduce opposition to its VLT program without losing machine revenue. The government also promised to increase support for problem gambling and to authorize charities to hold Texas Hold'em tournaments as fundraisers. At the same time, a destination-style casino and hotel complex was announced for the Moncton area, with a suggestion that some profits be allocated for the horse racing industry (p. 18). In the same year, the RCMP announced that it would partner with the New Brunswick government to establish a new gaming division in 2010 (Royal Canadian Mounted Police, 2008). The government passed the *Gaming Control Act* in 2008 (New Brunswick, 2008) and the new casino complex opened in the summer of 2010.

There has been little organized opposition to the casino. Although the 2001 referendum on VLTs was close, opponents bitterly complained that the government failed to ensure a fair campaign. The failed 2001 referendum could have reduced the casino opponents' expectation of success and their ability to mobilize. In addition, opponents may have faced difficulties arguing against concessions linked to the casino.

To recap, the *Criminal Code* of Canada permitted agricultural fairs and exhibitions to operate minor casino games such as wheels of fortune since 1925. When the federal government amended the *Criminal Code* in 1969, the provinces took a liberal interpretation of 'managing lottery schemes' and began licensing small charitable casinos. It is significant that these casinos first opened on the Canadian prairies where agricultural fairs were most abundant, possibly producing some traditional legitimacy and demand for casino-style games. Charitable casinos would also have provided some emotional legitimacy since the funds were going to 'good causes,' not unlike bingos held by the Catholic churches. Nevertheless, the *Criminal Code* prohibited gaming machines until 1985 which prevented potential American-style casinos until that time.

As in Australia, globalization had differential impacts on the Canadian provinces. And, as in Australia, regional economic decline and devolution do not tell the same story. For example, Manitoba, Saskatchewan, and Québec all faced similar economic problems between 1980 and 1990. Nevertheless, 83% of Québec's population is Catholic and approximately 6% report no religion. Moreover, secularization in Québec increased substantially during the 'quiet revolution' of the 1960s. Lastly, Montréal had always been a liberal city with wide-open gambling. Given these conditions, why did Québec not adopt first, or at least concurrently with Manitoba, and why did it take longer for British Columbia to develop casinos than Ontario, Nova Scotia, or Saskatchewan? Why has New Brunswick only recently legalized casinos? The answer is that although they all faced similar economic impetus, albeit, at different points in time, different political, social, and cultural conditions enabled some provinces to adopt before others.

Manitoba had already established a permanent charitable casino prior to opening up a small European commercial casino. It further established emotional legitimacy by allocating casino revenue to government operated 'good causes.' Significantly, no province had authorized video lottery terminals or slot machines; illegal machines operated openly in Québec under suspected links to organized crime. Consequently, while the economic conditions were ripe in Québec, the social problems associated with gambling and organized crime likely led the politicians to hesitate to open a casino.[45] In fact, the government of Québec attempted to legalize gaming machines outside of casinos in 1989 in a bid to control the crime associated with them.

Each province faced different social and cultural conditions. Those that decided to legalize commercial casinos faced varying levels of resistance and reacted in different ways: they either ignored the electorate, keeping the polity closed to challengers, or moved ahead cautiously with inquiries and public forums. Where the latter has occurred, segments of the population have managed to prevent the government from building commercial or charitable casinos in their communities. At times, concerned citizens gained access to the political process through the courts. A combination of moral obligations and/or grievances, combined with effective mobilization that provided access to the polity, influenced provincial governments' plans for casinos and forced them to consider their constituents during the development process. This is very similar to processes that have occurred in many American states.

United States

The economic impetus to adopt casinos was similar in the United States as in Australia and Canada; yet, just three of 23 casino initiatives between 1974 and 1989 were successful, and only 11 states had legalized casinos by 2006. To understand why the casino movement failed, we need to examine the unique conditions that constrained states from establishing casinos. Populist politics, perceived links between organized crime and gambling, and religion have all acted as barriers to casino adoption in many American states.

Legal casino gambling was restricted to Nevada for over four decades, a function of American attitudes toward gambling and the corruption and crime associated with slot machines and casinos.[46] However, public attitudes were softening by the late 1960s, and the image of casino gambling improved when capital became involved in the industry. Las Vegas's overwhelming success in tourism also garnered interest from other states' hospitality industries. As states faced economic crises many considered casinos and other forms of gambling as an alternative source of revenue and possible boon to tourism.

In the early 1970s, New Jersey relied on its deteriorating tourist industry for a substantial portion of state funds. Casino proponents argued that destination-style casinos would revitalize the industry and lobbied for legalization. The state held a referendum in 1974 for publicly owned and operated casinos, but voters soundly defeated it, fearing that tax payers would have to pay for their development. In addition, few wanted casino development in their community. The proponents were undeterred and continued to campaign for a referendum in 1976, however, unlike the 1974 fight, this time the political elite was firmly onside (Dombrink & Thompson, 1990). Along with private-sector business interests, they promoted the casinos as a painless revenue generator for the state, a way to revive the economy and tourism, a vehicle for undermining organized crime, and an assertion of personal liberties over state control (Schwartz, 2006).[47] In addition, supporters attempted to build emotional legitimacy by proposing that a portion of casino profit go to reducing property taxes and expanding health benefits for seniors and the disabled (Schwartz, 2006; Dombrink & Thompson, 1990). Opponents came from two fronts: church leaders who had successfully mobilized their adherents to help defeat the 1974 referendum, and law enforcement officials who argued that organized crime would quickly infiltrate the casinos – a realistic assumption given the history of crime and corruption in New Jersey. Other opposing groups – such as horse racing interests and individuals who had campaigned against the 1974 referendum – decided they would no longer oppose the move (Dombrink & Thompson, 1990). This may have had an impact on the primary opponents' ability to gain support.

Despite being outspent and a minor breakdown in the opposition's coalition, voters in New Jersey narrowly approved the second referendum. In an effort to prevent organized crime from infiltrating the Atlantic City casinos, New Jersey implemented a more restrictive regulatory model than that in Nevada.[48] Following New Jersey's success, the floodgates opened, and numerous other states unsuccessfully attempted to adopt casinos.[49] Many took place in the northeastern United States where conditions for casino adoption were ripe.[50]

Prior to the legalization campaigns of 1976 through to 1988, the northeastern states had experienced lower industrial growth and higher unemployment than the national average (Manley, Wysong, & Favero, n.d.) in addition to a recession and cutbacks in federal funding under the Reagan administration. New Hampshire launched lotteries in the mid-1960s, and they spread outward geographically across the United States beginning in the northeast. There were also a higher concentration of Catholics and a lower proportion of conservative Protestants than in the other regions.

However, several constraining factors were present. The political and business elite, including those from the media and competing gambling interests, were opposed. Casino proponents also failed to convince the public that casinos would not lead to increased crime and social problems. As a result, voters rejected casinos in those states that required referenda, and politicians rejected them in states that did not (Dombrink & Thompson, 1990).

In the late 1980s, the potential for casinos in the United States began to shift with the rise of tribal gaming. Congress passed the *Indian Gaming Regulatory Act* (IGRA) in 1988 that gave American tribes the right to operate casinos on reserve lands. This had several impacts important to the establishment of commercial casinos. When negotiating with state governments, tribes often made concessions that provided funds for state education or tax relief. Combined with arguments about economic development on impoverished Native American lands, tribal casinos became more politically palatable in some states. Class II and III gaming establishments sprang up almost immediately following passage of the IGRA, primarily in the midwestern and western United States where a majority of Native American reservations are found. This led some states to consider legalizing commercial casinos in response. Other states negotiated compacts to share casino profits with the tribes, thereby directly or indirectly, reducing the possibility of commercial casinos.

Following passage of the IGRA, Iowa established riverboat casinos in 1989, and the decision created a process of policy diffusion that led Illinois, Indiana, Mississippi, Missouri, and Louisiana to follow suit.[51] Legislators in Iowa decided to legalize casinos as a response to deteriorating economic conditions and the perceived impact of tribal casinos from nearby Minnesota and Wisconsin. No constitutional amendments were required, legislation was passed, and referenda were held in the counties where the riverboats were to be docked. To help ensure public acceptance, the legislation called for limited-stakes gambling while the riverboats were sailing; this was extolled as a way to limit social problems associated with excessive gambling (Mason & Nelson, 2001). In addition, proponents thought riverboats would appeal to the historic and romantic view of nineteenth-century riverboat gamblers (Nelson & Mason, 2003). Still, a low proportion of conservative Protestants and a substantial number of Catholics in the state may have led to reduced opposition among church groups and allowed politicians in Iowa to consider riverboat casinos.

Illinois was the second state on the Mississippi River to adopt riverboat casinos after it became clear that a large segment of Iowa's riverboat clientele would cross the river to gamble.[52] Unlike Iowa, Illinois was in a strong economic position during this period, and the state appears to have adopted casinos primarily out of competition. For instance, Illinois permitted unlimited stakes on its riverboats. When other Mississippi River states approved similar policies, a slow erosion of casino regulations in the region began (Mason & Nelson, 2001).[53]

Mississippi, with its long and colourful history with gambling, became the third state to permit riverboat casinos in 1990. In 1987, Mississippi's legislators contemplated permitting casino gambling on cruise ships along the coast, and approved a bill in March 1989 that would allow ships to operate casinos while in the Mississippi sound (Shepard & Netz, 1999),[54] and a bill permitting riverboat casinos the following year. Ironically, the state failed to establish lotteries at the same time, because they required both a constitutional amendment and a higher proportion of approval in both houses; not so for casinos

(Nelson & Mason, 2003). In addition, the lottery campaign preoccupied the public's attention while the casino bill gathered momentum.

In 1991, Louisiana became the fourth Mississippi River state to legalize riverboat casinos and the third state to legalize land casinos. Louisiana has a longstanding gambling culture and illegal gambling flourished throughout the state's history. Casinos operated by organized crime were widespread and prospered despite legalization of pari-mutuel horse racing in the 1970s and 1980s (Buchler, Buchler, Credo, & Raymond, 1999). When the economy deteriorated, and it became clear that potential gambling revenue might float up the Mississippi, the state's legislators turned to casinos for economic development and revenue generation. However, the transition was not without scandal. In 1998, Louisiana's governor, Edwin Edwards, who had supported establishment of casinos, was found guilty of racketeering and conspiracy in the awarding of riverboat casino licences (Sack, 2000, May 10). The news sent shockwaves throughout the industry and provided ammunition to anticasino groups nationwide (Buchler et al., 1999).

As with the others, Missouri and Indiana adopted riverboats out of economic need and competitive policy diffusion (Mason & Nelson, 2001). Unlike other Mississippi River states, however, Missouri's constitution required that voters decide all casino-related resolutions by referendum. The referendum passed easily in 1992 with 63% support (Missouri Gaming Commission, n.d.). However, Missouri's legislature could not authorize lotteries without a constitutional amendment, and a lawsuit was brought forward challenging the constitutionality of the vote.[55] The courts rejected the argument, but the legislature still had to pass additional legislation allowing Missouri riverboats to operate games of chance (Maxwell, Egbarts, & Stewart, 1999).

In 1993, Indiana became the sixth and last state to legalize riverboat casinos. Indiana required a constitutional amendment to establish lotteries, and when prohibition of lotteries was repealed in 1988, the task of defining acceptable forms of gambling for Indiana fell to the state's general assembly (Indiana Historical Bureau, 1995). In 1993, the assembly overrode a gubernatorial veto and passed legislation permitting riverboat casinos on the Ohio River, Lake Michigan, and Patoka Lake. Voters in each effected county had the option of consenting to the casinos through referenda, and seven out of 11 counties did so (Indiana Historical Bureau, 1995). Opponents also mounted a constitutional challenge to the legislation in 1994, but the state Supreme Court rejected it, and two riverboat licences were issued the same year (Braunlich, 1999).

Between 1989 and 1996, South Dakota, Colorado, and Michigan sanctioned land-based casinos. South Dakota was the first state after New Jersey to legalize commercial casinos. In the late 1980s, Deadwood, South Dakota, was a small and economically depressed city with seasonal tourism established around the city's historic sites, many of which required significant capital investment to prevent their collapse, but local business showed little interest (Ackerman, 1996). In 1986, a group of local citizens came together to promote limited-stakes gambling on the grounds that it would increase tourism and provide funds for preservation of the historic sites. The movement gained momentum when a fire destroyed part of the historic downtown area in 1987 and, in 1988, the town council financed a casino campaign and gained approval for a casino from a majority of the town's residents (Gromer & Cabot, 1993). The following year 64% of state voters approved casinos (Ackerman, 1996), and state legislators added their approval. Colorado followed South Dakota's example, in 1990, when 57% of voters approved an initiative to amend the state constitution and allow limited stakes gambling in the three historic mining towns of Black Hawk, Central City, and Cripple Creek (Nathan, 1999). Like Deadwood, all three towns relied on seasonal tourism that was rapidly declining, and each intended limited stakes gambling as a year-round attraction.

The last state to permit commercial land-based casinos in the United States was Michigan. During the 1970s, deindustrialization and deskilling in the automotive industry dramatically undermined the state's economy, and the public continuously rejected proposed constitutional amendments to increase taxes, leaving politicians to look for alternate sources of funds. When a constitutional amendment permitting lotteries was approved in 1972, it gave the legislature the authority to legalize casino gambling. Nevertheless, statewide referenda were required, and although numerous casino and slot machine parlour proposals were initiated between 1975 and 1987, voters rejected the few that made it to a ballot. The casino issue was dead by mid-1988 (Dombrink & Thompson, 1990). It might have remained that way had Ontario not legalized casino gambling in 1993 and opened a casino across from Detroit. The Ontario government's strategy to attract visitors from the United States was an enormous success, and it rapidly gained the attention of state and municipal officials. Soon after, local business interests joined state and municipal politicians in pushing for a referendum in Detroit, which local voters approved in 1994 amid reports Casino Windsor was drawing away monies that could be used to rebuild

Detroit's inner city. Although there was no constitutional prohibition against gambling in Michigan, and the legislature and governor could have enacted gambling legislation without a referendum, an initiative ensured the state put the question to a vote among the people (Bean, 2004). The initiative passed by a slim margin of 51.5% to 48.5% in 1996 (Zin, 2004).

In summary, similar conditions that drove casino adoption in Australia and Canada between 1970 and 1990 were at work in the United States, but different political and sociocultural factors reduced the likelihood of adoption. As in the two other countries, global recessions had differential regional impacts; states with struggling economies, facing urban decline, and attempting to grow tourism, looked to casino gambling as a remedy. Interstate competition also developed among the midwestern states. One factor that did not exist in Australia or Canada was the introduction of tribal casinos. Nevertheless, despite the parallel economic conditions across the regions of the United States, most casino campaigns failed and many states, particularly the Bible Belt states, did not attempt to establish casinos. Beyond poor market conditions, the threat of organized crime, corruption and/or conservative cultural and religious values were a more powerful constraint in the United States.

A strong association between organized crime, corruption, and all forms of gambling has existed in the United States since the prohibition era. The proliferation of illegal slot machines, numbers rackets, illegal casinos, and corresponding political corruption was common in many cities and towns. Although the casino industry tried hard to shake off perceptions of links between casinos, criminal activities, money laundering, and corruption, the issue was still at the forefront of the agenda in the 1990s. No other issue posed as many problems for the emotional and legal legitimacy of casinos as the spectre of criminal activity. Indeed, many a governor or legislator opposed casinos based on their opinion that casinos would attract crime and reduce the quality of life within their community (Dombrink & Thompson, 1990).

Religious and conservative social values also constrained the legalization of gambling in some regions of the United States. The evidence is less clear than for crime, but support exists for this assertion. In a 2004 study by Ham, Brown, and Jang (2004), Christian and Baptist survey respondents in Kentucky were significantly more likely to oppose a casino, and Baptists held the strongest views. Citing the same data,

Brown, Roseman, and Ham (2003) suggest that proponents of gambling legislation would be more successful in regions where a relatively large number of Catholics reside. Boehmke and Witmer (2004) found similar patterns with attempts to obtain approval for tribal-gaming compacts, and Satterthwaite (2005) showed that the presence of evangelical Christians was a negative predictor for the outcome of referenda in Oklahoma. Von Herrmann (2002) reached this conclusion for casinos in the United States as a whole. Evangelical churches in the United States enjoyed a revival in the post-war period and religious groups became more organized and politically involved (Caplow, Hicks, & Wattenburg, 2001). Many politicians in the south are personally opposed to gambling on moral grounds, and religious groups compelled the others to move cautiously or not at all. Thus, despite a long history of illegal gambling in several southern states, casino proposals have continuously been defeated at the ballot box or in the legislature.

As Dombrink and Thompson (1990) point out, however, religious attitudes do not stop casino campaigns – mobilization does. Campaigns to legalize gambling could be successful, even where there are large numbers of conservative Christians, if their leaders fail to raise opposition. One example is South Carolina where a majority of voters repealed a constitutional amendment prohibiting lotteries (Olson, Guth, & Guth, 2003). Religious and nonreligious individuals may also disagree on issues of faith, but often fall in line with local cultural norms. Accordingly, opponents could still mobilize more secularly minded individuals over moral issues such as social problems. This may be why the churches have dropped their public appeal to religion and taken up social causes in opposition campaigns; they still turn to moral arguments to activate their members.

Finally, casino proponents in the United States have encountered more political obstacles that, combined with sociocultural barriers, have reduced the likelihood of casino adoption. Legislators are often required to repeal sections of the constitution that prohibit lotteries, slot machines, or gambling. The people, one or more levels of government, the governor, or a combination thereof, may have to approve the amendment. In addition, unlike Australia and Canada where the ruling party makes a decision – often without input from the people – the American state political system opens up a variety of potential outcomes for casino adoption.

Proposals for casinos can come from the executive branch, congress, the senate, or through an initiative process. Each legislator may also vote his or her conscience or follow popular opinion of their district and is also more accessible to lobbying than in Australia or Canada. In addition, when referenda are required, legislators may opt for local community initiatives to accept or reject casinos; the latter allows for targeting areas most receptive to casinos. The governor can also veto legislation for casinos, which has happened numerous times (see Dombrink & Thompson, 1990), although a veto might be overridden. Taken together, the political system of the United States opens up the polity to both proponents and opponents, more so than in Canada and the United States. This often provides both sides with the opportunity to mobilize resources and influence the political process. Proponents tend to hold a financial and operational advantage, but competing gambling interests, local business interests, and members of the polity can add resources in assistance. In short, the American political system is considerably more open to success and failure of casino campaigns. The fact that so many campaigns have failed indicates the importance of social and cultural conditions in affecting political decisions surrounding the legalization of gambling in the United States.

In the final segment of this section, I examine the differences in casino gambling among aboriginal groups across Australia, Canada, and the United States. Limited sources do not permit analysis using the framework from Chapter 1, but they demonstrate very clearly the impact of historical contingency on gambling across societies. [56]

Aboriginal Groups

European settlers treated the indigenous peoples of Australia and North America in a similar fashion, subjecting them to acts of cultural genocide, attempts at assimilation, and segregation on reserves.[57] Nevertheless, the historical paths toward partial autonomy among the Australian Aboriginals, American Indians, and Canadian First Nations peoples diverged, allowing American Indians more control over their reserve lands. A United States Supreme Court act also helped pave the way for American Indians to develop gambling for profit on reserves. As demonstrated in Tables 3.1 to 3.3, these historical contingencies have significantly affected on-reserve gambling among the indigenous groups in the three countries: Aboriginal gaming exists in North America, but not in Australia.

When Europeans arrived in North America, the population density, political organization, and military strength of the indigenous peoples differed greatly from the original inhabitants in Australia. For, example, roughly 250,000 Mi'kmaq lived in the Canadian province of Nova Scotia alone (Paul, 2006) compared to a similar number of Aborigines spread out across the entire Australian continent (Australia Department of Foreign Affairs and Trade, n.d.; Nethery, n.d., p. 73). Many North American tribes were also organized politically within federations that could sign treaties with the Europeans. No such hierarchy or political order existed among the indigenous people in Australia (Council for Aboriginal Reconciliation, n.d.). As a result, British colonial policies in North America were the complete opposite of Australia. The *Royal Proclamation Act* of 1763 recognized North American tribes as autonomous and self-governing: they initially had exclusive use of their lands and could negotiate and sign treaties with the British Crown (Marenko, 2008). In contrast, Britain declared Australia *terra nullius* or an 'empty land,' and although the colonists acknowledged the presence of the Aboriginals, they did not accord them sovereign status since they considered them too primitive (Council for Aboriginal Reconciliation, n.d.).[58]

Following the American Revolution both the United States and British governments continued to acknowledge the diversity and sovereignty of the tribes. The United States government wanted both safe passage through Indian lands and assistance in times of war (for example, see Kappler, 1904); the British also required tribal allegiance to fight the French and, if necessary, the Americans. This quickly changed as colonization increased.

European settlement in all three countries led to armed conflict, but was most concentrated in the United States, where the heaviest influx of immigration occurred. Acting on pressures from the settlers, the federal government initiated policies to displace Indians from their tribal lands and move them to confined areas. The Cherokee Nation resisted and sued the state of Georgia in 1831 to stop the execution and enforcement of state laws on Cherokee lands. The case made its way to the Supreme Court which ruled that the Cherokees constituted a foreign nation but remained wards of the federal government as declared in the *Constitution*. The court also granted an injunction against Georgia, in effect removing the ability of states to pursue their interests on tribal lands without the assent of Congress or under exceptional circumstances (Supreme Court of the United States Judgement 30 U.S. 1 (1831)). This would have a profound impact on tribal gaming in the United States 150 years later.

In 1986–7, the *Cherokee v. Georgia* ruling aided the Cabazon Indians to argue successfully that they had a constitutional right to operate 'commercial gambling' on reserve lands (Supreme Court of the United States Judgement 480 U.S. 202 (11987)). The following year, Congress enacted the *Indian Gaming and Regulatory Act,* and tribal gaming has since proliferated in the United States. Nevertheless, the federal government restricts Class III gaming to tribal lands in states with existing forms of gambling or where agreement exists between states and tribes. Since few reserves exist outside these regions, this restriction has limited spatial distribution of Indian gaming to the western and midwestern states.

The British and later Canadian governments also pursued policies to relocate Canadian First Nations peoples to reserves and restrict their movement in specific geographic areas. In 1850, the government passed a statute that transferred Aboriginal control of reserve lands to the state (Saskatchewan Indian Cultural Centre, n.d.). Following confederation, parliament passed the *Indian Act,* which placed all First Nations lands under federal jurisdiction. More significantly, the act removed the people's autonomy by making them wards of the state, and it contained racist strategies designed to extinguish Aboriginal cultures and assimilate the people into mainstream Canadian society. Under the 1951 *Indian Act Revisions,* the Canadian government began slowly recognizing the distinct origins and cultures of Aboriginals along with minimal rights as a Nation (Canada in the Making, n.d.).

Despite the changes, and unlike the United States, First Nations bands in Canada have been constrained from opening tribal casinos without government consent. The federal government does not recognize First Nations political organizations as 'states within a state,' and even though the Canadian government formally recognized the treaty and land rights of Aboriginal peoples under the *Constitution Act* of 1982, the provincial governments hold exclusive powers to supervise, manage, and operate gambling. Since the provinces either own the casinos or provide monopoly rights to private corporations, there are no incentives to permit tribal casinos unless under revenue-sharing agreements. First Nations claims forced the issue in the Supreme Court of Canada in 1996, but the Court ruled that there was no historical precedent nor were Aboriginal rights to operate 'high stakes' gambling covered within the constitution.[59]

In contrast with Canada and the United States, Australian Aborigines do not operate or benefit from casino gambling on or off reserves, a result of variations in colonial and postcolonial policies toward the indigenous people. In essence, a lack of autonomy and paternalistic policies have precluded gambling on reserves; beyond that, most of the reserves are too remote and casinos would not be commercially viable.

As in North America, violent encounters with Europeans, new diseases, and the removal of mixed-race children from their families decimated the Australian Aboriginal population. In 1860, the South Australian government used frontier clashes and theories that the Aborigine race was becoming extinct to justify creating 'missions' where the people could 'disappear' in a 'humane manner.' Most other states had similar legislation in place by 1909 (Nethery, n.d, p. 74). Indeed, a constitutional refusal to count 'aboriginal natives' in Commonwealth or state censuses meant they were, for all intents and purposes, officially 'removed' from the Australian population (National Archives of Australia, n.d., p. 24). In 1951, the Australian government adopted a national plan of assimilation; it is noteworthy that this was when Canada started to formally recognize the cultural diversity and rights of First Nations. Although Australia instituted a formal policy of self-determination for the indigenous peoples between 1972 and 2005, Maddison (2008, p. 42) maintains it was rhetoric replaced with neo-paternalistic policies. This included a strong antigambling sentiment about permitting gambling on or near aboriginal communities.[60] Bradfield goes further declaring, 'Indigenous peoples in Australia enjoy less formal political autonomy than in any comparable settler society in the world' (2006, p. 80). Lastly, Stanley (2002) argues that a consistent feature of former reserves or areas obtained under land-rights acts is that they generally hold low commercial potential. Some areas might hold promise for developing tourism with gaming, but the attitudes toward Aborigines precludes development; even then, many indigenous communities are concerned about the social impacts and potential loss of cultural identity associated with gambling generally.[61]

The difference in tribal gambling on reserves is a prime example of the way historical contingency impacts gambling across and within nation states. From a political-economic perspective, American Indians, Australian Aborigines, and Canadian First Nations peoples have experienced different historical paths toward autonomy, leaving the American Indians with the strongest autonomy over gambling on reserve lands and the Australian Aborigines the weakest. The fiscal and economic problems faced by the Australian and American states and Canadian provinces pale in comparison to that found on most reserves and, like politicians, many tribal leaders have tried to pursue gambling for profit to deal with these problems. Whether they have been successful is contingent on a variety of enabling and constraining conditions, including their level of autonomy, commercial viability of the location, and social and cultural considerations.

Summary

Impetus for casino adoption was similar in different regions across Australia, Canada, and the United States. However, different internal circumstances dictated if, and when, a state or province adopted casinos. States and regions experiencing economic decline, increasing levels of unemployment, and/or a loss of public funds searched for models of economic renewal and alternative methods of revenue generation. Some states fared better than others. Those with robust economies generally resisted casino gambling until economic decline, fiscal problems, or interstate competition for gambling profit and tourist dollars compelled politicians to consider them. The state of the economy and interstate competition has been critical to casino adoption.

However, whether a state or province adopts casinos depends on many factors beyond economic. The right mix of sociocultural conditions must also be present to generate individual motives that will create support and limit opposition toward casino development. A perceived or real association with organized crime prevented states in Australia and the United States from adopting; it is less clear for Canada, but almost certainly was a factor in Québec. Strong adherence to conservative religious and/or moral values also derailed or delayed attempts to establish casinos in the United States and led to fierce opposition in a few Australian states and Canadian provinces. Motivations aside, mobilization is a critical component of a casino campaign's success or failure. Intense feelings toward an issue will move individuals to act, which is why religious, moral, and social issues are important in legalization campaigns. Nevertheless, the state and other groups can facilitate or impede collective action, and a mix of motives combined with resources available for mobilization will determine the outcome of proposed casino adoption. The combination of these differences combined with economic impetus is what led to variations among and within the three countries.

The political structures in Australia and Canada created situations where politicians could control the polity thereby influencing mobilization. At the extreme, premiers stopped casino proposals from moving forward within their cabinet; this also occurred with governors in the United States, but not within a closed polity. At times politicians in the ruling parties in Australia – less so in Canada – opted for commissions and inquiries in attempts to gain legal legitimacy for their intended actions. This tactic carried more risk when the government allowed submissions from opposing members or interest groups. As shown, the conscience votes in South Australia and referendum in Tasmania opened the polity, and casino proposals were defeated twice in South Australia and almost defeated in Tasmania. Australian and Canadian politicians rarely permit challengers open access to the polity through referenda, perhaps because access interferes with intended political actions; they may do so when they need to create legitimacy for a highly controversial move like a casino. Notice that, as challengers gained more access to the polity, the potential for successful casino adoption diminished, perhaps due to increased expectancy of success among opponents. There is little chance of success if the ruling party ignores the opposition, as happened in Nova Scotia, unless they move to litigation, but then the costs increase for the challengers. Finally, several Australian states and Canadian provinces have attempted to legitimize casinos by proposing allocation of some or all of the proceeds to public goods, creating a collective incentive for the majority.

The American political system is more conducive to mobilization, because the polity is generally open through lobbying and referenda. In addition, politicians can vote outside party lines, which means that they can align themselves with support or opposition groups and attempt to pressure others to follow. Accordingly, there are fewer barriers and lower costs to mobilize than in Australia and Canada. This is why more casino campaigns have been defeated, and legalizing gambling has been difficult to achieve in the southern states. Grassroots organizations can be successful when passions run high, and a vote is the only contribution required for success.

Ironically, there may have, initially, been higher demand for casino gambling in the United States than in either Australia or Canada. The economic conditions may also have been more conducive in some areas. Nevertheless, the political-economic, social, and cultural environments in which individuals were embedded dictated whether casino proposals were put forward and the outcome of the campaign. As with Aboriginal casinos, developments in Australia, Canada, and the United States have been highly contingent on historical events that have occurred in one time and place, but not others.

Conclusions

In this chapter, I explored the emergence of commercial casinos in Australia, Canada, and the United States using the analytical model from Chapter 1. The framework is comprised of combinations of conditions that produce different outcomes in the adoption and spatial distribution of gambling for profit. As I have shown, economic impetus compelled some political and business elites to attempt to adopt casinos. Nevertheless, success or failure of each proposal hinged on sociocultural and political-economic conditions based in historical narrative and conjunctures.

It is clear that economic factors drove casino adoption from 1970 forward. A series of global economic and fiscal pressures mounted as financial and industrial capital shifted from national to transnational forms along with exponential technological development. The resulting deindustrialization led to urban decline, decreasing revenue, and increased unemployment. The states and provinces responded by implementing neo-liberal policies and devolving economic responsibilities to lower-level polities. However, the negative impacts were uneven, and the economic viability, state fiscal autonomy, fiscal imbalances, and geography meant some regions were more vulnerable to economic shocks; politicians in these regions tended to look at casino developments first.

Nevertheless, if political-economic incentives were responsible for casino adoption, why did the pattern differ temporally and spatially? Canada and the United States had considerably higher levels of unemployment than did Australia between 1970 and 1980, and the United States had lower economic growth. Why did commercial casinos not emerge earlier in Canada and the United States? Macrolevel data hides mesolevel trends, but some regions in Canada and the United States must have experienced similar or worse economic conditions as did the early adopters in Australia. Indeed, many of the northeastern American states unsuccessfully attempted to introduce casinos concurrently with the Australian states' casino proposals.

To account fully for the variation in casino adoption, we need to consider combinations of political-economic and sociocultural factors bound in historical contingency. Different historical paths created conditions more conducive in some regions, and historical conjunctures meant outcome of specific events led to differences in adoption, which may have influenced patterns of legalization through legitimacy. In the remainder of this chapter, I use historical narrative and conjuncture to describe the conditions that created variations in casino adoption across the three countries.

Although Australia, Canada, and the United States are federal neoliberal states with a common British heritage, their historical courses diverged considerably. Each country formed during different time periods, under disparate political circumstances, and distinctive settlement patterns.[62] These factors later influenced the impetus to legalize casinos, responses to casino proposals, and likelihood of adoption.

To begin with, each country developed a unique federal system of governance upon formation that altered state and provincial political and fiscal autonomy. Unlike Australia and the United States, Canada developed a strongly centralized federal structure. The Canadian government enshrined gambling in the *Criminal Code* and a small Protestant elite prevented some Canadian provinces from establishing gambling for several decades. Conversely, gambling was under the control of the states in the other two countries. From colonization forward, the Australian states selectively authorized gambling, especially when it benefited community solidarity and good causes and did not threaten social disorder. The American states often took a laissez-faire position until crime and corruption associated with gambling led most to entrench prohibition within their constitution. Consequently, gambling continued to hold traditional, emotional, and legal legitimacy in Australia; adopting casinos generally involved building emotional legitimacy by reducing the threat of criminal involvement and social problems. While illegal gambling was rampant in the American states and Canadian provinces, it did not gain the same legitimacy among the middle class or highly religious. Consequently, while the Australian states were examining the introduction of casinos, most American states and Canadian provinces were either dealing with newly launched lotteries or had yet to legalize them.

The fiscal autonomy of the states and provinces also influenced the timing of casino adoption across the three countries. When the Australian Commonwealth government removed the states' ability to collect income taxes, it set Australia on a path different from Canada and the United States. The Australian states' reliance on gambling increased as their limited tax bases continued to decline, and as the

Commonwealth devolved responsibilities and reduced transfer payments, generating interstate competition for gambling revenue in the process. The American states and Canadian provinces were in a different position. The American states increased personal taxes almost threefold during the period from 1950 to 2000, but became increasingly reluctant to increase taxes and turned to alternative methods including casino gambling (Garrett & Mason, 2004, p. 14). Florida, Texas, South Dakota, and New Hampshire also collected limited or no personal income tax, which restricted their revenue generating capacity, and these states attempted to legalize casinos between 1978 and 1988. The Canadian provinces all have control over personal income taxes and other sources of tax revenue. However, even these were insufficient at specific conjunctures, for example, when Ontario and Québec faced steep reductions in public funds when their manufacturing sectors collapsed following the *North America Free Trade Agreement.* In short, McMillen (1993) clearly demonstrates that economic restructuring through tourism was the principle reason the Australian states legalized commercial casinos. The evidence further suggests that, compared with Canada and the United States, a lower level of fiscal autonomy exacerbated the economic situation in that country.

The ongoing immigration and settlement patterns also affected the adoption of casinos in a significant way. Immigrants to Australia, from colonization until the Second World War, were primarily British Protestants and Irish Catholics, as compared with British, Scottish, and northern European Protestants in Canada[63] and a diverse mix of religious immigrants into the United States. Religious groups have been key to mobilization efforts in all three countries, but less so in Australia than in Canada and certainly the United States. In addition, compared with the United States, patterns of immigration and settlement in Australia and Canada were modest and relatively orderly. The living conditions in American cities during the late nineteenth and early twentieth centuries created pervasive crime, political corruption, and social problems. At the same time criminals and fraudulent organizations more frequently controlled and operated large-scale lotteries, slot machines, and other forms of gambling. A real and reasonable fear of organized crime involvement in gambling appeared in many parts of the United States from the 1920s forward. Thus, the outcome of the immigration and settlement patterns across the three countries was that the United States had a substantially higher proportion of evangelical Christians than did Australia and Canada, and the latter two countries experienced significantly lower levels of traditional organized crime involvement with gambling or other activities. Motivation to accept or reject legal gambling proposals will be grounded in a person's socio-cultural environment and experiences with gambling. Those who are highly religious Christians, who are apprehensive of involvement of organized crime, or both, should contribute the most resources to mobilize against casinos. Based in historical contingency, people in the United States, particularly in specific regions, appear within these cat-egories more than in the other two countries. Canadians are also more likely to object to gambling on moral grounds than are Australians.

Even if motivation to oppose casinos was similar among Australia, Canada, and the United States, the American state polities provide better access for campaigns for and against legalized gambling. Upon state formation, Australia and Canada opted for Westminster parlia-mentarianism, whereas the United States chose a republican model. Republicanism provides citizens with increased access to the polity and it is higher in American states that use referenda to decide major political issues. The ability to have *some* direct influence in political decisions will influence mobilization efforts; it is no accident that few Australian states or Canadian provinces have used referenda to decide gambling adoption. Indeed, legal casinos in Nova Scotia may not have material-ized had the province held a referendum on the issue. In addition, the polity in the United States theoretically gives governors more power to control casino legislation than the other two countries.

Another significant divergence has been the treatment of indigenous people in the three countries. By declaring American tribes domestic-dependent nations within each state, the United States federal gov-ernment unintentionally constructed a situation whereby the Indians could seek to set up tribal casinos. The *Indian Gaming Regulatory Act* in the United States acted as a catalyst, prompting several states to adopt commercial casinos. This kind of legislation could not occur in Australia or Canada where historical and current sovereignty of the aboriginal people is different.

As McMillen (1993) points out, gambling practices reflect the political-economy of a given society. Only the political elite can autho-rize commercial casinos and has often done so after intense lobbying by capital. All the same, social institutions, cultural beliefs, and social practices must provide sufficient legitimacy to avoid political crises. Accordingly, when analysing gambling for profit we need to link polit-ical-economy with the sociocultural and the global with the local. As demonstrated here combinations of impetus, political institutions, socio-cultural influences, and ability to mobilize led to different outcomes in legalization of gambling for profit. Tracing the interactions among these determinants can inform us as to why casinos emerge in one area and not others.

A key distinguishing feature of casino adoption within Australia, Canada, and the United States has been the temporal and spatial variation in successful opposition of casinos. By examining motivational determinants, we can highlight local social and cultural aspects that give rise to internal and external motives to resist casinos. Analysis of the sociocultural and political institutions where struggles to introduce casinos take place, along with the resources groups bring to legalization campaigns, will further link the global to the local. People have historically opposed casinos out of religious beliefs and/or concerns about organized crime and social disorder. Consequently, proponents typically promote casino gambling under the rubric of economic development while claiming it will not increase crime or social problems. In some instances, particularly when proposed for areas in urban decline, this has worked. In other instances, it has not.

Once the political elite is onside, the critical determinant in casino adoption appears to be the capability to effectively mobilize.[64] Nevertheless, people must have strong motives before they will contribute to collective action and not become free riders. Feelings of moral obligation to self, family, and the community should produce the strongest inducements. This may be why mobilization in regions like the southern United States, where evangelical religious beliefs play a stronger role in people's daily lives, appears higher than elsewhere. A group's composition and resources will also help decide the likelihood of adoption, and access to the political decision- making process is crucial. Anticasino groups in the United States have had more success in preventing the introduction of casinos in large part because Australian and Canadian political institutions provide less access to the polity. However, challengers will force their way into the polity when the perceived threat to personal and collective values/material circumstances is strong enough.

In short, the business and political elite tend to be self-serving and will attempt to establish casinos when the move is congruent with their own values and they perceive the political conditions as suitable. Whether proposed casinos will materialize depends on the configuration of motives among various groups in society, and their ability to force their positions on others. Both are based in historical narrative and conjunctures and are embedded in culture, which I turn to next.

4 Lotteries and Gaming Machines in Australia, Canada, and the United States

Chapter 2 demonstrated that historical contingency shaped the political-economies of western states producing variations in gambling policies and practices. Broadly speaking, the neo-liberal Anglo countries have moved further into risk governance of gambling than the European welfare regimes. In Chapter 3, I examined differences in casino adoption among Australia, Canada, and the United States. Overall, Australia adopted commercial casinos earlier than did either Canada or the United States, arguably because the political-economic and sociocultural conditions were more conducive. Casino development has also been uneven in each country, the result of diverse economic pressures and public response.

In this chapter, I highlight culture as a single aspect of the framework outlined in Chapter 1, using lotteries and gaming machines outside of casinos (GMOCs) to illustrate my argument. Gambling for profit is unlikely to be legalized without a minimum of people – most importantly the elite – who accept the activity as legitimate, if for no other reason than it will not be commercially feasible. At the extreme, opposition groups will mobilize and delegitimize the polity. Since legitimacy is the major theme of this chapter, it is useful to revisit the concepts presented in Chapter 1.

Gambling holds traditional legitimacy when it produces shared positive symbols within a group's historical culture. However, traditional legitimacy may be absent, because of religious beliefs or negative symbols associated with gambling. When religious beliefs delegitimize gambling it reduces faith legitimacy; when people oppose gambling out of personal or collective deprivation it limits emotional legitimacy. Proponents of gambling activities could build both faith and emotional legitimacy through inevitability and legalization legitimacy. If people who resist on religious or emotional grounds perceive gambling adoption as inevitable, they may grudgingly give up because they see no chance of successful opposition. Politicians often attempt to promote gambling proposals through inevitable legitimacy by arguing that illegal gambling exists and/or surrounding regions have adopted it, and most people will engage in the activities outside the state. Groups struggling to define gambling may also attempt to invoke social-norm legitimacy to pressure others to support, or at least not oppose, their position.[1] Legal legitimacy occurs when a state legalizes gambling; however, a political legitimation crisis could arise when a state adopts gambling and it fails to attain legal legitimacy. Lastly, social disorder or scandals can quickly delegitimize the activity by creating negative symbols.

As shown in the previous chapter, a political elite wishing to introduce gambling must establish legal legitimacy by overcoming resistance based in faith and emotion, and they will accomplish this most readily in an favourable cultural milieu. Gambling gains traditional legitimacy once it becomes an accepted leisure pastime within a social institution. When the state proposes a second gambling activity, supporters can appeal to social-norm legitimacy among those opposed; for example, people in neo-liberal societies may pressure religious opponents to allow individual choice. Other issues may undermine these efforts, at which point the state must try to create emotional legitimacy by proposing regulatory controls, linking revenue to public goods, raising inevitability legitimacy, or shifting responsibility for potential social problems to other institutions or individuals.[2]

In essence, culture produces and directs motivations leading to mobilization in support or opposition of a proposed gambling activity. Accordingly, the culture of a region should be a strong predictor of the legalization of gambling for profit. Groups also reproduce cultures through historical narrative, which helps explain differences across regions; historical conjunctures transform cultures and are valuable in accounting for variations in gambling across time. Lastly, cultural attributes can be heterogeneous or homogenous at all levels. People can hold different religious beliefs, but still share strong bonds over their national culture. The variations in cultures, at different junctures and levels, help clarify struggles over the legitimization and definitional processes involved with gambling for profit.

Gambling as a Cultural Commodity

Focusing on the relationship between gambling and culture in no way diminishes the importance of political economy in the adoption of gambling for profit. To the contrary, culture is the dominant force in capitalism and drives the political-economic and social realms (Jameson, 1984; Lash & Urry, 1994). Culture is also the foundation of the new economy (Lash & Urry, 1994), gambling is an economic 'linchpin' (Nealon, 2006, p. 469), and lotteries and gaming machines are at the centre.

Lotteries and gaming machines are an important industry for the state and capital, and both derive substantial profit from them. Indeed, Australians spent $10.1 billion (AUD) on GMOCs in 2004–5, which represents 59% of gambling expenditures compared with 15.6% for casinos (Australian Gaming Council, 2007, p. 20). When combined, GMOCs and lotteries made up 92% of the aggregate gambling *taxes* collected by the Australian states; GMOCs brought in 65% of the total (p. 42). In 2004–5 gambling taxes were an important source of income for the Australian governments, ranging from 6.1% of total tax revenue in Western Australia to 15.1% in the Northern Territory (p. 39). In 2005, lotteries in the United States produced $53.2 billion (USD) in gross sales, of which $16.4 billion (USD) was profit (North American Association of State and Provincial Lotteries [NASPL], 2006).[3] Canadian lotteries garnered $8.4 billion (CAD) producing a return of just over $3 billion (CAD) (NASPL, 2006). All lottery revenue went to state and provincial governments. In 2003, GMOCs generated $4.4 billion (USD) in gross revenue in the United States and $4.3 billion (CAD) in Canada; the bulk of which went to commercial operators and state/provincial governments (McQueen, 2004, September).

Fiscal returns from these gambling activities link culture to political economy, but so do research and development used to generate profit. The continuous aestheticizing of lotteries and gaming machines makes them both cultural commodities and objects of political-economic decisions. That is, the production of gambling around which political decisions are made is part of the cultural economy. A case in point, Aristocrat, the largest gaming-machine manufacturer in Australia, spent $59 million (AUD) in 2004 on gaming-machine research and development (Australian Institute of Primary Care, 2006, p. 46). Gaming-machine manufacturers are also boosting machine profitability through artificial intelligence and ergonomics based on player's perceptions and habits (Schull, 2005).

The unprecedented involvement of states and capital in gambling for profit is a global phenomenon. Nevertheless, as shown in Chapter 3, there are important differences in structural characteristics, ownership, spatial organization, and level of dispersion and accessibility across Australia, Canada, and the United States. A private lottery has operated uninterrupted in Australia since 1881 and the first Australian state-operated lottery began in 1916. In contrast, private lotteries in the American states and Canadian provinces are illegal, and state-operated lotteries resurfaced in the United States in 1964 and started in Canada in 1970. Most Australian states and Canadian provinces have legalized GMOCs, but only a quarter of American states have done so. In addition, in 2004–5, Australia had four times more GMOCs per 10,000 people than did the United States and about eight times more than did Canada (Australian Gaming Council, 2007; Canadian Partnership for Responsible Gambling, 2005; McQueen, 2004).

We cannot explain these differences solely through political, economic, or social factors. States must build legitimacy to generate public acceptance or minimize resistance before a gambling activity can be legalized, and shared social values and positive perceptions of activities are central to this process. Gambling practices are signifiers (Abt et al., 1985; McMillen, 1996a) and interpreting the signs affects perceptions, which influence consumption. However, social and cultural milieus frame the symbolic value of gambling, embedding the meanings in individual and collective habitus. These differences in predisposition toward gambling combined with structural factors like populist electoral practices have established different contexts for successful legitimization and legalization of gambling for profit. Moreover, political-economic and social characteristics of societies that have shaped, and continue to shape, gambling practices are the result of historical political-economic choices fashioned within ideological frameworks.

It is possible for powerful groups or institutions to alter the symbolic value of gambling such that people accept legalization with little opposition. Any newly legalized gambling activity could soften up the public for future forms, but it will also provide a reference point by which people can judge each proposed gambling activity. Therefore, previous experience with gambling is important, but the *type* of experience associated with the *form* of gambling is key (Dombrink & Thompson, 1990), and the surrounding environment produces these experiences through individual habitus and cultural values. This is one reason why the adoption of gambling activities and participation in them varies temporally and geographically.

Finally, shifting attitudes during the past century have increased the public's approval of gambling.[4] More specifically, middle-class attitudes toward gambling became more positive (see Morton, 2003; O'Hara, 1988; Rosecrance, 1988). Nevertheless, responses to changes in gambling practices have been geographically uneven, because of ongoing differences in world views toward gambling, and certain types of gambling.

Gambling is a symbolic activity (McMillen, 1996a) and its meaning differs temporally and geographically, a function of individual and collective habitus. Culture, based in historical narrative and conjunctures, partly inculcates predisposition toward gambling, but political-economic and social conditions can still influence perception. People will not accept or participate in gambling activities they view illegitimate out of religious beliefs (faith) and/or social values and concerns about negative social impacts (emotion). But building faith and emotional legitimacy should be easier when the activities are positively valued through traditional/legal legitimacy. Where necessary, political elites will attempt to minimize faith issues by invoking social-norm legitimacy while building emotional legitimacy through inducements or claims the gambling activity is inevitable. Anything that increases the state's ability to cultivate legitimacy should lead to earlier adoption and higher participation. To be sure, political-economic factors, like a state's authority and electoral practices, have often determined where and when legal gambling has emerged. All the same, regional cultural features are present before considerations of legalizing gambling. Culture influences resistance, participation, and the manner in which both are undertaken.[5] Accordingly, local culture is critical to the emergence of gambling for profit, and Australia appears to have cultural attributes that, until the early 1990s, were more conducive to legitimizing gambling for profit than did either Canada or the United States. Diverse culture within each country has meant further variations in timing of adoption and/or participation in lotteries and GMOCs.

Cultural Differences among Australia, Canada, and the United States

Concepts of culture are elaborate, and differences in Australia, Canada, and the United States are too complex to develop fully here. Nevertheless, I provide some indicators of cultural differences that would affect the legitimation and legalization of gambling for profit. Australians have often been described as 'happy-go-lucky' gamblers who will bet on 'two flies going up the wall,' – an obvious stereotype. However, there are stark contrasts in Australian gambling practices, the absence of legal gambling, and moral opprobrium associated with gambling in Canada and the United States, throughout much of the twentieth century. As in Canada and the United States, historically, Australia attempted to control working-class and ethnic gambling (McMillen, 1993). Unlike the other two countries, from the time of colonization, the Australian states permitted some forms of gambling that gained legitimacy as leisure activities within social institutions (O'Hara, 1988).

Shared Social Values and Legitimacy Building

It would be a mistake to consider American, Australian, or Canadian culture as homogeneous instead of groupings of multiple identities and values across regions (see Phillips, 1996). Broad cultural differences exist, and Australians have historically shared social values that generated a more conducive cultural environment to legitimizing gambling. The process of legitimacy building in all three countries has been *political,* involving capital, social class, and religious groups. However, Australian culture has tended to emphasize nonconformity, egalitarianism, (Lipset, 1963) and communal values, more so than in Canada and the United States. Australians also took a different approach to gambling, alcohol, and sex-trade work. Conversely, American culture has been considerably less favourable to the introduction of legal gambling than have the other two countries. This seems paradoxical, since gambling, although illegal, was rampant throughout parts of the United States. Canada's culture lies between the other two countries, and lotteries might have been legalized sooner had the provinces held control. Most importantly, historical conjunctures in both Canada and the United States constrained earlier development of faith, emotional, and legal legitimacy.

In terms of legitimacy building, we can see a major indicator of the differences among Australia, Canada, and the United States in Inglehart and Baker's (2000) World Values Survey in which they examined longitudinal data of social values from 65 countries in 1981–2, 1990–1 and 1995–8, and categorized four ideal types of societies: 'traditional' versus 'secular-rational' (2000, pp. 23–5) and 'survival' versus 'self-expression' (pp. 23–8). They then segmented societies, based on world view, placing them on a global map with traditional/secular-rational on one axis and survival/self-expression on the other. In their findings, they described

Australians and Canadians as close neighbours in terms of social values, viewing Americans as quite distinct (p. 25).

According to Inglehart and Baker, *traditional social values* emphasize the following: an authoritarian outlook with a strong emphasis on religion, the family, and male dominance in economic and political life; a low tolerance for abortion, divorce, and differences in sexual orientation; and deference for parents and family. *Secular-rational values* comprise a liberal outlook with less importance placed on religion or the family; higher acceptance of abortion, divorce, sexual orientation as individual rights; and the challenging of authority.[6]

A second category of social values Inglehart and Baker mapped (2000, pp. 24–8) was *survival versus self-expressive*. People at the survival end are uncertain about whether they will obtain their material needs and hold low levels of comfort and security. This leads to materialism, low tolerance for foreign peoples or other cultures, and a strong adherence to traditional social roles and norms. Inglehart and Baker (pp. 24–8.) maintain that an intergenerational shift occurred toward self-expressive social values in the advanced industrial countries. People in these societies tend to emphasize postmaterial concerns that include subjective well-being and quality of life issues.

These two categories of social values could help explain differences in the adoption of legal gambling. Stronger resistance to gambling should occur when people develop objections out of faith, moral obligation, or a combination. We would expect that building faith legitimacy would be most difficult among those holding traditional social values, since they typically have strong religious and moral views, along with concerns of sanctity for family values.

The influence of survival versus self-expressive values on legitimacy building for gambling is less clear. People concerned with 'survival' are dissatisfied with their material circumstances and place more importance on income and material wealth. At some point, these could outweigh religious and moral objections, particularly if the state intends to allocate some or all of the proceeds to good causes. This could lead some to gamble, hoping to improve their lot in life, which would help account for higher participation in lotteries among the lower classes. Nevertheless, a materialist orientation, combined with the Protestant ethic, might also reinforce notions of hard work and frugality that would deter participation in gambling. A self-expressive culture comprises, among other things, overall satisfaction with personal finances, emphasis on the importance of leisure, and tolerance of new ideas.

Table 4.1   Rank Order of 'Traditional' and 'Survival' Social Values in Australia, Canada, and the United States 1981 & 1995

	'Traditional' Social Values		'Survival' Social Values	
	1981	1995	1981	1995
Australia	3	2	3	3
Canada	2	3	2	1
United States	1	1	1	2

Source: Inglehart and Baker (2000: 40)
1 = Most Traditional   3 = Least Traditional

These values should increase acceptance of gambling. Notice, however, that quality of life issues may lower emotional legitimacy if crime and social problems are associated with a specific form of gambling. Nevertheless, emotional legitimacy should be high where these issues are not present. Using Inglehart and Baker's (2000, p. 40) mapping of 38 countries, I compared levels of traditional values in Australia, Canada, and the United States at two points in time – 1981 and 1995. As shown in Table 4.1, the overall culture in the United States has been more traditional than that of Canada, which in 1981, was slightly more so than Australia's.[7] In fact, Americans had become more traditional by the 1990s. Canada and Australia began to take divergent paths, with Canada moving slightly beyond Australia in terms of secular-rational beliefs, right at the point when Canada began liberalizing its gambling laws. We can also see that Australia outranked Canada and the United States as a more self-expressive society between 1981 and 1995. The United States apparently surpassed Canada by 1995, but Adams (2003) observes that social values in the United States, between 1992 and 2000, became more survival oriented while Canadians continued to move toward self-expression.

The evidence from the World Social Values surveys provides one indicator that culture influenced the emergence of legal gambling in Australia, Canada, and the United States. Australia, initially, had the least traditional and most self-expressive culture and tended to adopt lotteries and casinos earlier. The findings further suggest that regions of the United States have not readily legalized different gambling practices, in part, because a strong traditional culture based in Protestant values has prevented state politicians from building faith legitimacy. This is in spite of the movement toward a more self-expressive society.

As noted in Chapter 3, some Australian states and Canadian provinces also had difficulty building faith legitimacy for casinos, although political elites restricted access to the polity and influenced the outcome.

However, Inglehart and Baker's (2000) cultural attributes of each country only take us so far. The World Values Survey does not allow us to account for regional differences. Furthermore, if these social values were the main predictors, we would expect the least traditional and most self-expressive countries (Sweden, The Netherlands, and Norway) to lead the world in gambling participation, and this is not the case. There are other cultural differences, important to legitimation of gambling, that the World Social Values surveys fail to capture. For example, although Inglehart and Baker (2000) consider Australia and Canada close cultural neighbours, Pringle argues that most English speakers would initially find Australia much like the 'Mother Country,' but would quickly discover it was much different:

> although it is true that ninety percent of Australians are of British descent, they were never, so to speak, an average sample. There were more Irish, Scotch, Welsh and less English, more Roman Catholics and less Protestants, more working class and less middle class. It was not a case of minnows scooped from a little pond and dropped into a big one, but of two cooks who use the same recipe to make a cake but mix the ingredients in quite different proportions. The result is very different cakes. (1959, pp. 14–16)

The difference in 'recipes' left Australians more egalitarian[8] and particularistic (Lipset, 1963), demonstrated by the concept of 'mateship,' described as 'volunteering, helping others and pulling together' (Phillips & Smith, 2000, p. 217). Mateship was important in the establishment of service and social clubs in Australia, which played a significant role in building emotional legitimacy for the legalization of gaming machines in New South Wales (see Caldwell, 1972; Hing, 2000, 2006). It is important to note, however, that corruption, crime, and social problems involved with poker machines in these clubs *reduced* their legitimacy, making it difficult to introduce the machines and/or casinos in some Australian states. Voluntary associations also exist in Canada and the United States, but appear more central to the Australian national identity (Phillips & Smith, 2000).

Australians also have a vernacular that most Americans and Canadians would find confusing. One colloquial expression some Australians use to describe themselves and their values is 'larrikinism.' Metcalfe

(1985) describes the larrikin culture of Australian coal miners in the nineteenth century as 'mock[ing] the values which respectable society [of the time] holds dear and . . . celebrat[ing] the very behaviour which draws bourgeois condemnation' (1985, p. 6). He further claims the miners approached life from a happy-go-lucky perspective full of hedonism and disregard for 'qualities achieved through education or organised religion' (p. 6). Some in Australia embrace individuals who embody 'larrikinism,' which is consistent with other aspects of Australian identity like 'giv[ing] it a go' and 'having a good time' (Phillips & Smith, 2000, p. 217).

The historical treatment of alcohol and sex-trade work provides further insight into attitudes held by many Australians over issues typically considered immoral in Canada and the United States. All three countries restricted the sale and consumption of alcohol to some degree following the First World War, but Australia restricted hours of consumption instead of total prohibition (Dupré, 2004); this had the unintended consequence of encouraging binge drinking (Fiske, Hodge, & Turner, 1988). In Canada, the federal government let the provinces decide, and all but Québec banned alcohol by 1916.[9] Most provinces repealed the legislation by the mid-1920s, although Prince Edward Island remained dry until 1948. In the United States, the federal government banned all commercial production and consumption of alcohol as part of the war effort in 1917. The *18th Amendment* to the constitution and the *Volstead Act* followed, and as of 1 January 1920, the United States prohibited the production, transportation, and sale of alcohol anywhere in the country. The laws proved too difficult to enforce and were repealed in 1933.

While the successful restriction of alcohol in Australia, and prohibition in Canada and the United States, were the direct result of powerful institutions and groups asserting their power over others, as with gambling, we can link the various outcomes among the three countries to social and cultural differences. The prohibition movement was driven by a Protestant, Anglo-Saxon, middle-class world view. As a result, the movement was less successful wherever the working classes and/or other ethnic or religious groups were strong enough to resist (Dupré, 2004). This is why prohibition went further in the United States. There was a larger population of evangelical Protestants who found support among capitalists wishing to maintain or increase workplace productivity. In contrast with the United States, a sizeable proportion of the population in Canada and Australia were Anglican and Catholic, and just as with gambling, these religious groups were opposed to banning alcohol consumption. Of the three countries, Australia had the highest proportion of Catholics and Anglicans, lower support from the business community, and the working class held more influence in the political realm (Dupré, 2004; see O'Hara, 1988). This combination would also have influenced the moral climate surrounding some forms of gambling.

It appears that the historical variations in responses to moral issues have lasted to this day. For instance, Australians seem more tolerant toward drinking and sex-trade work, whereas both have been associated, along with gambling, with vice in Canada and the United States. In one study, Berger, Snortum, Homel, Hauge, and Loxley compared Australian and American drinking habits and observed that, 'Australians cherish their hard-drinking, beer-swilling image, and drinkers are more likely to consume large amounts of alcohol at frequent intervals' (1990, p. 458). We find further indications that Australians hold a greater acceptance for drinking in World Health Organization (WHO) data. Of 85 countries, the WHO ranked Australia 35th (9.19 litres), the United States 41st (8.51 litres) and Canada 43rd (8.26 litres) in terms of total recorded per capita pure alcohol consumption for those over 15 years of age (World Health Organization, 2004, pp. 11–12). In addition, the rate of 'last year abstainers' among the adult population in Australia was 17.5% (2001) compared with 22% in Canada (1998–9) and 33.9% in the United States (p. 26). Australians also appear more tolerant when it comes to sex-trade work, which is legal in most states: the Australia Capital Territory, New South Wales, Queensland, and Victoria all permit brothels; the other states have a mixture of laws and regulations, some of which are similar to those of Canada.[10] Sex-trade work in Canada is legal, but brothels and public solicitation are not. In the United States, Nevada permits sex-trade workers but only in counties with less than 400,000 residents (Nevada Legislature, n.d.). Until recently, a loophole in Rhode Island legislation also allowed sex-trade work in private spaces. It is illegal in the remaining American states, and faces varying levels of enforcement.

Lastly, looking at attitudes toward nonmarital sexual relations at Table 4.2, we find a different pattern than the Australia – Canada – United States array above. In 1998, Australians were least likely to consider extramarital sex as 'always wrong'; Canadians held slightly more tolerant attitudes about sexual relations among those under 16 years of age and considerably more tolerance with regard to sexual orientation.

Table 4.2   Attitudes towards Non-marital Sex in Australia, Canada, and the United States – 1998

	Australia %	Canada %	United States %
Sex Before Marriage Always Wrong	13	12	29
Sex Before 16 Always Wrong	61	55	71
Extramarital Sex Always Wrong	59	68	80
Homosexual Sex Always Wrong	55	39	70

Source: Widmer et al. (1998: 351)

Americans displayed the most conservative attitudes about all four types of sexual relations.

The foregoing point to cultural variation among Australia, Canada, and the United States that suggests Australia had, and continues to have, a culture more conducive to the legalization and participation in gambling than do Canada and the United States. This began to change in the mid-1990s, but the evidence indicates that American culture – specified by region – is still the least open to legalized gambling. Australians are more likely to share nontraditional and self-expressive social values; they consume more alcohol per capita and are least likely to abstain; their legal culture displays a tolerance toward alcohol consumption and sex-trade work; and they hold more permissive attitudes toward sexual relations than do Americans. These factors, combined with convictions of nonconformity, egalitarianism, and the early acceptance of some forms of gambling as leisure activities, enabled the Australian states to legalize lotteries earlier than did Canada and the United States. The perception of gambling as a social institution has also meant higher access to gaming machines and increased participation in some gambling activities. Political, economic, and social factors have been important to legalization and participation, but primarily within the context of building legitimacy for each gambling activity. That is, historical events, like lottery fraud in the United States, delegitimized gambling activities; crime, social problems – and evangelical Protestants in many regions – made it difficult for political elites to build legitimacy thereafter.

In sum, the historically bound cultural trajectories of each country created different environments where groups struggled to develop legitimacy for specific gambling activities. In the remainder of this chapter, I examine the legalization of lotteries and GMOCs, with an emphasis on the processes of legitimation that enabled, or constrained, adoption in Australia, Canada, and the United States. Nevertheless, legitimacy building is entwined with the political realm, and the legalization of lotteries and GMOCs has been influenced by a complex arrangement of political-economic and sociocultural factors I cannot fully describe here.[11]

Adoption of Lotteries in Australia, Canada, and the United States

The legalization of lotteries in Australia, Canada, and the United States has involved minimizing religious and moral objections, and convincing the people that lotteries would provide communal benefits. The impetus to introduce lotteries has always been economic, but the capacity to build legitimacy for lotteries has differed in each country. Nevertheless, there are similar scenarios, keeping in mind that these are ideal types. In the first, states cannot produce faith or emotional legitimacy because of religious or moral opposition. This has occurred in the southern United States. In the second scenario, states ignore religious opposition, or undermine it, through promises of public goods that appeal to emotional legitimacy. Individuals who desire the collective good may try to produce social legitimacy by pressuring opponents to accept lotteries. The early adopting Australian and American states went through this process. In the third scenario, nearby states have legal lotteries, and other states try to overcome opposition by promising public goods and invoking inevitability legitimacy; that is, the state will continue to lose revenue if it does not adopt as well. Production of social-norm legitimacy is typically involved. A few Canadian provinces, several late adopters in Australia, and most late adopters in the United States have followed this course. In the final scenario, a majority accept lotteries as positive because tradition or examples from nearby states provide inevitable and/or legal legitimacy. Several of the last states and provinces to adopt lotteries among the three countries have followed this pattern.

The differential adoption of lotteries across the three countries is the result of historically contingent factors in Britain and the United States. In 1826, the British prohibited lotteries, which prevented the building of traditional legitimacy among the middle-class elite in Australia and Canada. One Australian state authorized a private sweepstakes in the late 1800s and state-operated lotteries followed over the next several decades. Canada closely followed Britain's example, and the federal government restricted the provinces from establishing lotteries. Given the opportunity, Québec would almost certainly have established state-operated lotteries at the same time as the early Australian adopters. Paradoxically, the American colonies inherited traditional legitimacy for lotteries from Britain, and they were widespread before corruption, scandal, and social problems led to delegitimization. Ongoing, illegal numbers rackets further reduced emotional legitimacy, and the American states have experienced the most difficulty introducing lotteries.

Lotteries in Australia

Although there was traditional legitimacy for wagering on horses among the Australian middle classes, it did not translate into acceptance for lotteries. However, sweepstakes can be organized around horse races, and wagering a small stake for a large prize fit with the working-class gambling culture of the day (O'Hara, 1988). In the 1880s, Tattersall's built up a successful sweepstakes operation in Sydney that quickly developed legitimacy among the players, a result of the company's honesty and respectability (p. 99). However, its success also attracted the indignation of evangelical Protestant reformers who successfully pushed to have Tattersall's outlawed in several Australian colonies. In 1895, Tasmania was first to authorize a lottery when it licensed Tattersall's to operate a sweepstakes from the state (p. 101).[12] When Tattersall's moved to Hobart, the Protestant churches were outraged. The Premier ignored the opposition and legalized Tattersall's operations while suppressing other gaming and betting; the state thereby controlled gambling by licensing those forms it deemed suitable (pp. 101–2). Despite attempts by the Commonwealth government to disrupt operations, Tattersall's flourished in Tasmania and several other Australian colonies.

Twenty years passed before another state established a lottery, in large part because of the Australian states' unwillingness or inability to develop faith legitimacy among evangelical reformers (O'Hara, 1988). Haig (1985) suggests that the states may have steered clear of the political risk, since public demand for sweepstakes was initially low. Nevertheless, Queensland took a chance in 1916, and established a lottery under the title the 'Golden Casket.' The first several draws provided funds for the war effort, and the state directed revenue to hospitals, presumably to build emotional legitimacy (see O'Hara, 1988). The Golden Casket soon caught on and Haig (1985) reports that Tattersall's and the Queensland state lottery were paying 29%

Table 4.3   Period of Introduction of Lotteries in Australia as of 2005

State	To 1970	1970–5	1976–80	1981–5	1986–90	1991–5	1996–2000	2001–5
Australian Capital Territory	1							
New South Wales	2							
Northern Territory				1	2			
Queensland	2							
South Australia	2							
Tasmania	1							
Victoria	1							
Western Australia	2							

Sources: Australian Institute for Gambling Research 1999; O'Hara 1988; State Lottery Agencies
1 – Commercial   2 – Public

and 25% of revenue respectively to the Tasmanian and Queensland governments (pp. 38–9).

Australia now had two operating models of lotteries, and states had proven that they could successfully manage both. Still, as O'Hara (1988) points out, Queensland demonstrated the state could morally justify its actions while obtaining additional revenue for general welfare purposes. Tattersall's, on the other hand, provided revenue to the state, but was on less morally defensible ground and lacked a nexus between the state, control of gambling, and projects deemed a worthy cause (Australian Institute for Gambling Research, 1999). In other words, Queensland's adoption of lotteries held a better promise of overcoming religious opposition through emotional and legal legitimacy.

New South Wales was the third Australian state to consider lotteries, after social institutions, including local hospitals, applied political pressure (O'Hara, 1988). Nevertheless, the government of the day thought the issue politically sensitive, and did not seriously examine it again until 1930, at which time it proposed a state lottery (p. 173). The idea drew immediate moral protests from the churches (New South Wales Lotteries, n.d.). The Premier overcame the opposition by appealing to emotional and inevitability legitimacy, proclaiming that the depression had reduced available funds for hospitals, and that if the state could not generate additional revenue through lotteries, he would have to close them (New South Wales Lotteries, n.d.). The New South Wales lottery began in 1931.

At this point, interstate policy learning spread to the remaining non-lottery states. Each state recognized it was losing potential income across state lines. Queensland and New South Wales had also proven that states could use lotteries as a politically safe and legitimate way to alleviate fiscal stress on the state by allocating the proceeds to 'good causes' (O'Hara, 1988). Accordingly, in 1933, Western Australia cited the depression as a reason to launch its own lottery to assist 'people in need.' In 1936, the South Australian government also wanted to introduce a lottery, but given the high number of evangelical Christians, it moved more cautiously by appointing a Royal Commission to examine the issue. The Commission recommended against a lottery, citing South Australia's small market and the overwhelming competition it would face from Tattersall's and the New South Wales lottery (p. 173).

In the 1950s, the state of Victoria made a deal with Tattersall's that saw the company relocate its headquarters to Melbourne in exchange for state authorization of Tattersall's products (p. 174). O'Hara (1988) observes that the establishment of a lottery in Victoria marked the end of government disapproval of lotteries. Still, it took the South Australian government a further 14 years to reconsider its position and it officially launched a lottery in 1967, but only after holding a referendum on the subject two years earlier (South Australian Lotteries, n.d.). The remaining two states resisted lotteries out of economic concerns. The Australian Capital Territory decided against a lottery because of its small population base. It then negotiated revenue-sharing arrangements with the NSW Lotteries Corporation and the Victoria government allowing NSW Lotteries and Tattersall's to market and distribute lottery products throughout the territory (ACT Gambling and Racing Commission, 2003). Tattersall's has also operated lotteries in the Northern Territory since 1978 (McMillen & Togni, 2000). In addition, a second lottery – the 'Territorian' – was established, but privatized in 1995. The lottery was unique to Australia in that it conducted its business through the mail (p. 93), but it was unprofitable and closed in 2004 (Personal contact – Joanne Boustead, Northern Territory Treasury, 2006).

To summarize, legal lotteries emerged in Australia during the late nineteenth century and slowly became institutionalized throughout the twentieth century. As O'Hara (1988) observes, the mainland state's experiences with Tattersall's led to a belief that lotteries were inevitable and, when Queensland linked lotteries to public welfare expenditure, it provided an example that the other states could follow. Nevertheless, lotteries were politically contentious (McMillen, 1993), particularly in those states with the highest percentage of evangelicals. In 1901, South Australia had the highest number at 40% followed by Victoria with 36%; the remaining states had between 22% and 26% (Author's calculations from New Advent Catholic Encyclopaedia, Retrieved February 15, 2010 from http://www.newadvent.org/cathen/02113b.htm). While this might lead to the conclusion that South Australia and Victoria – the two states with the highest percentage of evangelicals – were constrained by religious groups from adopting lotteries, all states experienced indignation from moral reformers over lotteries and other forms of gambling. The key was overcoming, or ignoring, religious objections and building emotional legitimacy, at times by invoking the inevitability of other lotteries, or the failure of welfare-state services without lottery revenue. Finally, the working classes strongly approved of lotteries, because they could win large sums of money from a small stake (O'Hara, 1988). Emotional legitimacy would have been easier to build and maintain once working-class cultural values surrounding gambling came to be seen as more 'Australian' than the predominantly middle-class culture of the reformers, which began to take hold in the 1920s (O'Hara, 1988).

Lotteries in Canada

As shown in Table 4.4, legal state-operated lotteries did not begin in Canada until 1970. As in Australia and the United States, the working classes approved of, and participated in, illegal lotteries. However, Protestant middle-class culture dominated the federal political process in Canada (Campbell, 1994; Morton, 2003; Osborne, 1989). A linguistic and geographically segmented cultural division was also present with Catholic francophone Québécois on one side and Protestant Anglo-Saxons on the other. Lotteries might have appeared earlier in Canada had Catholics been more geographically dispersed, and/or the provinces controlled gambling laws.

In 1892, Canada brought all laws regarding gaming and wagering under the *Criminal Code*, and few changes occurred with legal gambling over the next 80 years (see Morton, 2003). This is because a small, but dominant, Protestant elite had their religious and social world views entrenched in the *Criminal Code*, and they were successful in preventing major reform until the 1960s. The initial argument for prohibiting

Table 4.4   Period of Introduction of Lotteries in Canada as of 2005

Province	To 1970	1970–5	1976–80	1981–5	1986–1990	1991–5	1996–2000	2001–5
Alberta		2						
British Columbia		2						
Manitoba		2						
New Brunswick			2					
Newfoundland			2					
Nova Scotia			2					
Ontario		2						
Prince Edward Island			2					
Québec		2						
Saskatchewan		2						

Source: Provincial Gaming Agencies
1 – Commercial   2 – Public

games of chance fell within the realm of faith legitimacy: gambling undermined the Protestant work ethic and family values (Campbell, 1994; Morton, 2003). As the culture shifted from religious to secular values, gambling opponents argued that links with organized crime posed threats to public order and governance. This undermined efforts to build emotional legitimacy. By the 1960s, the federal government initiated public attempts to alter middle-class perceptions of lotteries by claiming state-operated lotteries would reduce criminal involvement, while providing revenue for the growing welfare state. Several provinces would use this same argument when introducing gaming machines outside casinos.

Gambling flourished in Canada between 1900 and 1969, because the laws were difficult to enforce, and the authorities applied them selectively and unevenly. The jurisdictional division of power was at issue: the federal government passed the laws and left the provinces to enforce them. Moreover, the police considered gambling a victimless crime, although they generally prosecuted working-class, Asian, and non-anglophone gamblers. The cultural environments in Québec, Manitoba, and British Columbia were also more open and tolerant toward gambling than those of Ontario or Nova Scotia (Morton 2003).[13] As illustration, Morton cites several examples of commercial lotteries in British Columbia and a large charitable lottery in Québec City that operated between 1905 and the 1920s. It was only when the operations became too successful, or widely known, that the authorities shut them down (p. 53).

As in Australia, the depression provided an opportunity for the Canadian provinces to generate legitimacy for lotteries, but the result was not the same. Municipalities and provincial governments attempted to introduce lotteries to provide revenue for hospitals and other social projects. Supporters argued that there was no clear consensus about the morality of lotteries, that existing laws were ineffective, that foreign lotteries were siphoning funds out of the country, and that it would be a voluntary tax which would provide revenue for hospitals.[14] Opponents cited church opposition on moral grounds, along with a British Royal Commission that rejected lotteries. They further argued that the Irish Sweepstakes were ineffective in capturing revenue and, although it might be a voluntary tax, it would place undue burden on the poor. In the end, the Protestant world view dominated attempts to build legitimacy for lotteries (Osborne, 1989; Morton, 2003).

Another chance for legitimation came in 1954, when a parliamentary committee sat to consider the issue, and lotteries inched closer toward legal legitimacy. After gathering submissions and reviewing the evidence, which included representation from Australia, the committee reached several conclusions. They maintained that illegal lotteries were popular, but difficult to police, and advocated a rigorous licensing system for legal lotteries. At the same time, they declared lotteries ineffective in raising revenue, and recommended against providing operational authority to the provinces. Osborne considered this a 'cautious and conservative' response to the issue, and it was not long before lottery proponents made another attempt (p. 51).

By the 1960s, the tide of legitimacy had shifted. Québécois widely approved of lotteries and the Québec government had tried unsuccessfully to establish a lottery for nearly a century. In 1969, Montréal experienced a fiscal crisis due to the World's Fair–Expo 67, and badly needed revenue for the 1976 Olympic Games. It was then that Québec began applying serious pressure on the federal government to permit lotteries in that province. Secularization in Canada had increased the potential for faith legitimacy and improved opportunities to establish emotional legitimacy. Specifically, a majority of anglophone Canadians was unwilling to pay higher taxes for an expanding welfare state and they now had members of Parliament willing to move on the issue (Morton, 2003).

Despite overall legitimacy for lotteries, the government still moved cautiously, because of the splintered cultural landscape and structure of the political system; small pockets of religious opposition in a single electoral district could mean an electoral defeat. Although several private members introduced bills calling for provincial or national lotteries, the government remained split on the issue and refused to act. In 1969, the federal government adopted an omnibus bill that decriminalized homosexuality and abortion and altered the status of lotteries within the *Criminal Code*. That lotteries were lumped in with such sensitive issues indicates the moral politics underlying lotteries at the time. The act passed, but lottery schemes remained within the *Criminal Code* to give the federal and provincial governments control over the authorization, conduct, and management of lotteries (Osborne, 1989; Morton, 2003).

Compared with Australia and the United States, the Canadian provinces acted quickly in adopting lotteries. Québec introduced lotteries almost immediately; there were high faith and emotional legitimacy, and a big economic impetus. The province held the first draw in 1970. Manitoba, another province with high legitimacy, tabled legislation shortly after Québec, and introduced a lottery that coincided with the province's centennial. The remaining provinces were slightly slower off the mark and required stronger legitimacy building (Morton, 2003).

Alberta, Saskatchewan, and British Columbia finalized legislation in 1974. Alberta had earlier permitted sweepstakes at fairs and exhibitions and had a history of charitable gambling. However, the province was socially and politically conservative, and it is plausible the politicians were wary of pushing too quickly, thereby eroding the existing legitimacy. Saskatchewan also displayed signs of political unease and earmarked all lottery proceeds for sports and cultural events. Once the western provinces had established lotteries, the remaining provinces followed suit – with some political manoeuvring. Ontario launched its lottery program in 1975 and allocated the profit to promote physical fitness, sports, culture, and recreational activities. The Atlantic provinces joined an interprovincial corporation in 1976 to offer lotteries, with the funds going to similar public goods.

The federal government also instituted a national lottery in 1974 to finance the Montréal Olympic Games and the 1978 Commonwealth Games (Canada Council, 1981). The national lottery caused provincial resentment, and the provinces moved their products into direct competition with Lotto Canada to force the latter out of the market

(Campbell, 1994). In 1985, the federal government gave sole jurisdiction to the provincial governments for lotteries and other games of chance, in exchange for an annual sum of $100 million that would initially be used to help fund the Calgary Olympic Games (Campbell, Hartnagel, & Smith, 2005).

The history of Canadian lotteries demonstrates that cultural legitimacy was easier to establish in a largely Catholic province (Québec, and to a lesser extent Manitoba) than in the remainder of Canada. Québec would have launched a lottery in the early 1920s, and other provinces might have adopted lotteries during the depression to pay for welfare projects, but the proportion of Catholics to Protestants is about 4/1 in Québec, and Winnipeg has the second-largest francophone Catholic population outside of Québec. There would be high faith legitimacy for lotteries among liberal Catholics, and earmarking revenue for public goods would have provided emotional legitimacy. However, a minority of Protestant middle-class reformers succeeded in codifying their world view in Canadian criminal law. Furthermore, given the difficult nature of governing a federation like Canada, it became politically infeasible to change the *Criminal Code* for one or two provinces. The law changed when it became clear to federal politicians that it was out of step with many (not all) of its constituents, and that lotteries could provide revenue for the welfare state. This is a sign of the cultural divide over lotteries in Canada (Morton 2003). How difficult legitimacy building for lotteries would have been in the more conservative provinces, before the 1960s, is largely unknown. This is less problematic for the United States, as demonstrated in the next section.

Lotteries in the United States

Despite some religious objectors, early American settlers were avid gamblers, and participation in lotteries was no exception. Although initially considered illegitimate by the authorities, lotteries played an important role in building the early colony. Lotteries might have continued, if not for the Protestant reform movement and corruption and scandals that plagued them during the late nineteenth century: both served to undermine the legitimacy of lotteries. The situation worsened when organized crime rings became the primary operators of illegal gambling.

American colonists transported lotteries from England, but the authorities initially tried to suppress them. Soon after, the colonies experienced massive immigration that required extensive infrastructure, yet taxation to raise revenue, and a banking system to distribute capital were non-existent (United States Commission on the Review of the National Policy Toward Gambling, 1976 [USC, 1976]). Consequently, the colonial governments reconsidered their policies, and lotteries burgeoned throughout the United States. Faith legitimacy was easily established, since most religious groups operated lotteries or profited from them. According to Asbury, lotteries were so common that 'the clergymen ... [to] the most besotted of bar flies,' purchased lottery tickets, and lotteries quickly lost the stigma attached to other forms of gambling (1969, p. 72). Approximately 2,000 lotteries were in operation by 1790, and legislators typically awarded at least one lottery grant to ensure their legitimacy (p. 76). Ticket sales approximated $2,000,000 a year during this period in New York and Philadelphia alone, a substantial wager per capita, since the cities had a combined population of 100,000 people (p. 77).[15] Nevertheless, moral reformers argued that lotteries were regressive, and generated most of the revenue from the poor.

When the financial difficulties associated with the growing colonies intensified, the authorities expanded local operations into statewide and national lotteries. This had three unintended consequences (USC, 1976). First, commercial interests hired to operate lotteries expanded and several merged into large companies that dominated the lottery industry (pp. 144–5).[16] Second, the sheer volume of lotteries across the United States and the mergers of lottery companies caused enormous competition and forced many into insolvency and/or to default on prizes (pp. 144–5). Third, corruption and fraud increased rapidly. These three factors delegitimized lotteries among the authorities and business people: lotteries were viewed as social institutions that would smother legitimate business, turn the populace into gamblers, and encourage corruption and crime. In the 1820s, the newspapers of the day exposed the corruption and fraud associated with lotteries, and public opposition developed immediately (pp. 81–2). Ironically, this failed to delegitimize lotteries among religious groups, perhaps because most held a stake in them. Nevertheless, legal legitimacy was lost, and all states, save Delaware, Kentucky, and Missouri, had constitutional bans or statutory prohibitions on gambling by the 1860s (Findlay 1986, p. 41).

Lotteries resurfaced in some southern states, following the civil war, as the region attempted to rebuild and deal with financial chaos. The most famous of these was the Louisiana Lottery, authorized in 1868 for 25 years (Asbury, 1969, p. 86). However, it quickly lost legal and emotional legitimacy. The organization was thoroughly corrupt and bribed legislators, governors, banks, newspapers, and other officials across the United States (USC, 1976). The people of Louisiana were also bitterly opposed, in part because of political corruption, and in part because the lottery preyed on the poor. Nevertheless, the Louisiana Lottery successfully continued to operate, despite antilottery legislation enacted by Congress between 1864 and 1876. Congress finally shut down the lottery by prohibiting advertising, prize descriptions, and the movement of lottery tickets and prizes across state lines (Asbury, 1969; USC, 1976).[17] This effectively ended lotteries in the United States, and *legal* lotteries would not return for over 70 years.

In the interim, the game of 'policy,' the 'lottery's illegitimate offspring,' slowly spread across the United States. Policy began in the lottery shops of London and offered the poor a chance to gamble without purchasing a lottery ticket. Gamblers would 'insure' a number on a lottery draw, and winning numbers received a prize. The game was popular between 1830 and 1900 but dropped off with the end of prohibition when Dutch Schultz, a notorious New York gangster, seized control of the 'numbers games' to replace his illegal liquor business (Wykes, 1964). Other crime bosses followed, and the games quickly spread across the United States.

As in Australia and Canada, the depression led to lottery proposals in New York City and 11 states, seven of which had large proportions of Catholic citizens.[18] The campaigns failed, seemingly because proponents failed to secure legitimacy for lotteries. Supporters argued that lotteries were not regressive, while opponents claimed they would place an unbearable burden on the working classes and poor who could least afford it. Nibert (2000) claims President Roosevelt's 'new deal' ended the debate by smoothing over tough economic times, and rising affluence following the war postponed the introduction of lotteries until the early 1960s. On the other hand, Moran (1997) argues that states refrained from introducing lotteries prior to the 1960s, because the public would not accept them. He claims Americans perceived gambling as a vice, detrimental to the poor, and a source of crime and social disorder. In other words, they held little legitimacy. He suggests that sociological studies used by governments helped alter these perceptions (p. 54).

The return of lotteries in the United States exemplifies the close connections between economic impetus, sociocultural intervening factors, and mobilization leading to adoption. The pattern of lottery adoption, in Table 4.5, suggests legitimacy building has been a major component.

Table 4.5 Period of Introduction of Lotteries in the United States as of 2005

State	To 1970	1970–5	1976–80	1981–5	1986–90	1991–5	1996–2000	2001–5
NORTHEAST								
Connecticut		2						
Maine		2						
Massachusetts		2						
New Hampshire	2							
New Jersey		2						
New York	2							
Pennsylvania		2						
Rhode Island		2						
Vermont			2					
SOUTHEAST								
Alabama								
Arkansas								
Delaware		2						
Florida					2			
Georgia						2		
Kentucky					2			
Maryland		2						
Mississippi								
Louisiana						2		
Oklahoma								2
North Carolina								2
South Carolina								2
Tennessee								2
Texas					2			
Virginia					2			
West Virginia					2			
MIDWEST								
Illinois		2						
Indiana					2			
Iowa				2				
Kansas					2			
Michigan		2						
Minnesota					2			
Missouri					2			
Nebraska						2		
North Dakota								2
Ohio		2						
South Dakota					2			
Wisconsin					2			

(*Continued*)

Table 4.5   (Continued)

State	To 1970	1970–5	1976–80	1981–5	1986–90	1991–5	1996–2000	2001–5
WEST								
Alaska								
Arizona				2				
California				2				
Colorado				2				
Hawaii								
Idaho					2			
Montana					2			
New Mexico							2	
Nevada								
Oregon				2				
Utah								
Wyoming								
Washington				2				

Source: Pierce and Miller (1999); State Lottery Agencies
1 – Commercial   2 – Public

The northeastern states adopted lotteries first, in response to fiscal stress, but these states have large numbers of Catholics and people with liberal social values. Political elites faced fewer issues with faith legitimacy, but had to overcome perception of potential corruption to build emotional and legal legitimacy. Once enough states had adopted, politicians could point to legal lotteries in nearby jurisdictions, and appeal to emotions by promising public goods and pointing to the inevitability of legal lotteries. This may have invoked social-norm legitimacy, but these tactics were less successful in the Bible Belt states with high percentages of conservative Baptists. It was 10 years after the first wave (1963–75) that these states began adopting lotteries. Four established them after 2000, and two still have no lotteries, despite strong legalization campaigns. Utah and Hawaii have also rejected lotteries. I unpack these observations in the remainder of this section.

In 1963, a slight majority of Americans favoured the introduction of lotteries (see Nibert, 2000; Nelson & Rubenstein, 2004). The state of New Hampshire also faced a dilemma: it badly needed funds for education but had no sales tax and by law could not impose income taxes. To solve the problem, the government proposed a 'sweepstakes,' and after fierce debate, on 30 April 1963, the Governor signed the first North American lottery in the twentieth century into law (New Hampshire Lottery Commission, n.d.). The lottery's opponents were undeterred and forced a local option referendum, but a majority of the districts voted in favour, (Nibert, 2000) indicating a high degree of legitimacy among the population.

Once New Hampshire demonstrated it could successfully create and operate a lottery, representatives in nearby states began campaigns to introduce lotteries. Nevertheless, Americans – or at least the political elite – resisted. It took three years for New York to propose a lottery, and it gained acceptance because the state pledged the proceeds for education. New York also connected its sweepstakes to an annual horse race. But neither New Hampshire nor New York had clearly thought through their business plans; the lengthy wait between purchasing a ticket and determining the winner dampened excitement, leading to a drop in sales in both states (Nibert, 2000). Enter New Jersey. In November 1969, 81.5% of New Jersey voters approved a state lottery; once again (New Jersey Lottery Commission, n.d.), the state proposed allocating funds to state government and education, both of which would reduce the tax burden. The governor of New Jersey purchased the first ticket in December 1970 (Nibert, 2000), an act typical among the early adopting states since it symbolized the lottery's respectability.

New Jersey's lottery was an immediate success, however, as shown in Table 4.5, just over half of the states failed to establish lotteries until after 1980. In addition, we can observe a distinct geographic pattern in the United States: the northeastern states established lotteries first, followed by the west and midwest, and then the south.[19] Moreover, as seen in Table 4.6 below, about half of the early adopters did not require referenda and campaigns in Georgia, Arizona, and Idaho almost failed to obtain majority support. This raises several questions. Why did most states wait to establish lotteries after New Jersey, and why did lotteries spread from northeast to west, midwest and then south? In addition, how can we explain the fact that many western states adopted before the midwest or southern regions but the west still has the highest proportion of non-lottery states in the country? Finally, why did some states, like Maryland, have overwhelming support, while others, like Arizona, did not? The answer to these questions lies in the enabling and constraining dynamics of lottery adoption in the United States.

Many consider fiscal stress on the state the key component, particularly among early adopters (Alm et al., 1993; Berry & Berry, 1990; Erekson et al., 1999; Garrett & Wagner, 2004; Mikesell & Zorn, 1988).

Table 4.6 Legislation / Results of Vote to Introduce State Lotteries in the United States

North East	Legislation/Vote	Midwest	Legislation/Vote
Connecticut	legislation	Illinois	legislation
Maine	61%	Indiana	62%
Massachusetts	legislation	Iowa	legislation
New Hampshire	legislation	Kansas	64%
New Jersey	81.5%	Michigan	67%
New York	61%	Minnesota	57%
Pennsylvania	legislation	Missouri	70%
Rhode Island	constitutional convention	Nebraska	63%
Vermont	66%	North Dakota	64%
		Ohio	legislation
		South Dakota	60%
		Wisconsin	65%

South	Legislation/Vote	West	Legislation/Vote
Alabama	no commercial lottery	Alaska	no commercial lottery
Arkansas	no commercial lottery	Arizona	51%
Delaware	legislation	California	58%
Florida	64%	Colorado	60%
Georgia	52%	Hawaii	no commercial lottery
Kentucky	60%	Idaho	51%
Maryland	80%	Montana	70%
Mississippi	no commercial lottery	New Mexico	54%
Louisiana	69%	Nevada	no commercial lottery
Oklahoma	68%	Oregon	66%
North Carolina	legislation	Utah	no commercial lottery
South Carolina	56%	Wyoming	no commercial lottery
Tennessee	58%	Washington	legislation
Texas	65%		
Virginia	57%		
West Virginia	67%		

Sources: Pierce and Miller (1999); State Lottery Agencies

Some go further and attribute the return of lotteries to the fiscal crisis of capitalism that began in the 1960s (Peppard, 1987; Nibert, 2000). Indeed, deindustrialization substantially lowered the living standards and increased unemployment in many of the early adopting states like Illinois and Michigan. Nibert (2000) contends individual fiscal problems sanitized lotteries as people came to view them as a chance for prosperity. These processes increased during the early 1980s when the federal government simultaneously devolved its responsibilities and reduced funding to the states. At the same time, in 1981, the United States experienced a major recession. Yet, only six states in the west and midwest established lotteries immediately following this period. Thirteen states – the largest number after the first wave of 1963–75 – waited roughly five years before launching their lotteries. What happened? When states faced reducing services or raising taxes, legitimacy arguably increased for politicians, the people, or both. Citizens were not amenable to tax increases during challenging economic times (Miller & Pierce, 1997). However, they were becoming more open to lotteries thanks to declining economic conditions. Individual deprivations could undermine religious opposition and alter emotional legitimacy; mobilization in support might follow. However, this would depend on the nature and degree of convictions held about lotteries.

Social values and religious beliefs have also affected the timing and dispersal of lottery adoption through legitimacy building. Proponents attempt to reduce faith opposition and create emotional legitimacy by altering symbolic elements or by suggesting lotteries are unavoidable. People who hold conservative social values and/or are fundamentalist Protestants tend to be more opposed to lotteries and other forms of gambling (Alm et al., 1993; Berry & Berry, 1990; Economopoulos, 2006; Erekson et al., 1999; Jensen, 2003; von Herrmann, 1999). It is harder to build faith and/or emotional legitimacy among these groups than with liberals and/or Catholics. Nevertheless, as Economopoulos (2006) notes, religious commitment is more important than denomination. Economopoulos found that potential economic benefit influenced mainline Protestants to support lotteries in 1975, but these same enticements failed to sway staunch conservative Protestants (pp. 281–2). This helps explain why states with large proportions of conservatives or evangelical Protestants have been opposed to lotteries. Pierce and Miller (1999) further argue that symbolic elements of lottery campaigns influence whether a legalization campaign is successful. Politicians earmarking revenue for education or other good causes are in essence creating positive symbolic values for the proposed lottery, and proponents use any symbolic capital that will neutralize the image of gambling as 'sin' or 'destructive behaviour.' A state is more likely to adopt a lottery when both the people and government consider it congruent with their belief system (Jensen, 2003). However, individuals may resign themselves to the introduction of lotteries if they consider it inevitable. Accordingly, when neighbouring jurisdictions adopt, it may create 'cognitive legitimacy,' which is where the public and government begin to take a policy for granted (2003, p. 524).

The introduction of lotteries in neighbouring states also increases competition and policy learning. Non-lottery states surrounded by those with lotteries lose revenue to the bordering states (Alm et al., 1993; Berry & Berry, 1990).[20] In addition, legislators in non-lottery states observe lotteries operating efficiently with little corruption while at the same time learning strategies to overcome opposition (Hansen, 2004; Jensen, 2003).[21] Alm et al. (1993) also assert that the probability of successful lottery campaigns increases with each new state lottery that operates efficiently and without scandal, since it enhances the overall legal legitimacy of lotteries (see Jensen, 2003).

The foregoing indicates that political-economic struggles are embedded in the cultural realm and influenced by individual habitus. Proponents and opponents of lottery campaigns attempt to frame the issue with symbolism that will appeal to either faith legitimacy, emotional legitimacy, or both. Allocating revenue to public goods and perhaps even individual incentives like tax relief may not be strong enough for highly committed conservatives and evangelical Protestants. It may be enough, however, to shift debates from moral issues to pragmatic ones, and this could lead to social-norm pressure. The capacity to invoke inevitability and legal legitimacy will also help. This suggests that late adopters of a controversial policy should face less resistance and reduced political risks and, as the number of adopting states increases, opposition and political risks should decrease. However, this does not guarantee adoption since other dynamics that affect mobilization are also involved.

Having examined factors associated with lottery adoption, I now return to the tables above and answer the three questions. The first was why lotteries started in the northeast and moved in a clearly defined geographic pattern. Jensen (2003) examined lottery adoption between 1962 and 1997 and found that early adopters comprised fiscally stressed states with large numbers of Catholic and Jewish constituents who held liberal attitudes. However, they did so through legislation as opposed to initiatives or referenda. As time passed, the legitimacy of lotteries shifted as public opinion became increasingly more favourable. This led to a second round of lottery adoption by states that were fiscally healthy, with a higher percentage of liberal minded Catholic and Jewish citizens. Finally, late adopters legalized lotteries after mainly Protestant voters, with conservative social values, approved the moves through referenda. These last states adopted lotteries, because sufficient jurisdictions had provided examples of legitimacy (often through the earmarking of revenue for education and other good causes) that the state could defend as a model to emulate (Jensen, 2003).[22]

New Hampshire, New Jersey, and New York – the first three states to adopt – allocated the revenue to education. Only 14 states, in total, do not earmark lottery revenue for education or some other good cause. Jensen's findings demonstrate that the institutional and cultural environment and passage of time can make a difference in policy diffusion. This is what we find in Table 4.5, and it helps explain the geographic dispersion of lotteries across the United States.

Turning to the second question (Why does the west have the highest proportion of non-lottery states?), some western states have not adopted lotteries because politicians did not see the need, proponents failed to establish faith or emotional legitimacy, and/or special interest groups successfully lobbied against lotteries based on religious grounds or out of commercial self-interest.

Alaska does not permit commercial lotteries, but has no economic need for lotteries since it has extensive oil revenue and is fiscally healthy. Alaska also does not border another region that might influence it through competition or policy learning.[23] Finally, Alaska is a relatively conservative state, although apparently not conservative enough to restrict gambling totally (as in Hawaii or Utah). Alaska permits 'charitable' gaming, and Alaskans wagered $355 million (USD) in 2003 (State of Alaska, 2003, p. 2), with the net proceeds going to good causes.

Hawaii is an interesting anomaly that provides a clear example of the importance of culture and contingency in gambling adoption. Gambling is illegal in Hawaii, and yet, the conditions that should have led to early adoption exist. The state has one of the highest tax burdens in the United States; it has a large Catholic population that leans toward liberal values; it does not use initiatives or referenda, reducing access to the polity; and it has a large tourist industry, which begs the question why casinos have not emerged. Gaming corporations have openly courted the governor, and state politicians have tried, on numerous occasions, to legalize gambling. Nevertheless, Hawaii is the only state where the majority of residents are of Asian or Pacific Islander descent, and Hawaiian culture is more Japanese than American. Indeed, it is a popular destination for Japanese tourists, who view it as an extension of their homeland (Agrusa, 2000). In 2008, Japanese tourists were ranked third (second to eastern and western American markets) in total visitor arrivals, visitor days, visitor expenditures, and 58% were repeat visitors (State of Hawaii, 2008, p. 21). The Japanese make up an important market for Hawaiian tourism and Agrusa (2000) theorizes that gambling has remained illegal because its presence would taint an otherwise idyllic and domestic experience. According to Agrusa, organized crime has strong links to pachinko (a form of Japanese gambling), and he found that 85% of Japanese visitors to Hawaii thought legal gambling would increase crime (Agrusa, 1998, p. 64). Rosenbaum and Spears (2006) provide partial empirical support showing that a majority of Japanese *and* American tourists felt negatively toward *casino* gaming in Hawaii. They further maintain that the Japanese are not averse to gambling, but Japanese visitors to Hawaii are. Thus, culture blends with the political-economic. Polling has shown a strong antigambling sentiment among Hawaiians, and opponents have offered tough resistance to any proposed legislation (Personal Contact – Malia Zimmerman, *Hawaii Reporter*, 2006). The Hawaii Coalition against Legalized Gambling – HCALG – is committed to preventing the introduction of legal gambling in the state and has, so far, been successful.[24]

Utah, like Hawaii, has no legal gambling, the result of strong religious opposition and conservative social values. Nevada is also a unique case. The casino industry has consistently lobbied the state government to forgo a lottery and Democratic politicians attempted, without success, to pass a lottery proposal in 2001, 2003, and 2005 (Stutz, 2005, January 27).

Finally, Wyoming is a conservative state with a high percentage of Protestants. With the exception of Utah, the states surrounding Wyoming have adopted lotteries. Still, the state has a small population spread across a large area, and beyond public resistance, politicians perceive lotteries as a risky economic venture (Personal contact – Bill McCarthy, 2009). Nevertheless, the state Supreme Court forced Wyoming to negotiate casino compacts with the local Indian bands, and some speculated a lottery would follow. Proponents failed to convince legislators in 2007, and again in 2009, despite attempts at legitimacy building through promises of funding for early education and assistance for the horse racing industry. The 2009 legislation would have permitted video lottery terminals at racetracks, a move that a majority of legislators were not comfortable with (McCarthy, 2009).

The third question, from above, asked why some states received strong support, while others barely passed in the referendum process. I have chosen to examine the two states with the widest margins of support that followed New Jersey's lead – Maryland with 80% support – and Arizona with 51% support.[25] Maryland had at least four favourable conditions for adoption in 1973. Maryland faced a fiscal crisis in 1968–9 and allocated lottery revenue solely to the general fund. Maryland's population is also comprised of mainly liberal Protestants, with nearly a quarter of the population Catholic. Religious legitimacy might not have been an issue if proponents used the right economic arguments (see Economopoulos, 2006). Maryland borders Pennsylvania, which had introduced a lottery the year before, creating competition and potential arguments about inevitability. Finally, Maryland had a 20-year history of legal slot machines that ended with prohibition in 1963 and staged removal by 1968 (Janis, 2004). This may have acted to legitimize lotteries among many in the population.[26]

Whereas Maryland had many preconditions for a lottery adoption, Arizona had few. Like Maryland, Arizona faced fiscal problems arising from the early 1980s recession. Nevertheless, the governor and the mayor of Tucson opposed a lottery. In addition, when Arizona launched its campaign, approximately 25% of the other states had embraced lotteries, and South Dakota was the closest lottery state to Arizona, limiting policy diffusion and legitimacy building. Utah, with its large conservative Christian population, also borders Arizona, and resources may have come across the border to assist the opposition. Finally, Arizona's population comprised a sizeable number of both Catholics and Protestants, but about two-thirds were politically conservative. It seems then that Arizona had the fiscal need, but lottery proponents had a tough time trying to legitimize a state-operated lottery, since there were no examples close by; in fact, easy access to Las Vegas may have caused limited support.

Summing up the history of lotteries in the United States, the early American colonies and states used lotteries to raise funds for public works and provide capital for nascent enterprises. When lottery schemes threatened the public interest, traditional, emotional, and legal legitimacy were removed *among the middle classes* and caused a moral panic. Most states responded by enacting constitutional amendments prohibiting lotteries, and the federal government closed the door on lotteries with further legislative measures. However, the poor and working classes continued to participate in illegal games, and organized crime took over operations. Some states tried, unsuccessfully, to resurrect lotteries during the depression years, arguably because the middle classes viewed them as illegitimate. Conditions for lotteries became more favourable during the 1960s, as growing secularization, the shift to a service economy, devolution, and deregulation led to extensive social and economic change that helped establish faith and emotional legitimacy. Lotteries also gained legal legitimacy as states began operating them profitably and without corruption. Lotteries slowly spread throughout the United States through processes of policy learning and interstate competition, often with the help of inevitability legitimization. Nevertheless, adoption was uneven, both temporally and geographically, and several states are still without lotteries. A wide array of political, economic, social, and cultural factors determined whether a state adopted a lottery, but issues surrounding legitimacy were central in those states that have tried.

Summary

Lottery adoption provides a good example of historical contingency and demonstrates the importance of culture in influencing societal gambling practices. As in Chapter 3, I want to account for the differential adoption of lotteries across Australia, Canada, and the United States. Many argue that political and economic conditions are the driving force behind the establishment and participation in lotteries. Modern states turned to lotteries as solutions to economic problems. Governments and powerful interest groups used lotteries to produce capital in nascent economies and, later, to alleviate taxes and produce public funds for state operations in shrinking economies. In addition, people participate in lotteries when they have limited opportunities or their ability to consume declines; both tending to occur during fiscal crises. Consequently, global and local economic conditions, devolution, and deregulation all directly affected lottery adoption. As with casinos, populist, democratic practices further influenced the spread of lotteries in the United States. While these arguments are valid and broaden our knowledge of lottery adoption, they tell only part of the story. To explain fully the variation among Australia, Canada, and the United States, we need to account for historical events and cultural processes that would have influenced individual motives to act for or against lotteries.

A comparison of lottery adoption across the three countries shows the Australian states were able to build legitimacy for lotteries earlier in the twentieth century than the other two countries, the result of the intersection of politics and culture. The situation in Canada and the

United States might have differed, had historical events not constrained lottery adoption until the early 1960s.

When Tattersall's established a private lottery without corruption and set up operation in Tasmania, it demonstrated that lotteries could operate without scandal. Yet, lotteries held low legitimacy among the middle classes and political elite who resisted until economic conditions pushed them to reconsider. The first state lottery in Queensland built emotional legitimacy and gave the other states a model they could implement in a morally defensible way. Once New South Wales introduced a lottery, the other states recognized the political utility of the prospective lottery revenue and need to build legitimacy by allocating revenue to public goods. As each successive state adopted, it increased both legitimacy and inevitability that lotteries would arrive in other regions regardless of legality. All the Australian states faced religious opposition, and some governments simply ignored it; social-norm legitimacy among lottery proponents prevailed. As in Canada and the United States, the holdout states could not build faith legitimacy, deemed lotteries economically unviable, or both.

The Canadian provinces faced a different set of political circumstances that prevented lottery adoption. A small group of Protestant elite ensconced its moral culture in the Canadian *Criminal Code,* and decades passed before their position weakened enough for lotteries to win support. It is clear, however, that lotteries held faith and emotional legitimacy in Catholic Québec long before provinces with large conservative Protestant populations. Accordingly, the historical conjuncture that created the political situation in Canada hindered an earlier introduction of lotteries, at least in Québec. Several other provinces may have followed during the depression years, since faith legitimacy should have been easier to build among the destitute liberal Protestants and Catholics. Without the political restriction, it is plausible that Canada may have taken a route similar to Australia with lotteries.

Ironically, traditional, emotional, and legal legitimacy for lotteries existed in the United States long before Australia or Canada. However, lotteries were delegitimized among the middle classes because of scandal, corruption, and the threat of corporate dominance in an emergent economy. Faced with a public backlash, the political elite suppressed lotteries through constitutional amendments. As with the prohibition of alcohol, this later opened the door for organized crime to operate illegal lotteries on a massive scale. Ongoing corruption and crime, associated with the numbers rackets, further reduced emotional and potential legal legitimacy. When state politicians united to propose lotteries, they had to build faith and emotional legitimacy; this was less complicated where there were liberal Catholics and pressing economic issues, and most difficult in regions with conservative Protestants. Nevertheless, most states tried to increase emotional legitimacy by linking lottery proceeds to public goods. This did not work in the highly religious Bible Belt until their citizens began to purchase lottery tickets from bordering states. Politicians have been unable to build faith and/or emotional legitimacy in four holdout states, and the remainder have not adopted for economic reasons.

In sum, like casinos, economic conditions generated the impetus to establish lotteries and, like casinos, sociocultural circumstances have been critical to adoption. The political elite and the people must be convinced that a gambling activity is legitimate and individual and collective habitus bound in culture determines how they will act.

Gaming Machines outside Casinos

> No other machine was ever invented from which the profits derived were so fabulous on so small an investment, and with so little effort. (Anonymous, 1950, p. 62)

In the remainder of this chapter, I examine gaming machines outside of casinos (GMOCs) from a cultural perspective. I am not precluding political, economic, and social factors, but I intend to focus on the cultural significance of the development of machine gambling and patterns of adoption in Australia, Canada, and the United States. The introduction and development of gaming machines illustrates the ongoing rationalization of gambling in society, the shift from modern to postmodern technologies, and the integration of gambling into the cultural economy. The spatial distribution and ownership of GMOCs in the three countries also highlight the structural and cultural divergence that led to different forms and availability of gambling. The sociohistorical research on gaming machines is sparse and, for this reason, I provide a more detailed historical overview than for either casinos or lotteries.

The 'nickel-in-the-slot machine' (Fey, 1983) first appeared in the United States in the late 1880s, and it is a testament to the machines' popularity and profitability that they had spread around the globe within a decade. Whereas casino table games developed out of private gambling between individuals (Falkiner & Horbay, 2006), early gaming-machine inventors set out to rationalize commercial gambling through the automation of pre-existing casino table games.[27] Charles Fey revolutionized this process in 1895 with his 'Liberty Bell' machine, which was an instant hit among players and machine owners alike: it was more entertaining, easier, and quicker to play, provided substantial profit, and did not require attendants to pay out prizes. Fey's success prompted other companies to begin manufacturing similar machines, and the industry rapidly expanded (Anonymous, 1950). Slot machines were soon made illegal throughout the United States and many other countries, however, American gaming-machine manufacturers thrived since several states permitted manufacturing and sales, but prohibited slot-machine gambling (Anonymous, 1950).[28]

The introduction of gaming machines represents one of the earliest efforts to develop gambling for mass consumption and corresponds with the wider push to commodify working and middle-class spaces of leisure. It is also significant that the appearance of gaming machines coincided with the advent of Fordism and Taylor's scientific management of production[29] – capital began cultivating and rationalizing spaces of leisure at the same time as spaces of work. In this sense, we can consider the emergence of gaming machines as the McDonaldization of gambling, even though the earliest machines predate the fast-food chain by decades.

Ritzer (2004) argues that McDonaldization is one aspect of the ongoing rationalization of society and that it encompasses increases in efficiency, calculability, predictability, and control through the substitution of human interaction with machine technologies. We find all of these elements in the evolving industry. Gaming machines constitute an efficient form of gambling since they increase the speed of wager, reduce human interaction, and often restrict the use of money during a gambling session. Machine operators hold a greater degree of calculability through means that allow for precise payouts. They can also manipulate the structural characteristics and prize schedules, thereby enhancing their control over players. Indeed, machine manufacturers have consistently explored new designs and methods to broaden efficiency and influence players' behaviour, thereby extracting higher profit (see Schull, 2005).[30] Gaming machines are also predictable, in that operators can accurately predict profit for each hour of play. Lastly, gaming machines are somewhat standardized, and players could adapt to most machines within a reasonable amount of time.

If gaming machines signal the growing rationalization of gambling, they are also symbolic of the shift from a modern to postmodern society. The earliest gaming machines reflected the new realities of an industrial and mechanized age. Gambling was modernized through the transformation of traditional casino games, previously the preserve of the elite and upper classes, to homogenized games produced for mass appeal; gaming machines were hugely successful in attracting the working classes.

The rationalization of machine designs coincided with postindustrialization, computerization, and an increasing emphasis on research and development to drive profit. Since the early 1960s, manufacturers have continued to merge technology with machine aesthetics turning the industry into 'an engine for experimentation and innovation with emergent digital capabilities' (Schull, 2005, p. 66). This began with a move to electromagnetic slot machines that facilitated higher payouts, increased reliability, and improved security. Mechanical slot machines were susceptible to manipulation by operators and cheating by players, which created problems for both owners and regulators. By the 1980s, the industry had completely transformed gaming machines with the introduction of video screens and digital microprocessors. Programmers could now install numerous games into a single machine and reliably control its functions. Manufacturers also introduced devices that accepted bills, and many machines now operate solely with tokens, debit, and credit cards.[31] These new features enhanced machine aesthetics, while increasing profit and broadening security (Schull, 2005).[32]

With discoveries and advancements in other sectors, the technological evolution of gaming machines continues to intensify, and manufacturers seek to develop machines that automatically adapt to individual psychological characteristics and tastes (Schull, 2005). Thus, despite the rhetoric of creating machines with 'responsible gambling features,' manufacturers and operators are putting earnings ahead of players' welfare. More than ever, gaming machines allure and captivate many, pulling them into a dissociative state players call 'the zone,'[33] which increases the frequency and duration of play, while generating higher profit. Beyond the use of technology, the gaming-machine industry has used pop culture, pastiche, and spectacle to single out and target weak and non-existent market segments.

The continuous research and design of gaming machines to increase profit is a clear example of capital invading the cultural sphere through the symbolic economy (Zukin, 1998), which progressively turns information and aesthetics into a business proposition.[34] Combined with changes in the social and political realm, gaming machines are now an integral part of the cultural economy.

While manufacturers and operators attempt to increase legitimacy of machine gambling by transmuting its image from 'gambling' to 'entertainment,'[35] other societal change has stimulated demand for this form of gambling. Increased access to credit altered attitudes toward money, leading to hyperconsumption and gambling as the ultimate act (Reith, 1999). The social realm has eroded, as people take up individualistic pursuits (Putnam, 2000) that fit nicely with the new digital and hyperreal aesthetics of gaming machines. In fact, many players choose machine gambling because they want to be alone, cut off from the social world, and one with the machine (Schull, 2005, p. 73).

At the same time, the political realm fragmented into numerous groups, splitting resources for social and political movements, undermining resistance to the expansion of gambling into everyday spaces. A shift to neo-liberal governance gave corporate interests and technocrats considerable power in decisions over the economy and other important spheres of social life. Although the state ultimately decides whether to legalize gaming machines, corporate elite and technocrats have a strong influence over the spatial configuration of this highly controversial form of gambling. It is through these processes that capital and the state have successfully integrated gaming machines into the new culturally based economy. Indeed, the fusion of gambling with technology and marketing schemes, which in turn influences perceptions of gambling and entertainment, heralds significant changes for gambling and the ability of the industry to expand its influence.

In short, the introduction, development, and expansion of gaming machines provide a prime example of the political-economic and sociocultural shifts that have taken place during the nineteenth and twentieth centuries. As discussed below, the middle classes refused to accept gambling generally, but machine gambling was particularly singled out because of problems controlling the games' integrity, crime, and corruption. Excessive gambling also threatened the social fabric of communities. Accordingly, the machines remained illegal in many jurisdictions for decades. Nevertheless, GMOCs proved very popular with the working classes as they offered entertainment and a chance to win modest prizes or sums of money for a small stake. The enormous profitability of the machines also made them very attractive to organized crime, particularly in the United States. And, since American manufacturers could legally produce gaming machines, they constantly altered the designs to stay one step ahead of the law.

In sum, it is no accident that gaming machines are the dominant form of gambling in western countries. Along with online gambling, gaming machines represent the most rationalized and McDonaldized type of gambling. They are predictable, calculable, and require little wage labour to operate. Gaming-machine manufacturers continually strive to make the machines more efficient (profitable) through ergonomic alterations, while inserting postmodern spectacle aesthetics. Development and introduction of other technological versions of traditional casino games are on the way. The intersection of these games and the move toward socially isolated leisure activities holds the potential to radically transform gambling practices.

Adoption of GMOCs in Australia, Canada, and the United States

Politicians have sought to legalize gaming machines for political gains, when not opposed for religious or other personal reasons. Nevertheless, success or failure have depended on their ability to build legitimacy among other elites and the public. Most Australian states and all Canadian provinces have legal GMOCs, whereas numerous American states have attempted adoption but less than one quarter have been successful. In addition, ambient machine gambling is widespread in Australia and most provinces in Canada,[36] compared with the United States where GMOCs are usually at racinos.[37] Australian and American states have typically appealed to emotional legitimacy by linking legal gaming machines to public goods or individual incentives; however, the presence of organized crime delegitimized machine gambling in both countries, often preventing adoption. Conversely, many Canadian provinces used the spectre of organized crime to legitimize the introduction and state control of GMOCs. As shown in Table 4.7, Australia has a substantially higher number of legal GMOCs, per capita, than do either Canada or the United States. Slightly over half are in New South Wales, approximating the number found in the United States and almost double that of Canada. GMOCs in Australia were initially legalized for and concentrated in non-profit clubs, but commercial operation in hotels and other ambient sites are increasing and, in some cases, surpassing that of clubs.[38] The pattern in Canada is public ownership and operation, and most GMOCs in the United States fall under a private model. These findings are not surprising given the cultural differences in each country,

Table 4.7   Gaming Machines outside Casinos in Australia, Canada, and the United States as of 2005

	Australia		Canada		United States	
Adult Population of States / Provinces with GMOCs	13,791,817(a)		30,285,694(b)		31,402,000(c)	
Number of Machines	187,896(d) (2005)		48,901(b) (2004–2005)		107,590(e) (2004–2005)	
	71,110 Hotel	116,786 Club	38,585 VLT	10,316 Racino	70,781 VLT	36,809 Racino
Number of Venues	5,871(d)		7,503(b)	25(b)	11,710(e)	31(e)
Estimated Number of Machines per 10,000 Adult Population	136		16		34	
			13 VLT	3 Racino	22 VLT	12 Racino

Sources:
(a) Australian Bureau of Statistics Cat. (2006) – population 20 years and over (data grouping constraints), excluding Western Australia
(b) Canadian Partnership for Responsible Gambling (2005) – population 18 years and over
(c) Estimate for 2005 derived from U.S. Census Bureau (n.d.) – population 18 years and over in states with gaming machines
(d) Australian Gaming Council (2007)
(e) McQueen (2004); State Gaming Commissions

expressed through political choices and the manner in which political decisions are made. There are four models of ownership and operation in Australia, Canada, and the United States (Tables 4.8, 4.9, 4.10, 4.11): non-profit, commercial, state owned and operated, and state owned and vendor operated.[39] These differences are a product of regional cultural variation that has facilitated the adoption of GMOCs at different points in time across regions. The presence, or absence, of legitimacy, especially among elite groups, have strongly influenced tolerance of gaming machines outside casinos and the regulatory models chosen.

Gaming Machines outside Casinos in Australia

Gaming machines first appeared in the Australian colonies in the mid-1800s (O'Hara, 1988). The early machines were mechanized poker games and Wilcox (1983) claims the term 'poker machine' was used as early as 1932, but became entrenched as an Australian legal term when introduced in the New South Wales' *The Gaming and Betting (Poker*

Table 4.8   Ownership and Operations of Gaming Machines outside Casinos in Australia, Canada, and the United States

---

Non-Profit Owner /Operator (NPOO): A non-profit organization owns, maintains, and operates the machines for charitable purposes. The non-profit organization may provide a percentage of the win to the state, the state may levy taxes based on the turnover or win, or it might charge licencing fees to permit legal operation. The state may choose to monitor the operations or subcontract monitoring to a corporate body.

Vendor Owner/Operator (VOO): A commercial venue owns, maintains, and operates the machines. The commercial entity may provide a percentage of the win to the state, the state may levy taxes based on the turnover or win, or it might charge licencing fees to permit legal operation. The state may choose to monitor the operations or subcontract monitoring to a corporate body.

Corporate Owner/Operator (COO): A gaming company owns and maintains the machines while another vendor (profit or non-profit) provides facilities for their operation based on leasing arrangements, a fixed fee, or percentage of the turnover or win. The state may charge licencing fees to the commercial entity, and it might either take a percentage of the turnover or win from the vendor or levy taxes based on the turnover or win. The state may choose to monitor the operations or subcontract monitoring to a corporate body.

State Owner/Operator (SOO): The state owns and maintains the machines while a vendor (profit or non-profit) provides facilities for their operation for a fixed fee or a percentage of the turnover or win. The state may choose to monitor the operations or subcontract monitoring to a corporate body.

State Hybrid Owner/Operator (SHOO): The state owns the machines and leases them to a vendor (profit or non-profit) who operates them on behalf of the state for a fixed fee or a percentage of the turnover or win. The state may choose to monitor the operations or subcontract monitoring to a corporate body. The state may also provide maintenance for the machines or leave the maintenance to the operator.

(Adapted from Texas Legislative Council, 2004)

Machines) Act, 1956. Gaming machines in Australia are also referred to as 'EGMs' (electronic gaming machines).

Illegal poker machines were well established in New South Wales in the 1880s, Victoria, South Australia, and Queensland by the 1920s, and the Australia Capital Territory and Western Australia by 1945 (Australian Institute for Gambling Research, 1999; Caldwell, 1972; O'Hara, 1988; Wilcox, 1983). Nevertheless, the association between gaming machines, non-profit clubs, and organized crime in New South Wales influenced the emergence of legal GMOCs in Australia.

Gentlemen's clubs in New South Wales established poker machines in the early 1900s, but the authorities did not enforce the laws because of the clubs' exclusive and restricted membership (Hing, 2000, 2006).

Table 4.9   Period of Introduction of Gaming Machines outside Casinos in Australia as of 2005

State	To 1970	1970–5	1976–80	1981–5	1986–90	1991–95	1996–2000	2001–5
Australian Capital Territory			1					
New South Wales	1					3		
Northern Territory							9	1,3
Queensland						9	1,3	
South Australia						1,3		
Tasmania							5	
Victoria						5		
Western Australia								

Sources: Australian Institute for Gambling Research, 1999; O'Hara, 1988; State Gaming Agencies
1 – Non-Profit Owner/Operator   2 – Vendor Owner/Operator (Racino)
3 – Vendor Owner/Operator (Other)   4 – Corporate Owner/Operator (Racino)
5 – Corporate Owner/Operator (Other)   6 – State Owner/Operator (Racino)
7 – State Owner/Operator (Other)   8 – State Hybrid Owner/Operator (Racino)
9 – State Hybrid Owner/Operator (Other)

The machines burgeoned across the state between 1921 and 1955 due to an ambiguity in the law that arose from differing interpretations between the Supreme Court in 1921 and a Royal Commission in 1932 (O'Hara, 1988; Wilcox, 1983).[40] By the 1950s, working-class registered clubs were using the profits from poker machines to subsidize drinks, meals, and other amenities, in addition to providing community benefits through charitable acts (Caldwell, 1972). The presence and tolerance of the poker machines, and their association with good causes indicates legitimacy among some segments of the population, but New South Wales legalized GMOCs out of economic interest not because the political elite regarded them as legitimate (O'Hara, 1988).

The New South Wales government tolerated poker machines on and off for years; yet it legalized them when it became apparent the clubs were making substantial profit (O'Hara, 1988). In 1956, the government authorized poker machines solely for use in non-proprietary clubs and subject to licensing fees. The public, church groups, and the hotel industry immediately objected (Wilcox, 1983) forcing the government to attempt to build legitimacy for its decision. It appealed to collective emotions by linking the poker machines to positive symbols and arguments of inevitability. First, it allocated a portion of revenue to a hospital fund expected to yield between $500,000 and $750,000 per year (Caldwell, 1972, p. 100). Second, the government prohibited access among women and children by restricting the machines to men-only sporting, social, and Returning Servicemen League Clubs (p. 102).[41] Third, government ministers claimed the clubs which provided individual and community benefits would collapse without the machine funds (p. 102). Wilcox (1983) argues the government avoided further controversy by excluding private interests. In the end, the popularity of poker machines among the working classes (O'Hara, 1988; Hing, 2000) and, the link between machine revenue and good causes, paved the way for the institutionalization of poker machines in New South Wales (Hing, 2000, 2006). This association would prove important to the emergence of GMOCs in several other Australian states.

When poker machines gained legal legitimacy in New South Wales, the Australian Capital Territory's registered clubs began losing revenue across the border (Wilcox, 1983). They subsequently lobbied for poker machines using the inevitability argument: the clubs would lose members and income without legal machines. These claims did not garner sufficient legitimacy, evident in that the government's refusal to act until 1975, when it legalized poker machines despite opposition from its own ministers, the public, and church groups. As in New South Wales, the state tried to build emotional legitimacy by confining poker machines to licensed clubs and directing the proceeds to charitable and community purposes (ACT Gambling and Racing Commission, 2002; Wilcox, 1983).

In 1984, the government decided to test the waters for private operations and established an inquiry in part to determine whether poker machines should be legalized for pubs and hotels. The *Edmunds Report* recommended continued prohibition of gaming machines in commercial and liquor-licensed establishments out of concern over widespread access. However, the government ignored the report and legalized 'approved amusement devices' (AADs) for specific licensees (ACT Gambling and Racing Commission, 2002; see also South Australia Independent Gambling Authority, n.d.). AADs are slower and less profitable, and Hing and Breen (2002) claim that AADs in commercial venues have never seriously threatened club interests.

The Australian Capital Territory was the only state to legalize gaming machines between 1956 and the early 1990s. The surrounding states' clubs lost revenue to New South Wales, and the potential income for clubs and public coffers was not lost on Queensland and Victoria (Australian Institute for Gambling Research, 1999; Wilcox, 1983). New South Wales' clubs garnered roughly $8 billion (AUD) between 1964 and 1986; the state government also took in $2.7 billion (AUD) in licensing fees and taxes from 1957 to 1989 (Author's calculations based on Hing, 2000, p. 66). Given the negative economic impact and potential revenues for Queensland and Victoria's clubs and hotels, why did these states not legalize poker machines until the 1990s? The answer is that strong opposition, arising in part from criminal activities and corruption in New South Wales, reduced the possibility of building emotional and legal legitimacy.

The New South Wales legislation of 1956 provided no regulatory oversight for poker machines beyond ensuring payment of licensing fees, and machine gambling involved large amounts of uncontrolled cash that facilitated fraud, skimming, stealing, and infiltration by organized crime. The limited sophistication of the machines also allowed players to cheat. In response to these problems, the government convened a Royal Commission (*The Moffitt Inquiry*) in 1974 to investigate allegations of criminal activities. This was, arguably, done to shore up legal legitimacy. Nevertheless, Justice Moffitt delegitimized the industry in New South Wales and the other states by concluding that inadequate regulations and oversight had made the clubs a prime target for fraud, and that machine manufacturers were colluding with organized crime syndicates in the United States. Indeed, Moffitt's report and New South Wales' problems controlling the poker-machine industry constrained the other states from legalizing poker machines for the next 15 years (Wilcox, 1983).

In the early 1980s, clubs and lobby groups in Queensland, Victoria, and South Australia began pressuring governments for poker machines,[42] but Queensland's and Victoria's premiers opposed legalization (Australian Institute for Gambling Research, 1999). As the fiscal crises in the states deepened and spread, the Victoria government considered introducing GMOCs. Yet, given the moral climate, concern over social disorder, and the *Moffitt Report*, it needed to legitimize any proposed legislation. Hence, in 1983 the government established a public inquiry, headed by Murray Wilcox, QC, to examine the feasibility of legalizing gaming machines. Wilcox reported that, while many Victorians would enjoy playing poker machines, and it could generate significant revenue for the clubs, criminal activities and social problems would increase along with negative impacts on existing businesses and gambling operations, and he recommended against legalization (Wilcox, 1983).

The *Wilcox Report* dramatically reduced the ability of proponents in other states to build legitimacy for poker machines (Australian Institute for Gambling Research, 1999). A combination of other public inquiries and social-norm pressures among the public, churches, and powerful individuals and groups further hindered support. Opponents used negative symbols to undermine legitimacy by citing New South Wales' experience with social problems, organized crime, and inability to effectively control operations.[43]

Nevertheless, several factors later provided the non poker-machine states with openings to legitimize and legalize GMOCs. Poker machines had become popular in Australia during the 1980s, and clubs were struggling financially, which created difficulties for low-income groups that had traditionally relied on them (Australian Institute for Gambling Research, 1999). Problems with regulatory control and fears of organized crime had also faded with the introduction of new technologies that improved surveillance and oversight (McMillen, 1997).

The main reason for adoption, however, was economic. The ongoing pressures produced by global recession and the downloading of federal fiscal responsibilities forced the state governments to look for new revenue sources (Smith, 2000). Queensland and Victoria re-evaluated their positions first and authorized GMOCs for clubs and hotels in 1991, but the politicians chose different avenues of legitimation. Whereas proponents in Queensland maintained legal gaming machines would assist community organizations, the Victoria government justified the move by claiming gambling revenue would limit the fiscal crisis and that poker machines would be a draw for tourists (Australian Institute for Gambling Research, 1999; Doughney, 2002). Queensland also initiated a public inquiry and allowed public debate on the introduction of GMOCs,[44] a move not taken in Victoria, possibly to prevent the *Wilcox Report* from resurfacing. Interestingly, the premiers in Queensland and Victoria, who had personally opposed gaming machines, had either resigned or been defeated in the polls (Australian Institute for Gambling Research, 1999). As in New South Wales and the Australian Capital Territory, the state governments allocated a share of the proceeds to good causes. They additionally allocated funding for gambling problems and implemented strict regulatory controls to limit criminal activities.

Upon seeing that Queensland and Victoria could successfully regulate and control poker machines, the South Australian government also moved to adopt. However, strong opposition forced the government to resort to several legitimizing tactics. First, it claimed gaming machines would help stabilize the club and hotel industry, a major part of tourism (*Advertiser Sunday Mail*, 2007, April 22).[45] The state also attempted to create emotional legitimacy through the *South Australia 1992 Gaming Machines Act*, where poker machines were authorized for clubs, and a wide assortment of community groups were given collective incentives to support the move: $3.5 million (AUD) was allocated to sport and recreation, $4 million (AUD) went to a charitable and social welfare fund, and $20 million (AUD) was allocated to community development (South Australia, 2002). The last strategy used to minimize political risk was a conscience vote, which readily passed in the lower house, but squeaked by with just one vote in the Legislative Council (Parkin, 2005; South Australia Independent Gambling Authority, n.d., p. 12).[46]

Tasmania and the Northern Territory were the last two states to have legalized poker machines in Australia to date. Although Tasmania adopted casinos first it did not permit gaming machines. This changed in 1993 when the Tasmanian government granted a monopoly over poker machines in the state to three subsidiaries of the Federal Hotels group of companies (Tasmania, 1993). The rationale for legalizing poker machines was economic, but the government used the promise of public goods and selective incentives to reduce opposition. Government ministers also maintained that without gaming-machine revenue, the state would have to increase taxes or cut services (Tasmania, 2002). Public protests to the proposal were seemingly minimal (Australian Institute for Gambling Research, 1999), yet, as in the other states, the government introduced a community support levy for sports.

In the Northern Territory a small number of poker machines were allowed in the casinos in the early 1980s. The clubs and hotels complained about the situation when poker machines began appearing in other states and sought legitimacy by claiming they needed poker machine revenue to remain solvent (pp. 184–5). The casinos lobbied to prevent the introduction of the machines in clubs and hotels, and the government used negotiations to resolve the issue (p. 185). Public opposition was also present, but it is difficult to gauge its saliency.[47] In 1994, the state announced it was legalizing poker machines in community settings. After the fact, and ostensibly to minimize public resistance, the legislature tasked committees with determining the impacts of legal GMOCs and to advise on regulatory matters. The committees examined the issues, and the legislation was passed in 1995, with poker machines becoming legal in 1997. The government repeated the other states' arguments for legalization, allocated revenue to benefit community organizations, and set aside funds for research and treatment of problem gambling (see Northern Territory, 1995 [2005], *Sect 36 & Sect 150*; Northern Territory, n.d.).[48]

Gaming machines in Western Australia have been legalized solely for casino operations under *Section 22* of the *Casino Control Act 1984* (*Western Australia Gaming and Wagering Commission Act, 1987* [2007], p. 95). All poker machines outside casinos are proscribed under *Section 85, 1(a)(b)* of the *Gaming and Wagering Act 1987* (pp. 95–6). In 1996, cashless video lottery terminals were introduced into the state and are operated by non-profit organizations. With the exception of the casino, all forms of gaming in Western Australia are meant to generate proceeds for non-profits. Politicians and community groups in Western Australia appear united in opposition to GMOCs (Western Australia Parliament, 2006, November 1).

In summary, poker-machine adoption in the Australian states reveals several important points about the legalization of GMOCs in that country. Although the impetus was economic, legitimacy building was crucial to adoption. Regardless of demand, states did not legalize poker machines where opposition existed among influential political, business, or social leaders. For example, both Premier Bjelke-Peterson in Queensland and Premier Cain in Victoria opposed introducing poker machines based on personal values (Australian Institute for Gambling Research, 1999). Second, politicians who supported legalization had to contend with corporate, church leaders, and/or segments of the population who were opposed. When legalization became an option, it forced the issue of legitimacy, which was manufactured through appeals to individual and collective emotions by linking machine gambling to social institutions, public goods, and inevitability. Each successive government that adopted poker machines did so for economic reasons and had to justify their decision; the connection between clubs and gaming machines helped establish a base of emotional legitimacy to build upon. Indeed, five state governments argued adoption was necessary to assist clubs to continue to provide social benefits to the community. All Australian states that adopted GMOCs further allocated a portion of machine revenue or taxes directly to public goods. Nevertheless, gaming-machine venues have increasingly become corporatized and profit driven, and the number of machines in hotels in the later adopting states are equal to or higher than those found in clubs, suggesting that political-economic goals prevail once legal legitimacy has been established. Third, several states avoided potential legitimacy crises by setting up public inquiries or conscience votes; these mechanisms indicate politicians are assessing or reducing the political risk involved in controversial policy decisions. Government commissions and inquiries can increase legitimacy while distancing politicians from the policy. However, the Moffitt and Wilcox inquiries exposed crime and social disorder that accompanied machine gambling in New South Wales and the potential for it elsewhere. Consequently, these two inquiries constrained the emergence of gaming machines in the Australian states. Fourth, GMOCs have lost some legitimacy in Australia because of problem gambling, and state governments have continued to use commissions, inquiries, and studies to protect an important source of income. Finally, resistance to poker machines has continued, and in some instances strengthened, despite attempts to reinforce emotional and legal legitimacy through increased regulation and responsible gambling practices.

The legalization and legitimacy building of GMOCs have been much different in Canada from that of Australia or the United States. Unlike Australia, no Canadian jurisdiction had experience with legal GMOCs, and unlike the United States, the association of gaming machines with political corruption and organized crime was not as widespread. Consequently, the Canadian public had little reason for concern when provinces first began legalizing video lottery terminals (VLTs) and most provinces did so in short succession. However, social problems surfaced almost immediately, fuelled by intense media scrutiny, which delegitimized the machines for those provinces that tried to introduce them a few years later.

Gaming Machines outside Casinos in Canada

Table 4.9 showed that legal poker machines first emerged in Australia in the mid-1950s, but did not spread to most states until the early 1990s, and that clubs and hotels owned and operated them. Table 4.10 provides a different picture for GMOCs in Canada. The adoption of GMOCs in ambient settings, such as corner stores, began in 1990, and eight of ten provinces established VLT programs between 1990 and 1994.[49] Moreover, most provinces chose models of state ownership with various operating arrangements.

Gaming machines were first introduced into the Canadian *Criminal Code* in 1892, and the definition caused much confusion in law and enforcement (Robinson, 1983). It also appears that different levels of

Table 4.10   Period of Introduction of Gaming Machines outside Casinos in Canada as of 2005

Province	To 1970	1970–5	1976–80	1981–5	1986–90	1991–5	1996–2000	2001–5
Alberta						6, 7		
British Columbia								6, 7
Manitoba						6, 7		
New Brunswick					3			7
Newfoundland						7		
Nova Scotia						7		
Ontario							6	
Prince Edward Island						3		6, 7
Québec						7	6	
Saskatchewan						7		

Sources: Provincial Gaming Agencies

1 – Non-Profit Owner/Operator
2 – Vendor Owner/Operator (Racino)
3 – Vendor Owner/Operator (Other)
4 – Corporate Owner/Operator (Racino)
5 – Corporate Owner/Operator (Other)
6 – State Owner/Operator (Racino)
7 – State Owner/Operator (Other)
8 – State Hybrid Owner/Operator (Racino)
9 – State Hybrid Owner/Operator (Other)

legitimacy existed for this form of gambling. For example, Alberta established a slot machine licensing fee of $50 in 1923 (Hunt, 1925, pp. 36–7) while other provinces followed a 1915 Ontario ruling and restricted or banned them (Robinson, 1936; Morton, 2003).[50] Robinson (1983) argued the federal government was slow to clarify the law because gambling was considered a victimless crime, and threats to public order, following the First World War, were more pressing. Nevertheless, the government amended the *Criminal Code* in 1924 when the authorities linked slot machines with American gangsters in Montréal and Toronto (pp. 110, 117). The provinces continued to face difficulties interpreting and enforcing the law, and gaming machines burgeoned (Morton, 2003).[51] By the mid-1930s, most provinces considered the laws unenforceable and enacted their own legislation prohibiting slot machines; Saskatchewan went as far as to declare slot machines government property (Ford, 1936; Robinson, 1936; Robinson, 1983).[52] Ontario and Québec waited until 1944 and 1946 respectively to pass slot machine acts (Robinson, 1983).

The prevalence of gaming machines in Canada after this period is unknown, but Robinson (1983) maintains enforcement between the

1930s and 1950s was sporadic, since the police considered gambling a low priority. However, overall enforcement of illegal gambling increased in Ontario and Québec following the movement of organized crime into Montréal and Toronto during the 1950s (p. 118). Illegal gaming-machine operations continued, and some operators attempted to skirt the law, at times, with rather imaginative attempts.[53]

By the 1960s, the Canadian public's attitude toward gambling was changing, and the federal government saw lotteries as a way to support welfare-state activities. However, the fact that the government left gaming machines out of the 1969 *Criminal Code* amendment, suggests that GMOCs were not legitimized to the same degree as lotteries. For decades, pinball and other amusement machines had been widespread in bars, corner stores, and other convenience locations. Computerized poker machines also spread throughout Canada in the late 1970s. The machines were popular and legal as amusement devices; however, machine owners began paying cash prizes for jackpots to induce play. The provinces could have introduced GMOCs as of 1985, but did not do so until compelled to by fiscal problems.

There is no question that economic impetus led the provincial governments to legalize video lottery terminals (VLTs) in quick succession. The recession of the early 1990s produced severe economic difficulties across the country, and Ontario and Québec were reeling from the deindustrialization associated with liberalized trade agreements. Even oil-rich Alberta was coping with declining oil prices (Nikiforuk, 2006). Given this scenario, it is not surprising that eight provinces established VLTs in just over three years. It is significant that the expansion of VLTs produced little opposition or public debate, primarily because the social impact was unknown to the public, and the early adopters closed access to the polity. Nevertheless, VLTs in Canada quickly lost emotional legitimacy, the result of widely publicized media stories concerning gambling related harm linked to the machines. Provinces that waited to establish VLTs faced fierce public opposition.

The introduction of GMOCs in Canada took place without public inquiry that would have alerted the people to the government's intent and allowed churches, community groups, and other stakeholders to advance their positions on the issue. More importantly, most provinces used the Order in Council (OIC) process to establish machine gambling.[54] Although legislative debate often precedes an OIC, the process does not allow for full parliamentary deliberation. The lack of public inquiry and use of OICs suggest government ministers saw little need to build faith or emotional legitimacy for VLT programs in their respective jurisdictions. Two pieces of evidence support this position. First, British Columbia and Ontario tried to adopt after the other provinces, but politicians were forced to heed intense public opposition and either backed down or introduced VLTs in restricted settings.[55] Second, unlike Australia or the United States, few in Canada proposed or defended the legalization of VLTs for charitable causes or other public goods. Most political elite claimed legalization was necessary to deal with illegal machines, that prohibition was not a viable solution, and legalizing and regulating the machines would alleviate the problem while providing revenue to government (for example, see New Brunswick, n.d.). Nevertheless, claims that illegal machines were widespread and uncontrollable are questionable.[56] A better explanation is that governments needed the income, were unable or unwilling to provide the necessary resources to enforce the laws, and crown prosecutors found it difficult to obtain convictions (see HLT Advisory, 2006, p. 30; Robinson, 1983).[57]

In 1990, New Brunswick became the first Canadian province to establish GMOCs claiming 5,000 to 7,000 machines were operating unlawfully throughout the province (Azmier, Jepson, & Patton, 1999). It further tried to increase legitimacy by directing the proceeds to community groups and other eligible organizations, but the revenue was reallocated to the general government fund within two years.[58] The province was seemingly unconcerned about organized crime, evidenced by its choice of regulatory model. Upon implementing its program, the government chose the New Brunswick Machine Coin Operators Association to manage and operate the VLT network, despite some members' involvement in the illicit market (McKenna, 2008; Ormaechea, 1995, July 28).

The vendor-owner-operated model resulted in a rapid increase of GMOCs in neighbourhood settings (McKenna, 2008), but the machines did not initially attract much attention. However, the public began voicing concerns over accessibility and increasing social problems by 1995, which threatened the legitimacy of the VLT program. The government re-evaluated its policies in 1996, but opposition to VLTs and demands to restrict them to age-controlled sites continued to mount. During an election campaign in 1999, the Conservative Party pledged that it would hold a binding referendum on VLTs if elected. After gaining power, the Conservative government was forced to convene a referendum, and in 2001, 46.9% voted to prohibit VLTs and 53.1% supported the status quo (New Brunswick, 2001, 2003).[59] In 2003, continued public opposition forced the New Brunswick government to relocate VLTs to liquor-licensed venues, reduce the number of sites and machines, and to shift management and oversight of operations to the Atlantic Lottery Corporation.

The remaining Atlantic provinces initiated their VLT programs within a year of New Brunswick's using the same justification of illegal machines to establish legitimacy for legalization.[60] Newfoundland and Labrador was the second Canadian province to establish GMOCs, but unlike the other Atlantic provinces, it passed legislation – as opposed to using an OIC – and put the machines in age-restricted liquor-licensed venues. Newfoundland also chose a state-managed/vendor-operated regulatory model. Newfoundlanders were at first ambivalent toward VLTs, but the public's mood had changed by 1995. In response to the mounting opposition, the government issued an OIC that restricted advertising, the number of machines at each location, and prohibited the use of credit. Beyond this, the government did little over the next decade to address public concerns.[61] However, the legitimacy of the VLT program was again in question by 2005, forcing the government to react by placing a cap on the number of machines, promising a 15% reduction over five years, and in addition, providing more funding for problem gambling.

Nova Scotia authorized VLTs through an OIC just months after Newfoundland and Labrador, legitimizing the move by asserting a need to control illegal machines throughout the province. The ownership model was similar to Newfoundland's, with the exception that VLTs were located in non-age-restricted premises. Whereas opposition built slowly in New Brunswick and Newfoundland, condemnation of VLTs came swiftly in the more conservative province of Nova Scotia, arising within a year of legalization. By 1993, VLTs had lost emotional and legal legitimacy and, in an attempt to quell the opposition, the government relocated the machines to age-controlled establishments and pledged $500,000 (CAD) annually for problem gambling treatment. This failed to stem the ongoing delegitimization. The government responded by holding three public inquiries in two years, which further reduced legitimacy by criticizing the government's decision to legalize VLTs and highlighting the slight majority of opposition.[62] In 1995, the Nova Scotia government announced plans to introduce commercial casinos and the ensuing debate removed the VLT issue from the forefront, but it did not disappear. In 1998, the government passed the *Video Lottery Terminals Moratorium Act*, which set a cap on the number of VLTs in the province and mandated completion of a socioeconomic impact study within one year. Nevertheless, the pressure continued,[63] and in 2005 the Conservative government announced a new gambling strategy, which included a reduction of VLTs to one-third the number permitted under the moratorium.

Prince Edward Island legalized VLTs concurrently with the other Atlantic provinces. It also chose a regulatory model similar to New Brunswick's, with vendors owning and operating the machines in ambient settings. Although VLTs quickly proved controversial in the rural and conservative province, successive governments were slow to respond.[64] In 1997, citizens in the provincial capital, Charlottetown, voted by 79% to prohibit VLTs across Prince Edward Island (Manitoba Gaming Control Commission, 1998, p. 20; Wigginton, 1998).[65] The opposition's successful entry into the polity forced the province to reconsider its policies. Following the vote, the government moved VLTs to age-controlled establishments, assumed ownership, and placed the Atlantic Lottery Corporation in charge of operations. Notwithstanding this shift in policy, it launched GMOCs at the Charlottetown raceway in 2005.[66] McKenna (2007) describes the process and concludes that fiscal pressures on the state, strong industry lobbying, political influence, and ineffective opposition allowed the province to establish GMOCs at the raceway.

Although Manitoba's VLT program coincided with the Atlantic provinces', the government used a different route to legitimize machine gambling, claiming that VLTs would boost rural economic development by assisting the ailing hospitality industry and provide entertainment for tourists (Manitoba Gaming Control Commission, 1998).[67] The province established a state-owned/vendor-operated regulatory model and placed VLTs in age-controlled liquor-licensed venues throughout the province, but not in the provincial capital of Winnipeg to avoid competition with the new state-owned and operated casino. In 1993, Manitoba expanded its casino operations and simultaneously introduced VLTs in Winnipeg. As gambling opportunities grew, so too did public opposition, along with questions of legitimacy. The Manitoba government's initial response was to announce a moratorium on VLT gambling[68] and launch a public review of its gambling policies. In 1995, the Manitoba Lottery Policy Review Working Group released its report (*Desjardins Report*, 1995), and recommended a series of initiatives, ostensibly designed to limit opposition and rebuild legitimacy. Upon accepting the report, the government announced it would allow local plebiscites over VLTs; however, communities that prohibited the machines would also lose associated municipal grants. The *Gaming Control VLT Local*

Option Act passed in 1999, and the thinly veiled threat of losing VLT revenue appears to have worked. Just one town in Manitoba prohibited VLTs and lost its grant in the process.[69]

Alberta officially launched its VLT program in 1991 under a trial that was clearly not intended to assess public opinion. Although the Minister of Gaming promised that he 'would ask for public reaction ... [and would] evaluate the social impact' (Alberta Legislative Assembly, May 23, 1991), the results of such inquiries, if they occurred, were never made public (Smith & Wynne, 2004). In 1992, the Alberta government legalized VLTs through an OIC and tried to build legitimacy by claiming the revenue would benefit non-profit organizations, would prevent criminals from setting up illegal operations, and would provide Albertans with a new entertainment option (Alberta Gaming and Liquor Commission, 2001). Opposition to VLTs developed quickly, compelling the province to take ongoing measures, including a public review in 1995. One recommendation the government implemented gave communities a share in VLT profit – with a catch; communities that prohibited lotteries using a local plebiscite option would lose their share (Alberta Lotteries Review Committee, 1995, pp. 22–3). Between 1997 and 1998, 40 municipalities held plebiscites, and the outcome in some cases was close. For example, the citizens of Edmonton chose to keep VLTs by a margin of 485 votes (Alberta Gaming and Liquor Commission, 2001, pp. 14–17). In total, seven communities voted to remove VLTs, and the machines were immediately moved from two municipalities that had banned them. The government acted slowly on the remaining binding resolutions (Alberta Gaming and Liquor Commission, 2001: pp. 14–18). In 2003, the province reduced the number of VLT sites, but has continued to expand GMOCs by permitting slot machines at racetracks.

Saskatchewan borders two Canadian provinces and one American state with legal GMOCs, providing competition for Saskatchewan's hospitality industry. In 1993, the government passed an OIC authorizing VLTs for age-restricted venues, using Manitoba's economic rationale to legitimize the move. The provincial government immediately faced legitimacy issues and announced major changes just 18 months after launching the program (Government of Saskatchewan, 1995, January 27). The new plan called for a reduction and cap on machine numbers and increased funds for problem gambling treatment, research, and education. Following Alberta and Manitoba's example, municipalities were to receive a share of VLT profit. The government later cancelled the arrangement, purportedly because the municipalities could not agree on distribution (Azmier et al., 1999). In 2002, the Saskatchewan government increased the number of VLTs by 400 machines. The Saskatchewan Gaming and Liquor Authority (SGLA) claimed the move was to aid the hospitality industry, and was an outcome of newly released provincial research on problem gambling (Government of Saskatchewan, 2002, March 22). The SGLA further maintained it would balance state revenue with additional resources for problem gambling treatment. Yet, following the 2007 release of a report examining the relationship between problem gambling and gaming machines, the province reduced the number of VLTs to 2003 levels (Government of Saskatchewan, 2007, March 16).

Québec was the last province to introduce VLTs in ambient settings. Although this might seem peculiar, given the more tolerant and permissive culture in the urban areas of Québec, video poker 'amusement' machines were widespread in the late 1970s, and organized crime had long been associated with slot-machine gambling (Robinson, 1983). In 1979, the National Assembly passed legislation authorizing Loto-Québec to operate video lotteries (Québec – A, n.d.),[70] and during the 1989 provincial election, the Liberals pledged to place gaming machines under the direction of Loto-Québec (Panetta, 2002). When the party gained power, it stopped licensing video-poker amusement machines and directed the provincial police to seize them. The Québec Superior Court declared the machines unlawful, and the case went to the Supreme Court of Canada where the court denied leave to appeal (*R v. Laniel*, 1991 in Supreme Court of Canada, 1994 *R v. Kent*, [1994] 3 S.C.R. 133, 1994: cases cited, disapproved). Following the collapse of the amusement operator's case, the police estimated between 25,000 and 40,000 illegal machines existed across the province (Loto-Quebec, n.d.; Panetta, 2002). The Québec Liberal government seemingly used this to legitimize the introduction of its video-lottery program despite the fact that provincial legislation had authorized it 14 years previously.[71] Although Loto-Québec could have operated VLTs without legislative amendments, the government felt additional controls were needed because of 'the nature of the activity and the perception of concern regarding criminal activity' (Personal Communication – Service à la clientele, Loto-Québec, 2007). Consequently, the government passed a law in 1993 that provided a new legislative framework for VLTs.[72] Profit from Québec's GMOCs jumped from 93.7% to 141%, between 1994 and 2001(Loto-Québec, 2004, p. 18),[73] and ambivalence became intense opposition. Following a series of highly publicized suicides, the government announced it would remove 1,000 VLTs and place the remainder in less visible locations (CBC News Online, 2001, May 31).[74] Within a year, a class-action suit was also launched against Loto-Québec on behalf of an estimated 125,000 problem gamblers who allegedly suffered from VLT addiction and wanted redress from the province (Canadian Press Newswire, 2002, May 6). By 2004, Loto-Québec reacted to the credible threat posed by the lawsuit, issuing a series of recommendations to the government.[75] Among the many implemented, the province began moving VLTs from neighbourhoods to racetracks.[76]

British Columbia and Ontario were last to attempt to legalize VLTs in convenience settings, but neither province could build emotional legitimacy for GMOCs in ambient settings. Opposition was stronger than that of the other provinces, due to negative experiences, and publicity surrounding GMOCs in other regions acted as a frame of reference. Public pressure also forced open the polity in both provinces through public hearings and plebiscites. Finally, the police in British Columbia hindered legitimacy building by questioning whether legal VLTs would have any impact on VLTs operated by organized crime.

British Columbia began looking at VLTs in 1992 (British Columbia Legislative Assembly, June 9, 1992) but waited to adopt until 1994. The government tried to establish legitimacy with a tactic that had been successful elsewhere; members of the political elite claimed organized crime was operating illegal gaming machines. However, the police undermined this position by suggesting legalization would not solve the problem (Canadian Press Newswire, 1995, March 1). At the same time, citizen and church groups had banded together to fight the expansion of all forms of gambling; thirty-nine municipalities enacted by-laws where gaming machines would be prohibited without council approval.[77] Having recognized that VLTs held little emotional and legal legitimacy and, that legalization would be a risky political move, the government abandoned its plans in 1995. However, some municipalities did agree to allow slot machines in casinos and, in 2002, the government declared its authority to site and control slot machines at casinos, bingo halls, and racetracks in communities that agreed to host them. Throughout this period, the horse racing industry had been unsuccessful in lobbying for gaming machines at racetracks, primarily because municipalities would not permit them. This changed in 2003, when Surrey agreed to slots at Fraser Downs raceway. Vancouver followed in 2004, but several other communities continue to resist.[78] The issue of VLTs in ambient settings appears a dead issue in British Columbia.

Ontario tried to introduce VLTs in 1996; however, deep opposition led to mixed success. In the early 1990s, Ontario faced slow economic growth and one of the sharpest increases in unemployment in the country (Baldwin et al., 2004). Perhaps anticipating resistance, the New Democratic Party government displayed little interest in adopting VLTs. (Ontario Legislative Assembly, May 11, 1992). It established a casino in Windsor instead, which attracted little opposition because of promises of economic development and revenue from the United States (Klassen & Cosgrave, 2009). In 1995, Ontarians elected a Conservative government which immediately undertook efforts to adopt GMOCs. The plan was to introduce VLTs, beginning with permanent charitable casinos, followed by racetracks, and then liquor-licensed venues. The premier endeavoured to establish legitimacy by claiming permanent charitable casinos and age-controlled sites would reduce the estimated 20,000 illegal machines in the province and provide better control (Ontario Legislative Assembly, November 5, 1996). He further appealed to traditional legitimacy by arguing that gambling was a historical feature of racetracks and that GMOCs would help the tracks survive the hard times they had fallen on. The government would help out charities, the horse racing and hospitality industries, while simultaneously confronting the problem of illegal machines it had linked to organized crime.[79] Notwithstanding these tactics, the people and competing business interests put up substantial resistance.[80] The premier had made an election pledge to allow local plebiscites for casinos, and opposition groups applied it to VLTs forcing the premier to keep his promise. Just three of 33 municipalities voted in favour on municipal election ballots (Laframbroise, 1998). Smith and Rubenstein (2009) further cite two events that dissuaded the government from adopting GMOCs. First, a Toronto law firm hired by the Ontario Lottery and Gaming Commission recommended against legalizing VLTs, and second, the Ontario minister for gambling received advice from his counterpart in Alberta that such a move would be a mistake (p. 27). The culmination of these proceedings reduced the legitimacy of adoption, and the Conservative government withdrew plans for VLTs in ambient settings and 44 permanent charity casinos, although it still managed to establish four charity casinos and several racinos across the province.

In summarizing the Canadian experience with GMOCs, there has been a mixture of policies as each province responded to cultural differences and contingencies. Gaming machines that paid cash prizes were illegal for a century, but this changed with an amendment to the *Criminal Code* and a global recession. All the provinces introduced GMOCs between 1990 and 1996, the result of fiscal imperatives and/ or efforts to appease the hospitality and horse racing industries. There was also weak initial opposition in the provinces that were first to legalize GMOCs. Governments limited debate and access to the polity through the Order in Council process, and when legislation was put forward the public had little information about the potential negative impacts of gaming machines, which left church groups to speak out. This is why three of four Atlantic provinces could establish VLTs in highly accessible settings without public resistance. As the media and concerned citizens groups began highlighting the associated problems, it prompted several provinces to relocate them to liquor-licensed premises or to opt for a different regulatory model. More importantly, eight of 10 provinces directly or indirectly used the spectre of illegal machines, operated by organized crime, to try and create legitimacy, despite the fact that law enforcement had never been a priority. Several other provinces associated GMOCs with economic development and non-profit organizations. British Columbia and Ontario tried to introduce gaming machines after they had become controversial, but failed to build legitimacy and faced stiff resistance as a result. Continuing questions of legitimacy have meant ongoing efforts to regenerate acceptable VLT policies. Nevertheless, opposition and government responses have differed regionally, because of differing moral values and political cultures. For example, in 1999, 41% of Canadians thought VLTs should be banned, but nearly two-thirds of Atlantic Canadians felt this way (Azmier, 2000, p. 53). Those most opposed were regular participants in religious activities and/or were against gambling (p. 53). Easy access to GMOCs has also been a primary concern. When asked in the 1999 survey whether 'Video Lottery Terminals should be limited to Race Tracks and Casinos,' 70% agreed overall, 49% strongly (p. 52). Even though the provinces have implemented a wide range of policies designed to (re)build legitimacy for GMOCs and minimize resistance, opposition persists. At issue is the governments' refusal to remove VLTs from easily accessible community settings, which has weakened legal legitimacy in the process. Politicians and bureaucrats have instead altered the discourse to responsible gambling and linked revenue to government programs and/or charitable causes.

Gaming Machines outside Casinos in the United States

An examination of the emergence and ongoing presence of gaming machines in the United States reveals different conditions than those in Australia and Canada. Six states legalized slot machines before 1970, and four subsequently prohibited them before a state or province in the other countries had adopted GMOCS. The evidence also shows that illegal gaming machines were (and still are) widespread, and that organized crime involvement and corruption have been more pervasive in the United States.[81]

Gaming machines first emerged in the United States in the mid-nineteenth century (Fey, 1983). As with lotteries, social disorder caused strong opposition and created legal legitimacy issues for the industry. Following the First World War, the antigambling and temperance movements were successful in delegitimizing slot machines and the political elite took steps to prohibit them. However, Congress unintentionally helped the industry by prohibiting alcohol. The speakeasy proved the ideal environment for slot machines,[82] and organized crime began to control operations, forging an inexorable link between the two (Engler, 2004). Indeed, the connection between slot machines and gangsters like Al Capone and Lucky Luciano led to the label of 'one-armed bandits' (Tamony, 1968, p. 122).

To evade the laws during this period, manufacturers, owners, and operators colluded with public officials and the police, still a problem in some states.[83] They also changed machine designs for amusement or gambling (King, 1964; see also Drzazga, 1963). The new machines were highly lucrative, immediately attracted organized crime, and led to further corruption among public officials.[84] The addition of free games, and inability to distinguish between slot and pinball machines, also made it difficult to interpret and enforce the laws. By the mid-1930s, commercial and non-profit venues offered various types of legal and illegal machine gaming, and a patchwork of state regulations and differences in tolerance and degrees of enforcement ensued.

With the exception of Nevada, the states of Florida, Montana, and Washington authorized gaming machines during the depression years for good causes or to provide funds for charities. Idaho and Montana legalized slots as fraternal organizations within each state began competing with each other (Drzazga, 1952, 1963; Peterson, 1949; *Time*, 1953, March 2). Gaming machines seemingly gained some emotional and

Table 4.11   Period of Introduction of Gaming Machines outside of Casinos in the United States as of 2005

State	To 1970	1970–5	1976–80	1981–5	1986–90	1991–5	1996–2000	2001–5
NORTHEAST								
Connecticut								
Maine								4
Massachusetts								
New Hampshire								
New Jersey								
New York								8
Pennsylvania								4, 5
Rhode Island						8		
Vermont								
SOUTHEAST								
Alabama								
Arkansas								
Delaware						8		
Florida	3 ■							4
Georgia								
Kentucky								
Maryland	1 ■				1			
Mississippi								
Louisiana						3, 4		
Oklahoma								
North Carolina								
South Carolina						3	■	
Tennessee								
Texas								
Virginia								
West Virginia						8		1, 3
MIDWEST								
Illinois								
Indiana								
Iowa						1		
Kansas								
Michigan								
Minnesota								
Missouri								
Nebraska								
North Dakota								
Ohio								
South Dakota					3			

(*Continued*)

Table 4.11   (*Continued*)

State	To 1970	1970–5	1976–80	1981–5	1986–90	1991–5	1996–2000	2001–5
Wisconsin								
WEST								
Alaska								
Arizona								
California								
Colorado								
Hawaii								
Idaho	3 ■							
Montana	1 ■			3				
New Mexico							1, 3	
Nevada	3							
Oregon						6, 7		
Utah								
Wyoming								
Washington	1 ■							

Source: Drzazga, J. (1952); McQueen (2004) Montana Department of Justice (n.d.);
Time (1953); State Gaming Agencies.

1 – Non-Profit Owner/Operator	2 – Vendor Owner/Operator (Racino)
3 – Vendor Owner/Operator (Other)	4 – Corporate Owner/Operator (Racino)
5 – Corporate Owner/Operator (Other)	6 – State Owner/Operator (Racino)
7 – State Owner/Operator (Other)	8 – State Hybrid Owner/Operator (Racino)
9 – State Hybrid Owner/Operator (Other)	■ – Legalized then prohibited

legal legitimacy when legalized for good causes and crime and/or corruption were not involved. However, control was a serious issue leading to legitimacy problems in most early adopting states.

In 1935, Florida became the first state outside Nevada to authorize slot machines under the auspices of funds for public projects and social services (Florida Committee on Regulated Industries, 2004, p. 6).[85] However, crime and corruption associated with slots were rampant (Drzazga, 1963), and Florida repealed its law in 1937 after referenda demonstrated widespread public opposition (Peterson, 1949).

Just as Florida was rejecting slots, Maryland turned to machine gambling to augment state income; although the legislation had a 'sunset' clause for 1939, the state passed bills to permit operations through local option for several decades (Maryland Department of Legislative

Services, 2004, p. 1). Slot machines gained legitimacy in a few counties, but Maryland banned them in 1963 when organized crime became associated with the operations (Janis, 2004, January 12). Nevertheless, fraternal organizations continued to openly use gaming machines for funds, and the state again chose to permit local options for non-profit organizations in 1987 (Maryland Department of Legislative Services, 2004, p. 1).

Washington State also authorized slot machines for non-profit clubs and fraternal organizations during the depression (Perkins, 2004). However, the Washington Supreme Court ruled, in 1952, that the constitution did not permit a lottery, that slot machines were lotteries, and therefore illegal (pp. 75–6). Montana passed laws similar to Washington's in 1945 (Drzazga, 1952),[86] but crime and social disorder quickly increased. In 1947, the governor declared he had made a mistake signing the legislation and was determined to have the laws repealed (Peterson, 1949). The public was also opposed to slot machines as illustrated by a 1950 referendum where 72% voted against the machines (see Montana Initiative and Referendum Issues, n.d.). In the same year, Montana's Supreme Court ruled slot machines and punchboards illegal under the state's constitution (Montana Department of Justice, n.d.).

Idaho was in proximity to three states with legal slot machines – Montana, Nevada, and Washington – and by 1947 the significant monies pouring into the neighbouring states prompted legislators to legalize gaming machines for non-profit clubs on a local option basis (Drzazga, 1963; Time, 1953, March 2). Within two years, organized crime, corruption, and social problems had forced Idaho's larger cities to forbid them (Drzazga, 1963), and the governor sought a state-wide ban, but slot machines across state lines and potential lost income constrained prohibition until 1953 (Time, 1953, March 2).[87]

Following the depression, slot and pinball gambling machines were prolific across the United States and politicians and law-enforcement agencies had difficulty maintaining control. In 1941, the federal government imposed a stamp tax of $10 on amusement machines and $50 on gambling machines (Anonymous, 1950; King, 1964; Frey, 1998).[88] The act allowed close scrutiny on the slot-machine industry, since each legal machine required an official stamp, and each owner had to maintain public records. The illegal industry flourished nonetheless, and the federal government again intervened in 1950 with the *Johnson Act*, which made it a federal offense to transport gaming machines into states where they were illegal. However, the legislation was flawed[89] and effective laws were not passed until 1962. *Lawful* gaming machines in the United States began disappearing by the mid-1960s.[90] Nevada was the last state with legal slot machines but illegal machine operations continued elsewhere and, in many cases, states and law enforcement agencies openly tolerated them (King, 1964).

For analytical purposes, I have divided the resurgence of legal GMOCs in the United States into three segments: 1985 to 1991; 1992 to 1997; and 2001 forward. The main distinguishing feature between the latter two periods is that an increasing number of states attempted adoption after 2001. Examining the early regulatory models, it is noteworthy that six of the seven early adopters legalized GMOCs for ambient settings, whereas the majority of states after this period located the machines at racetracks. In addition, several states in the first wave faced immediate opposition, which coincided with establishment of The National Coalition against Legalized Gambling in 1994. These factors prompted other political elites to either bypass constitutional issues by introducing GMOCs as part of voter-approved lottery programs and/or propose GMOCs for racetracks.

Siting gaming machines at tracks has proven the most effective tactic for legalizing GMOCs in the United States, because it uses a combination of traditional and emotional motivations to build legitimacy. Proponents of racinos appeal to tradition by claiming that GMOCs will save ailing horse/dog racing industries. Where applicable they use inevitability legitimacy by maintaining slot machines at tracks are necessary to eliminate illegal operations and prevent gamblers from going to bordering states. They argue that racinos will encourage economic development and tourism without the same capital investment as destination-style casinos (Christiansen, 2005). Lastly, they propose assigning the proceeds to county governments, education, and other public goods. Accordingly, racino supporters maintain that GMOCs will support a valuable – and often historic – industry at modest expense, and without spreading gambling throughout the state. In addition, the gaming machines will provide public benefits. For these reasons, racino proposals have been more successful than proposals for ambient settings.[91]

The first wave of the revival of legal GMOCs in the United States began in Montana in 1975.[92] Montana's voters changed the constitution in 1972, authorizing the legislature to approve gambling in the state (Montana Department of Justice, n.d.) and video keno was introduced soon after. Video-poker machines could be found throughout the state by the early 1980s, and when the State Supreme Court declared them illegal in 1984 (*New York Times*, 1984, February 5), the legislature passed the *Video Poker Machine Act* (Montana Department of Justice Gambling Control Division, 2002). Montana restricts GMOCs to age-controlled sites, and opposition groups have so far failed to generate effective resistance along faith or emotional lines.

South Dakota borders Montana and was first to introduce a video lottery, thereby providing an example for other American states and Canadian provinces.[93] When the state initiated a lottery in 1987, it immediately began considering a video-lottery program. The first attempt to legalize GMOCs took place in 1988 and failed by one vote. The measure was reintroduced and passed the following year. It is unclear how the government justified the VLT program but it did not consult the electorate; voters had approved lotteries through a constitutional amendment, and the state legislated video gaming as a form of lottery (South Dakota Lottery, n.d.). Still, opposition to VLTs has been constant, and efforts to repeal the legislation have been close.[94] In 1994, South Dakota's Supreme Court ruled video lotteries included casino-style games and violated the constitution (Hattori, 1994, September 6). The state proposed a constitutional amendment authorizing VLTs and the initiative narrowly passed (South Dakota Secretary of State, 1994), which led the government to appeal to emotional legitimacy by using VLT revenue to reduce property taxes, a strategy that has worked so far. Nevertheless, the video-lottery program remains controversial.[95]

GMOCs were also legalized in Maryland and South Carolina during the mid-1980s; however, the experiences in both states have been much different than the remaining jurisdictions. Maryland authorized gaming machines for non-profit clubs by local option in 1987, allowing a small number of clubs to operate a modest number of machines (Maryland Department of Legislative Services, 2007). In 2003, the governor tried to gain authorization for commercial GMOCs, but the measure failed. Then, in 2008, Maryland voters approved a constitutional amendment 59% to 41% permitting 15,000 VLTs at five locations around the state (Maryland Budget and Tax Policy Institute, 2008; Maryland State Board of Elections, n.d.). Proponents drew upon the same arguments that appeal to tradition and emotion and have been successfully used in lottery and gambling campaigns elsewhere: save the horse racing industry, and provide funds for education while preventing gambling dollars from leaving the state (Maryland Budget and Tax Policy Institute, 2008, p. 9).

South Carolina prohibited all gambling, but the State Supreme Court ruled in 1984 that video poker only constituted gambling if the machines paid out cash prizes (Ulbrich, 1998). In 1986, a senator attached a provision to a budget bill legalizing payouts on video-poker machines (Plotz, 1999, October 15). Since the original legislation did not include any restrictions, the industry remained unregulated and, at one point, 7,000 establishments had over 30,000 machines (Stedman Weidenbener, 2004, December 13). There was apparently some legal legitimacy since the General Assembly passed legislation in 1993 to license and monitor the machines. However, the 1993 legislation also provided for a statewide referendum and local option to prohibit GMOCs. A referendum to ban GMOCs passed in 1994 but the South Carolina Supreme Court subsequently ruled it unconstitutional, finding the state had no power to institute referenda (Olson et al., 2003). In 1998, opposition continued to grow and the governor championed a successful effort to ban the machines, yet the State Supreme Court again overturned the decision ruling that video poker was not a lottery (Goddard, 2000). Finally, in 1999, the General Assembly voted to hold a referendum to prohibit video poker from the state that included a proviso: if the courts found the referendum unconstitutional, a ban would come into effect (Plotz, 1999, October 15). South Carolina's Supreme Court found the referendum unconstitutional, and video poker became illegal in 2000 (Firestone, 1999, October 15).

In 1990, West Virginia became the sixth state to legalize GMOCs when the state's lottery commission authorized video lotteries at racetracks without legislative approval (Cogar, 2001). The State Supreme Court later ruled the commission had acted in excess of its powers and declared the program illegal (*State ex rel. Mountaineer Park v. Polan*, 438 S. E. 2d 308 [W.Va. 1993]). Soon after, the legislature passed the *Racetrack Video Lottery Act*, which authorized publicly administered and privately operated VLTs at racetracks, subject to local option. To obtain legitimacy, the state divided VLT profit among the tracks, the counties where the tracks were located, and other public funds (West Virginia Legislature, n.d.). In 2001, the legislature passed the *Limited Video Lottery Act* to permit VLTs at liquor-licensed lounges and non-profit clubs. The legislators used inevitability and legal issues to build legitimacy: illegal machines had proliferated across the state, and legal VLTs would combat the problem (*Club Association of West Virginia, Inc. v. Wise*, 156 F. Supp 2d 599 [S.D.W.Va. 2001]). In 2003, two antigambling groups petitioned West Virginia's Supreme Court to prohibit all lottery operation, but the court dismissed the petition ruling the state was acting in the public's best interests (*Greenbrier County Coalition against Gambling Expansion, et al., Petitioners*, 2003). The state currently directs the proceeds from video lotteries to education, seniors, and the promotion of tourism (American Gaming Association, 2006).

Louisiana legalized video-poker machines during the 1980s, along with lotteries and casinos, to reduce fiscal stress on the state following the collapse of the petrochemical industry. The main obstacle to legalization was the state's constitution stating that the legislature should define and suppress gambling (see Louisiana, n.d.; Louisiana State and Local Government, n.d., Chapter 2). The state legislators moved around this obstacle by passing the *Video Draw Poker Devices Law* (1991) that declared video poker to be *gaming* (Supreme Court of Louisiana, 2001). The appeal to emotional legitimacy was that introducing GMOCs would increase economic development and tourism, thereby benefiting the welfare of the citizens (Louisiana State Legislature, n.d., RS 27, 2). By 1992, video-poker devices were at racetracks, liquor-licensed lounges, and truck stops around the state. In 1996, just over half the parishes in Louisiana voted to prohibit the machines (Rose, n.d.) and GMOCs remain in those parishes that voted to keep them.

In 1984, Oregon voters approved a constitutional amendment permitting the state to operate lotteries, and in 1991 the General Assembly approved 'games of chance using video devices' (Oregon State, 2005). Proponents may have obtained legitimacy by claiming 10,000 illegal machines were operating throughout the state (Oregon Lottery, n.d.) and by allocating 3% of gross revenue for the treatment of problem gambling (Volberg, 1997). However, numerous protests and legal challenges quickly ensued when video-poker devices appeared at liquor-licensed establishments in 1992 (p. 2). Some politicians also introduced motions prohibiting video poker. All of these efforts failed and despite ongoing resistance, the lottery commission approved the introduction of VLTs in 2005 (*Lottery Post*, 2005, January 27).

Four states legalized GMOCs during the second wave of legalizations: Rhode Island (1992), Delaware (1994), Iowa (1994), and New Mexico (1998). In 1973, Rhode Islanders voted to permit a lottery and authorized the government to regulate them. As in South Dakota, legislators used this to establish a video lottery without voter approval, and VLTs opened at two racetracks in 1992. The electorate rejected this reading of the law and amended the constitution in 1994 to prohibit further forms of gambling. Although opposition continued to grow, the lottery commission voted to increase the number of VLTs at the tracks. The governor resisted and the Rhode Island Supreme Court heard the case and ruled in the commission's favour (Driver, 1999). The cities with racetracks also appealed to the State Supreme Court, but the

General Assembly passed legislation in 2005 overriding the governor's veto and endorsing the expansion (*Gaming Law Review*, 2005b). The state directs video-lottery revenue to the general fund, and the state gets approximately 11% of its revenue from gambling (Donnis, 2003, September 19–25).[96]

In 1994, the Delaware legislature passed the *Horse Racing Development Act* to place VLTs at three racetracks. The justification was to provide assistance to the state's racing industry through economic development and increased purse sizes. Like many other states with video lotteries, Delaware prohibits slot machines, and the General Assembly circumvented the constitution by calling the machines 'video devices' even though the definition in the constitution included electronic slot machines (*Delaware State Lottery Office Video Lottery Regulations*, 2005). The racing industry initially prospered with VLTs at the tracks, but competition from other jurisdictions with GMOCs forced Delaware to increase the number of machines (Brand & Egan, n.d.) and, in 2009, the state added 24-hour alcohol service.

Iowa provides an interesting case of what Parvin and Koven (1995, p. 434) call the 'inversion of the private sector's market test for expansion' to legitimize the introduction of slot machines at Iowa racetracks. The state legalized pari-mutuel gambling in the 1980s, and some counties guaranteed loans for racetracks to stimulate economic development (p. 422). By the early 1990s, the state's tracks were in decline with several facing bankruptcy, and one county had to cover its loans and operating expenses. When given the opportunity for tax relief through a racino, the electorate approved the measure 62% to 38% (p. 433). Three counties, in total, voted for slot machines at tracks owned by non-profit organizations and operated by private operators. The slots have been a windfall for local charities and governments (*Supreme Court of the United States 02-695*, 2003). Legitimacy was achieved, in part, by allocating public revenue to the state for education, the environment, state infrastructure, and problem gambling.

New Mexico did not permit lotteries until 1996 and, had it not been for political manoeuvring, it is unlikely the state would have legalized GMOCs. Following his election in 1994, the governor signed compacts for tribal casinos, but the compacts were ruled illegal (Rose, 2002). A bill was introduced in 1997 to reinstate them. The state's racetracks were foundering and charities felt threatened by the prospect of casinos (Webb, 2003, January 31). The governor compromised by permitting slots for fraternal organizations, charities, and tracks, with the taxes going to the general fund and problem-gambling treatment.

Between 2001 and 2010, 14 states introduced proposals for GMOCs (Prah, 2004, May 18), but only five have been successful. New York led the third-wave push for GMOCs in 2001 following the terrorist attack on the World Trade Center (Francis & Keilin, 2004). Facing a huge deficit, the legislature directed the state lottery to license VLTs at eight racetracks (p. 3). The rationale for the bill was that it would prevent people leaving the state to gamble, while increasing revenue for tracks and state education (New York State Senate Standing Committee on Racing, Gaming and Wagering, 2005). However, opponents successfully challenged the legislation, pointing out that the constitution instructs that all lottery proceeds be used for education (Francis & Keilin, 2004). In response, the state passed a bill providing funds for the tracks from general revenue (*Rochester Downtown*, September 2005). In 2004, the governor of New York proposed opening eight additional sites with VLTs outside of the tracks, but the legislature rejected the plan and, in 2005, a group opposed to VLTs tried to have them banned, by arguing they were not lotteries and therefore unconstitutional (Francis & Keilin, 2004). The Court of Appeals ruled 5–2 in favour of the state (*Dalton et al. v. Pataki*, 2005).

In 2004–5, Maine, Oklahoma, Pennsylvania, and Florida joined the other 11 states with legal GMOCs.[97] Voters in Maine approved the introduction of slot machines for raceways in 2003, by a narrow margin of 52.9% to 47.1% (Maine Secretary of State, n.d.). The town of Scarborough, Maine later prohibited slots within its town limits. The track attempted to relocate, but failed to obtain support in two local-option votes (Peters, 2004, October 15). In 2006, the General Assembly passed further legislation authorizing a second racino in the state and setting up local options for county approval. After the governor vetoed both bills, the Secretary of State announced a referendum on the issue in the 2007 November election (Maine Secretary of State, 2007, April 26). Nevertheless, opposition to gambling expansion in Maine has been strong and constant, and an antigambling coalition initiated a second referendum question, calling for the prohibition of slot machines across the state (Canfield, 2006, November 6), but lost. The proceeds from Maine's slot machines are allocated to the horse racing industry, health care, education, and the host community (Center for Policy Analysis, University of Massachusetts, 2007).

Pennsylvania authorized up to 61,000 slot machines for resorts, racetracks, and slot parlours in 2004 (Barnes, 2005, January 2). The Democratic governor proposed the legislation in 2003, and despite strong resistance from Republican legislators, it passed in 2004 (January 2). The governor obtained public support by claiming that GMOCs would benefit the horse racing and hospitality industries and promising the revenue for tax relief and education. However, political manipulation was also involved: a bill to regulate the horse racing industry was amended to include slot machines just prior to introduction and pushed through the house and senate. Antigambling groups challenged the constitutional validity of the legislation in 2005 (January 2) but Pennsylvania's Supreme Court ruled in the state's favour (*Supreme Court of Pennsylvania, 2005, J-19*). In 2006, the government linked GMOC profit to tax relief for homeowners and senior citizens, which may have strengthened support for machine gambling (Commonwealth of Pennsylvania, n.d.).

In Florida, the governor was opposed to GMOCs and had several allies in the House and Senate. Despite their efforts to stop a constitutional amendment permitting GMOCs, a ballot measure passed in 2004, giving Broward and Miami-Dade counties the local option of approving slot machines for pari-mutuel facilities (Hallifax, 2004, November 5). Floridians had rejected proposals for gambling expansion three times since 1978, but the 2004 measure promised a proportion of slot revenue for the state's schools, which garnered support from the teacher's union, school boards, and administrators (November 5). In 2005, Broward County voted in favour of GMOCs and Miami-Dade rejected the proposal (Baró Diaz, 2005, March 10). Following the vote, legislators opposed to GMOCs unsuccessfully tried to stall the move and restrict the machines to electronic bingo (Kleindienst, 2005, March 25). Governor Bush signed the bill permitting slot machines in Fort Lauderdale, while declaring his objection and constitutional obligation to sign it into law (*Canada Newswire*, 2005, December 8).

As shown in this brief historical overview, several developments led to continued condemnation of GMOCs in the United States for most of the twentieth century. The introduction of slot machines led to widespread social disorder, and middle-class moral reformers pressured politicians to ban them early on. Nevertheless, the prohibition of alcohol and lucrative slot-machine operations attracted organized crime. Ongoing illegal operations, fraud, corruption, and social problems with both slot and pinball machines curtailed attempts to build legitimacy. These factors, and the lack of public acceptance, despite the allocation of revenue to good causes, led early adopting states to quickly reverse legalization. Yet, illegal gaming machines flourished and are still found in many states, primarily because operations were prohibited, but manufacture, sales, and/or ownership were not. A few states also permitted gaming machines for fraternal and non-profit organizations until the 1960s provided local communities did not organize resistance. Law enforcement intensified after the 1951 *Kefauver Inquiry* highlighted organized crime involvement in the industry (*Nevada Observer,* n.d.).

As state-operated lotteries re-emerged, confidence that gambling operations could operate efficiently and without corruption increased. Furthermore, middle-class Americans' attitudes toward gambling softened, and states began looking to additional forms of gambling to generate revenue. Many states have tried to establish GMOCs in ambient settings or at pari-mutuel venues, but most have been unsuccessful; of 14 states that legalized GMOCs between 1985 and 2005, 12 did so through legislation alone. Numerous others have failed to secure voter approval. Furthermore, six states implemented video lotteries to avoid constitutional conflicts, and two passed legislation through what might be termed 'backdoor' legislation. These points highlight the difficulties states have had in building legitimacy for GMOCs.

As in Canada, the early adopting states that sited GMOCs in ambient settings faced immediate opposition. Other states paid attention through policy learning and restricted GMOCs to pari-mutuel and slot facilities, partly as a result of perceived or real opposition and partly from lobbying by the pari-mutuel industry. In most cases, antigambling organizations have challenged the state's legitimacy in legalizing GMOCs, but the courts have typically sided with the state and capital. Finally, all states attempting to introduce GMOCs have sought traditional, emotional, or inevitability legitimacy either initially or thereafter. Most have cited threats to the horse race industry, lost revenues to bordering states, and/or the presence of illegal machines, while promising increased revenue for public goods, or individual incentives like tax relief. The recent fiscal crises should lead to many more proposals and, perhaps, adoption in states where citizens are faced with cuts to services or increased taxation. The key issues will be the political will and capacity to legitimize the move.

Summary

Machine gambling represents the first concerted effort to commercialize gambling for the general masses, which predates many other incursions by capital and the state into the cultural realm.[98] However, the associated crime and social problems quickly led states and communities to prohibit them. For decades, gaming-machine manufacturers created innovative designs to circumvent the laws and were largely successful; lawmakers, the courts, and the police often had difficulty determining if a gaming-machine's features fell within the law. Once demand for GMOCs grew, the industry focused on aesthetics and has increasingly used leading-edge technologies to drive profits. In fact, gaming machines are at the epicentre of the gaming industry's research and development and are clearly integrated within the new cultural economy. States and provinces are aiding these processes through attempts to shift the symbolic elements of machine gambling to entertainment and by sanctioning and/or introducing prototypes without fully examining their impact on individual gamblers.

GMOCs in Australia, Canada, and the United States were, for the most part, prohibited for much of the twentieth century. This was the result of moral disapproval among the middle classes and ruling elites. Nevertheless, crime, corruption, and social problems delegitimized GMOCs more than any other factor. The involvement of organized crime and corruption has also been more pervasive in the United States than elsewhere. Technological developments during the 1980s provided potential for better regulatory and legal control, which helped legitimize GMOCs among lawmakers. Once GMOCs were introduced, social disorder surrounding problem gambling became key, which is why resistance has been pronounced when the machines are placed in ambient settings; easy access is one contributing factor to gambling-related harm.

As with casinos and lotteries, many state and provincial jurisdictions have attempted to legalize GMOCs to augment state revenue in response to global and local political-economic pressures. Yet, this does not fully explain variation in the timeline of adoption, models of ownership and operation, dispersion, and participation. The social and cultural environment of a region has clearly influenced legitimacy building for GMOCs.

Australia's culture and clubs assisted adoption in several states. Lobbying by the hotel and gaming-machine industries led to further expansion. It would be a mistake to assume that GMOCs were introduced in Australia without public opposition. All the same, the historical connection between clubs and illegal gaming machines in New South Wales established a strong link between these entertainment centres and gambling providers (O'Hara, 1988; Caldwell, 1972; Hing, 2000, 2006). The clubs also became institutionalized as support networks for local communities. The combination of the two allowed the New South Wales government to build legitimacy for legal GMOCs. The criminal activities and social problems that followed delegitimized GMOCs and created a political disincentive for other Australian states to consider introducing poker machines.

These deterrents were reduced by financial problems experienced by the states and other Australian clubs, a softening of public attitudes, and technological developments conducive to tighter regulatory control. As each state attempted to adopt GMOCs they used similar legitimizing tactics that had worked in the other states: they appealed to collective emotions and Australian tradition by claiming the clubs would inevitably decline without poker-machine revenue and by offering public goods. Where the state wished to introduce commercial GMOCs, it added economic development and tourism to enhance proponents' arguments. Given Australia's egalitarian culture, it makes sense that the social institution of the club, and/or promises to fund other good causes would legitimize GMOCs. Still regional cultural differences and political-economic factors led to diverse levels of opposition, efforts to legalize, and the configuration of ownership and operation of GMOCs in that country.

Comparing Canada and the United States with Australia, organizations similar to the Australian club that might have been used to validate GMOCs were not as numerous or well-established (see also Caldwell, 1972).[99] Politicians had to find other ways to legitimize introduction, and they used promises of public goods, control of crime, and/or preserving the historic horse racing industry. Still, as in Australia, variations in culture, the perceived social problems associated with GMOCs, and political-economic dynamics, in each region, strongly influenced adoption. The Canadian provinces were also constrained by federal legislation dating back to the late nineteenth century.

Historically, illegal gaming machines existed in Canada, but their numbers and the extent of organized criminal involvement is unclear. Following the 1985 *Criminal Code* amendment legalizing 'mechanical gaming devices,' most provinces quietly established GMOCs without public debate and rationalized the move after the fact. Although the real reason was economic, the majority of politicians and bureaucrats used justifications that would resonate with the Canadian public: maintenance of law and order. The 'problem' would only be curtailed through legalization, and the *Criminal Code* directed the provinces to manage and operate GMOCs. The contention that illegal machines would exist despite enforcement may have further created inevitability legitimacy through a sense of certainty.[100] Proposals to use VLTs to encourage rural economic development were used in Manitoba and Saskatchewan since it would help overcome opposition among rural constituents (and the machines would be hidden from view in urban areas).

The provincial governments tried to further validate the introduction and/or presence of gaming machines by pointing to proceeds that could be used for public expenditure and tax reductions. These attempts at legitimation were initially successful among the provinces that did not wait to establish VLT programs. However, the public's ambivalence turned to collective anxiety when anecdotal and media stories of social disorder associated with gaming machines surfaced. Although early adopters of lotteries often paved the way for other provinces by establishing emotional, inevitability, and legal legitimacy, the reverse has occurred with GMOCs; and British Columbia and Ontario illustrate this point. Both provinces waited to establish VLT programs, and the proposals were met with media attention and public concerns that prompted most communities to refuse GMOCs or consent to establishment at racetracks or charitable organizations. This occurred despite promises of public goods or individual benefits. In short, Canadians accept government intervention in the social sphere more readily than in the other two countries, but the perceived social disorder associated with GMOCs increased resistance, and ongoing public pressure has forced governments to reconsider policies and/or offer different models of ownership and operations.

In the United States, the history of gaming machines is more closely associated with crime, corruption, violence, and social problems. The clear link between gaming machines and organized crime, combined with regional moral opposition, contributed to stronger vocal opposition at the state and national levels. Consequently, as in the other two countries, political elites in the United States deliberately avoided public debate and attempted to limit access to the decision-making process. Nevertheless, securing political and electoral consensus has proven difficult in states where referenda or plebiscites are required. Politicians and proponents also learned from early adopters that proposals for GMOCs in ambient settings were doomed to failure. They instead turned to legitimacy building using traditional, emotional, and inevitability legitimacy. In states where pari-mutuel industries were in trouble, proponents of GMOCs used the familiar argument of saving a historic industry while supporting economic development and promoting tourism. To secure additional legitimacy, many politicians also promised that the profit from GMOCs would go toward tax relief; interestingly, unlike lotteries, few states have earmarked the funds for public goods like education. To date, a large number of proposals for GMOCs have been unsuccessful, the result of a failure to obtain legitimacy for legalization. The example set by South Carolina's prohibition on gaming machines suggests that the presence of GMOCs is not guaranteed in any of the American states.

Finally, the earlier emergence of legal GMOCs and ongoing presence of illegal machines in the United States underscores the assertion that Australia's culture has been more conducive to the *legalization* of GMOCs. Six American states legalized slot machines before 1970, and four subsequently prohibited them before an Australian state or Canadian province adopted GMOCs. However, the American states have faced more difficulties legalizing gaming machines than has Australia, as a direct result of three cultural differences. First, a stronger culture of organized crime and political corruption exists in the United States, which played the most crucial role in both countries in constraining the legalization of GMOCs. Second, the Australian culture of egalitarianism and 'mateship' created a historical juncture where social and fraternal clubs became an important part of Australian society. It is interesting that several of the early adopting American states either legalized or continued to authorize GMOCs for fraternal and non-profit clubs. Finally, as noted above, Americans tend to hold more traditional values than Australians and the religious reform movement in Australia collapsed before that of the United States. On the whole, the evidence indicates that Australians are more preoccupied with controlling social problems than with moral issues, whereas the reverse is true in many American states. GMOCs might have spread across the United States earlier had these cultural conditions matched up.

Conclusions

Culture is fundamental to the emergence of gambling practices within societies. Political-economy is a necessary component, but local cultures both influence and affect political decisions. Historical conjunctures set one region on a path different from others. The state and capital have played crucial roles in altering the symbolic value of gambling in late modernity. Nevertheless, inter- to intra-national cultures create sites of ongoing conflict between individuals, groups, and social institutions (van Elteren, 1996). This is as true for gambling as for other political challenges, and it is what connects gambling across the political, economic, and social realms. As demonstrated in this chapter, many

governments, often prompted by elite interests, have tried to introduce gambling for profit, but success has been contingent on the ability
to cultivate legitimacy for adoption. Since culture is both antecedent
and wrapped up in struggles over legitimacy, individual habitus and
regional cultural differences have strongly influenced the outcomes.

Gambling activities are socially constructed and each form, and
acceptable consequences associated with them, are a reflection of the
moral codes found within a given society. These codes produce signs
interpreted differently by individuals according to their habitus, and
gambling is more likely to emerge when a group collectively accepts or
tolerates it. Furthermore, the symbolic value and reading of a gambling
activity can be transformed through direct or indirect experiences and/
or changes to objective social and cultural conditions. Consequently
regional variation in adoption, participation, and ownership and operation are due in large part to individual and collective perceptions and/or
experiences with a form of gambling, but most importantly, the power
to establish a dominant discourse that either increases or decreases
legitimacy.

The emergence of one form of gambling can raise the legitimacy for
the introduction of subsequent forms. If the symbolic value is positive,
or made to appear positive, it can alter perceptions of gambling, generally, and should make it easier to introduce new forms. On the other
hand, resistance arises when a gambling activity is viewed negatively
or gains disapproval over time. This process can involve conflict within
local cultural contexts, influencing perceptions and reactions to the
discourse, in addition to the choices made. That is, different cultural
frameworks affect various groups' ability to control and steer narra-
tives that affect political actions. Historical paths alter social institutions and cultural predispositions that later affect future governments'
capacity to establish gambling for profit. The emergence of lotteries and
GMOCs in Australia, Canada, and the United States is illustrative of
these points.

Early lotteries in Australia operated without major scandals, whereas
fraud and corruption among lotteries in the United States were rampant and led to the constitutional abolition of lotteries in all but three
states. The American experience with lotteries led to middle-class disapproval, and a historical conjuncture in the form of the Protestant
reform movement helped to sustain it. A similar development occurred
in Canada when Protestant reformers successfully dominated French
Catholics to define jurisdiction over lotteries and enshrine gambling in

the Canadian *Criminal Code*. Thus, Canadian provinces and American states were hindered from establishing lotteries for decades, the result of politics wrapped in historical contingency and cultural differences. Political leaders could not persuade other polity members to change the legislation that restricted them from establishing lotteries; the people were unwilling to support lotteries through populist practices – or both. In contrast, the Australian states did not face the same obstacles. Similar efforts were short lived and failed to delegitimize all gambling practices, leaving church groups and evangelical Protestants to resist lotteries. The government in Queensland established a lottery to generate revenue and linked it with public welfare, creating a discourse that forced those opposed to tolerate the decision. Clearly mobilization and other political factors were involved, but the state's authority would have been called into question without legitimacy. Queensland provided an example for other states to follow. In all three countries, inevitable and legal legitimacy increased as more states introduced lotteries; yet all have used selective and/or collective incentives such as tax breaks or state welfare programs to ensure support.

Legitimacy building has been considerably more difficult with GMOCs, a result of crime and social problems associated with machine gambling. In every instance, political-economic imperatives have driven attempts to legalize GMOCs. Yet, cultural differences bound in historical events across and within Australia, Canada, and the United States created different conditions for adoption. In Australia, egalitarianism, communal values, and a connection between sporting, leisure, and fraternal activities led to the establishment of clubs that became a significant part of the community social fabric. Illegal gaming machines were tolerated in New South Wales' clubs because the revenue provided patron amenities and community benefits. Nevertheless, social disorder and crime delegitimized poker machines, constraining the other states from considering GMOCs for their own clubs. Opposition to GMOCs transpired in all of the Australian states, but the degree of resistance depended on local cultural circumstances. Poker machines were introduced into most of the states during economic crises after technology increased control and attitudes toward GMOCs had changed. Political elites then used the social institution of the club and/or economic development to appeal to collective emotions for legitimacy and to reduce potential mobilization. It is noteworthy, however, that once established, several states that initially legalized GMOCs only for clubs, authorized commercial operations that have increasingly been dominating the market.

American states legalized slot machines before Australia or Canada. However, prohibition created a situation ripe for organized crime to dominate and control the illegal gaming-machine market. This reduced the legitimacy of GMOCs and led most states that had introduced them to reverse their decision. It is significant that GMOCs were tolerated longest when authorized for fraternal and non-profit organizations. It is also important to note that machine gambling was revived through legislative procedures and legitimized after the fact. States following the early adopters have resorted to a combination of legitimizing tactics to overcome faith and emotional issues surrounding GMOCs.

Canadians did not initially have the same frame of reference to judge GMOCs. Although crime associated with GMOCs existed, it appears to have been confined to Québec. None of the provinces held public inquires, as was done prior to legalization in Australia; in fact, eight of the 10 provinces legalized gaming machines within three years, most through a legislative process that precluded any debate. The public's initial reaction was ambivalent, but soon changed when social problems associated with video lotteries began to appear. Still, some provinces experienced a backlash earlier than others, despite the same rationale used to introduce GMOCs. This was due to cultural differences, as evidenced by variations in the levels of resistance over time. Furthermore, the two provinces that waited to adopt faced a public that refused to accept the justification used elsewhere, and they had no choice but to establish GMOCs in non-ambient settings.

In short, historical contingency and regional cultural differences and experiences combined to influence individual perceptions of lotteries and gaming machines. Lotteries, GMOCs, and other forms of legal gambling emerged first in regions where opposition was replaced by support or indifference by a majority of the population. This occurred earlier in Australia because historical events created a culture more accepting of legal gambling; there was opposition to lotteries and poker machines, but the political elite could provide enough legitimacy to soften resistance, some quicker than others.

Regardless of the temporal and geographic dimensions, the transformation did not occur by chance; it has been a reflection of social change, but more importantly the desire by political and business leaders to introduce gambling for profit. Nevertheless, both the state and capitalist enterprises require legitimacy to survive, and the introduction of gambling for profit has been accomplished through ideological struggles, which have included undermining public debate and manipulating the symbolic meaning attached to each form. The intent has been twofold. The state and capital have employed one strategy to shift attitudes from opposition to indifference, and indifference to participation. Proponents have also linked lotteries and GMOCs to individual and collective incentives intended to weaken mobilization against legalization. These strategies have not always been successful, as demonstrated by the American states that have not legalized one or more forms of gambling. It has also not worked in that some forms of gambling are increasingly seen as emotionally offensive and/or legally illegitimate. In response, the state and capital have undertaken tactics to protect the industry and reinforce legitimacy. These include a discourse of individual responsibility that precludes any state/provider responsibility for gambling problems and adding responsible gambling features to gaming machines. Both heighten the focus on prudentialism, and counter attacks on the legitimacy of gambling practices the state relies so heavily on for revenue.

5 Historical Contingency in Political-Economic and Sociocultural Contexts

The liberalization of gambling for profit has expanded across western countries in a jagged fashion over the past four decades, the result of different practices shaped by historically contingent preconditions. Many scholars have accounted for this expansion using political-economic explanations: politicians and economic elites promoted legal gambling as a response to economic crises that threatened state legitimacy while facilitating capital accumulation. Others have highlighted sociocultural characteristics that made the introduction of legal gambling opportunities possible. Both approaches have provided valuable insight into gambling in late modernity, but, as McMillen (1996a) points out, they are presented as universal, tend to be static and ahistorical, and are incomplete.

This book has demonstrated that to understand the production of gambling practices we need to combine past and present interactions of the political-economic and sociocultural contexts where it takes place. Gambling for profit only emerges with the right mix of political, economic, social, and cultural factors. Furthermore, different configurations of these conditions produce variations in timing of adoption, regulatory arrangements, types of gambling legalized, and structural characteristics of each form. Since these conditions are grounded in contingencies, we must reject universal explanations of the manner in which legal gambling develops and evolves. We need to instead build conditional theoretical models based in historical preconditions and current events.

In Chapter 1, I presented an analytical framework for the adoption of gambling for profit. It is meant to be reflexive, and some important variables may be missing. Additionally, the analysis throughout the book has, necessarily, been broad. Nevertheless, the findings support the framework developed so far.

I theorized that the legalization process begins with an impetus that is further influenced by welfare regime, polity type, and degree of state centralization. The likelihood of adoption is then contingent on the outcome of struggles among groups to define the meaning of gambling activities and successfully mobilize their collective resources. The sociocultural context within which these campaigns occur determines the group's capacity to legitimize the proposed form of gambling, which in turn drives motives to contribute resources for the cause. The more resources a group holds, which includes membership in the polity, the greater its ability to control the outcome.

Politicians must be amenable to the introduction of gambling for profit and can be motivated by their own, or other, elite interests, those of the people, or a combination thereof. Nevertheless, politicians make decisions within their own habitus, although self-interested individuals will generally set aside their beliefs and values when the public supports or opposes legalization and it threatens their position. Once the decision to legalize gambling has been made, ruling elites may still be prevented from doing so. Governments must have the legal authority to enact legislation, but the degree of organized resistance and capacity to successfully challenge adoption will largely determine the outcome. Social and cultural features of societies give rise to opposition, and political-economic arrangements determine its success.

Weber (1930) argued that culture acts like a railway-yard switch, directing social action down one path instead of another. Cultural acceptance of gambling is crucial for both the emergence and the forms of gambling for profit. Gambling in western countries has often been viewed as sinful or immoral, and legalization campaigns have foundered or failed in regions where the majority of people are conservative Protestants, hold strong traditional social values, or both. Some gambling activities also generate public concern because of associated crime and social problems. Whether groups who oppose the legalization of gambling are successful or not is contingent on their ability to mobilize and influence the polity.

Any factors that enable mobilization can facilitate or constrain the introduction of legal gambling. Attitudes toward gambling are central, and individual habitus, based in local social and cultural conditions, predisposes people toward ambivalence, support, or opposition. Previous collective experience with gambling becomes important, because it can increase or decrease traditional legitimacy, and may create social-norm pressures to accept or reject. All the same, public views of gambling can be altered, which is why opponents and proponents appeal to faith and emotion in attempts to undermine or build legitimacy. Opponents point to moral decline and social costs, whereas proponents usually link proposals to increased individual or public goods, control of crime, social problems, and/or the inevitability of legal gambling, especially when the state borders or is nearby other states with gambling.

In the end, the political-economic conditions within a jurisdiction govern the adoption of gambling for profit. Groups who wish to change the legal status of gambling face more challenges when they have limited access to the polity; it may reduce their expectancy of success, affect contributions and lead to demobilization. Members of the polity have unfettered access and advantage. However, the structure of the polity and political practices can lower barriers and, at times, members align themselves with challengers, opening the polity and increasing a group's chance for success.

In short, the empirical findings throughout this book show that the adoption process of gambling for profit is fluid and dynamic, and although it begins and ends in the political realm, it is strongly shaped by existing regional circumstances that have been forged in historical narrative and conjuncture.

The Analytical Framework: Comparing Australia, Canada, and the United States

A comparison of Australia, Canada, and the United States in Table 5.1 allows for a more detailed elaboration of the framework, keeping in mind that I am considering patterns of liberalization within each country.

A central question, posed in Chapters 3 and 4, is why such variation exists in gambling for profit across and within Australia, Canada, and the United States. All three countries are Anglo, federal, neo-liberal states that faced similar economic conditions between the 1970s and 1990s. In addition, demand for illegal gambling was high among segments of the working classes. Yet, Australia established lotteries and casinos earlier than did Canada and the United States; Australia also has a higher rate of participation with gaming machines outside of casinos, and the Australian states obtain considerably higher profit from gambling than the American states or Canadian provinces. Using Table 5.1 and the analytical model help explain the variation across the cases.

Table 5.1 Likelihood of Adoption of Casinos, Lotteries, and Gaming Machines outside Casinos in Australia, Canada, and the United States

Likelihood of Adoption: ● = High O = Medium ⊙ = Low

Political	Status	Australia	Canada	United States
Welfare state	neoliberal	●	●	●
Type of polity	federal	●	●	●
Degree centralization at state formation	low	●	⊙	●
Constitutional/Criminal Code Amendment	no	●	⊙	⊙
Bordering State with gambling	yes	●	●	●
Policy learning among states	high	●	●	●
Use of populist electoral practices	low	●	O	⊙
Degree of organized resistance	low	●	●	⊙
Access to polity by challengers	low	O	O	⊙
Economic	*Status*			
Impact of global economic recessions	negative	●	●	●
Regional economic decline	high	●	●	●
Degree of devolution	high	●	●	●
State's ability to generate tax revenue	low	●	⊙	⊙
Gaming industry resources available	high	●	●	●
Gambling provider competition	low	O	O	⊙
Consumer demand	medium +	●	O	O
Social	*Status*			
Catholic / Liberal Protestant	yes	O	O	⊙
Pre-existing favourable legal gambling	yes	●	⊙	O
Organized crime involvement	low	O	O	⊙
Gambling a traditional social institution	high	●	O	O
Cultural	*Status*			
Perception of gambling as leisure	high	●	⊙	⊙
Gambling as a moral issue	low	●	⊙	⊙
Traditional shared social values	low	O	O	⊙
Self-expressive shared values	high	●	O	⊙
Political culture	liberal	O	O	⊙

Australia has the most enabling political-economic conditions and the United States has the least. Australia also has more sociocultural factors that enabled adoption than did Canada, and both are clearly different from the United States. In essence, social and cultural differences are strong intervening factors that help determine whether or not gambling is accepted and becomes legal. In addition, some political-economic, social, and cultural conditions have played a more critical role than others.

Impetus to Adopt

The impetus to adopt casinos, lotteries, and GMOCs in all three countries was, for the most part, economic. Global recessions deflated economic growth, caused regional decline, increased unemployment, and reduced state income, all of which posed problems for the legitimacy of the state. In some cases, but not all, politicians responded by proposing lotteries, casinos, and/or gaming machines outside of casinos to revitalize economies and increase state revenue. Nevertheless, some national and subnational units were better equipped to deal with globalization and recessionary periods. By chance, many regions had strong industrial bases or the ability to sell natural resources, and others were shielded by revenue redistribution from the federal government. The economically vulnerable states and provinces were generally more likely to propose and legalize gambling for profit, but other economic factors also played a role in the timing of adoption.

As states moved toward neo-liberalism, national governments devolved political, economic, and social responsibilities, and reduced fiscal transfers to regional and local governments. This put pressure on the lower level by exacerbating the economic difficulties, especially among those performing poorly. Regions that remained economically healthy could attract or retain capital investment whereas the remainder faced increased pressures to adopt gambling for profit as they ran out of economic and fiscal options.

The federal governments in all three countries shifted responsibilities to the lower-level polities. But the Australian Commonwealth transferred its administrative responsibilities to the Australian Capital Territory and Northern Territory and dramatically reduced federal funding to the Australian states. The first move helped push the territories closer toward introducing casinos, and the second forced the states to look at maximizing gambling taxes for badly needed revenue. The Australian states' minimal fiscal autonomy made them more vulnerable during the recessions. Beyond the need for economic renewal, this was a further reason why the Australian states established urban commercial casinos overall before either Canada or the United States.

A second explanation can be found in consumer demand. Australians initially displayed little interest in casino gambling, but demand grew as casinos opened. The country was also concurrently experiencing increased tourism that the states could theoretically tap into with casinos, or lose without them. Thus, some Australian states faced stronger economic incentives: economic decline and a reduction in financial transfers from the Commonwealth government combined with an opportunity to regenerate their economies through tourism. Nevertheless, these conditions cannot adequately explain why American states and Canadian provinces, experiencing similar or worse economic conditions, did not adopt gambling for profit at the same time – or earlier.

Welfare Regime/Polity/Degree of Centralization

I argued in Chapter 2 that western states have moved to some degree from the 'alibi' to 'risk model' of governmentality. Under the alibi model, states intervene to control illegal gambling and ensure that revenue is directed to 'good causes' through strict regulation, monitoring, and taxation. When governments move toward the risk model, they liberalize and deregulate their gambling policies to minimize social problems and reduce the risk of a public backlash, while diverting gambling profit from 'good causes' to state coffers and corporate interests. As I have shown in Chapter 2, the pattern has been for neo-liberal welfare regimes to shift their policies furthest into the risk mode of governance. Thelen maintains that 'institutions rest on a set of ideational and material foundations that, if shaken, open possibilities for change. But different institutions rest on different foundations, and so the processes that are likely to disrupt them will also be different, though predictable' (1999, p. 397).

The political-economic institutions in the liberal states were established on different principles. Although western countries have implemented some neo-liberal principles, the Anglo countries established the most deregulated market-driven policies and the United States moved furthest in this direction. We would, accordingly, expect the American states to have legalized gambling for profit earlier and more aggressively than did Australia and Canada, but this did not happen. The Canadian provinces and American states were constrained by a requirement to amend the *Criminal Code* or state constitutions.

Unitary polities can exercise greater regional control over gambling policies than federal polities. When a subnational unit in a federal state legalizes gambling for profit, there is an increased potential for bordering states to lose revenue while facing mounting social problems. Policy sharing should occur more frequently among federal subnational units, the result of similar cultures and interactions in commerce. Australia, Canada, and the United States are all federal states with intraregional competition, and gambling for profit emerged in some regions out of cross-border competition and policy learning. However, these factors explain little of variation across the three countries. Until 1969, the Australian and American states held more power to decide gambling policies than did the Canadian provinces, which is linked to the historical conjuncture of centralization during state formation.

Australia and the United States were more decentralized than Canada, giving the Australian and American states more powers than the Canadian provinces. When the Canadian federal government prohibited lottery schemes in the *Criminal Code*, it substantially reduced the likelihood of adoption. Provinces like Québec would almost certainly have introduced lotteries, but the federal government prevented them from doing so. Most American states used their powers to enshrine the prohibition of lotteries and/or slot machines in their constitutions, thereby requiring an amendment to authorize them. Additionally, many American states have faced the constraints of highly organized resistance that can gain easier access to the polity through populist electoral practices.

Access to the Polity

Struggles over political decisions are played out within the polity. Members – political, business, and social elite – have direct access, which means they can more easily influence gambling adoption. Challengers could support legalization in states where members are reluctant to do so, or oppose legislation where legal gambling is introduced. Challengers can gain access to the polity through populist political practices, public commissions and committees, conscience votes, and the courts. The likelihood of adoption is most unpredictable in lower-level polities and/ or when the people have a direct say on proposed legalization. Even when the polity is closed, challengers can force their way in with the right resources, which would include structural, human, and symbolic elements; for example fiscal reserves, highly credible members of the polity in their camp, and the ability to offer public goods.

As shown in Table 5.1, one of the main factors that has limited the expansion of gambling for profit across the United States is access to the polity through populist practices, combined with robust organized resistance from church groups, citizens and, at times, competing business interests that included gambling providers. Australia and Canada also experienced opposition to casinos, GMOCs, and, in a few instances, lotteries, leading to delays or failure to launch them. Several Australian states used Royal Commissions and other public forums to examine proposals for expanded gambling, which allowed public debate; South Australia also permitted conscience votes. At times, these developments constrained the introduction of gambling for profit. Most of the Canadian provinces introduced gaming machines in ambient settings quickly, quietly, and through the Order in Council process, thereby heading off potential confrontation. The provinces that waited faced organized opposition that forced its way into the polity; in these instances, gaming machines were restricted to racetracks and/or casinos. It is noteworthy that easy access to the polity in the United States could have had the opposite effect on the expansion of gambling for profit. High levels of support, translated through populist practices, may have forced politicians to adopt in many more states, but sociocultural barriers prevented this from occurring.

The Sociocultural Contexts of Adoption

The state may, and often does, impose legal gambling where the public is ambivalent, or a small majority openly opposes it. Nevertheless, politicians will typically not risk introducing gambling for profit where it threatens the legitimacy of the state. Politicians and corporate elites have been most successful in regions where the public accepted the move, was indifferent, or could not effectively mobilize. Wherever public tolerance has been low, and state, commercial, or charitable interests have been high, elite groups have attempted to manufacture consent and generate demand. However, this must be accomplished and maintained through legitimation.

Building legitimacy is crucial for convincing both politicians and the people that legalizing gambling activities will benefit individuals and the community. In fact, legal gambling would not exist without perceptions that the activities hold *some* legitimacy. This makes local social and cultural features crucial to the emergence of gambling for profit. Regions with pre-existing favourable gambling activities that form part of the community's cultural and social fabric should be predisposed to accept new forms of gambling because of their historical and legal legitimacy. Conversely, people who consider gambling as morally inappropriate, because of religious faith, shared conservative and traditional values, or perceived social disorder, will be inclined to reject proposals because they lack faith or emotional legitimacy.

To understand fully the mechanisms involved, it is necessary to outline the possible configuration of relationships in the process. To begin with, historically determined conditions, such as settlement patterns, combine with contemporary situations to produce variations in social institutions and cultural beliefs. These create individual and collective habitus, which affect motives to support or oppose gambling. Conservative Catholics and Protestants, who hold traditional social values, have been shown to display less tolerance and higher degrees of moral opprobrium for gambling practices than liberal Catholics with self-expressive ideals. The outcome is regional divergence in gambling practices that may or may not be condoned by the authorities. A second contingency is the presence of crime and corruption linked to gambling. When highly visible, it will reinforce the view among conservative and religious groups that gambling should not be tolerated, and may cause others to take stock, perhaps prohibiting one type or stepping up enforcement. In the end, regions with a majority who tolerate gambling should come to accept the activity as leisure and part of the group's culture.

The public comprises many ethnic and social groups that are often at odds when it comes to gambling. Political and economic elites are embedded in these communities and act as both participants and arbitrators of these struggles. Gambling has, historically, been the preserve of the working and upper classes, but the middle classes have controlled the polity. Until recently, the middle classes have generally eschewed gambling as either morally offensive, unproductive, and/or socially disruptive. As a result, governments frequently and selectively prohibited working-class gambling, particularly among women and non-European ethnic groups, in an effort to protect middle-class interests and purportedly to protect the lower social orders from themselves (McMillen, 1993, 1996a). Nevertheless, the laws have differed temporally and regionally.

Table 5.1 demonstrates that Australia had more enabling sociocultural conditions than did Canada and the United States. European settlers to Australia brought horse racing with them, and wagering at the track became legitimized as a part of Australian culture that exits to this day. For example, Australians are greatly preoccupied with the yearly Melbourne Cup horse race and areas in Victoria and the Australian Capital Territory celebrate it as a public holiday. Protestant resistance to gambling did emerge in Australia at the turn of the twentieth century with resultant prohibitions on many forms. But to sustain their own gambling opportunities the upper classes pressured the state to permit some working-class gambling, which helped reinforce an Australian working-class gambling culture. The Protestant churches persisted and were more successful in some regions than others, but from this point forward, gambling per se was considered less from a moral perspective than one of social control over diverse segments of the population (O'Hara, 1988). In addition, as shown in Chapter 4, the culture in Australia is much different than that of Canada and the United States. Australians appear more tolerant of issues that invoke moral politics in other jurisdictions, especially the United States. Yet, perceived social disorder and the real threat of organized crime made casino adoption difficult in a few states and prevented the establishment of poker machines beyond New South Wales and the Australian Capital Territory for some time. Thus, while traditional legitimacy existed for horse racing and built with each new form of legal gambling, further liberalization required legitimacy building through promises of public goods, selective incentives, and assurances of social control.

Canada shared many of the sociocultural enabling conditions as Australia. Indeed, the country also had a long history of horse racing and small-stake gambling at agricultural events. However, legitimacy building for legal gambling was more difficult among *members of the federal polity*, which controlled the *Criminal Code* in Canada, and a large segment of the Canadian Protestant population also considered gambling morally inappropriate. Québec had a disproportionate number of Catholics, but the population was deeply religious and held conservative, traditional social values until the 1970s. Even so, had the province had the authority, it is plausible that Québec would have instituted lotteries as early as did Queensland in Australia.

The United States makes for an interesting case, since it had legal gambling before the other two countries, and illegal gambling was rampant across the country. Pari-mutuel wagering did emerge in many states, and casino gambling was well established·in Nevada by the end of the Second World War. Yet, the American states have faced the most difficulty in legalizing gambling for profit compared to their Australian and Canadian counterparts. Settlement patterns, and historical narrative and conjunctures related to fraud, corruption, and organized crime, have played a critical role in constraining the development of legal gambling. Of the three countries, the United States has the highest proportion of evangelical Christian denominations, which created stronger faith-based resistance and moral opprobrium. The urban social conditions for immigrants also produced more social chaos than that of Australia or Canada, ultimately leading to higher levels of – or at least more visible – organized crime and the potential for political corruption. The combination of Protestant reform movements, conservative religious beliefs, fraudulent lottery practices, and criminal activities gave politicians the moral authority to prohibit all, or most, forms of gambling. When state politicians later proposed gambling for profit they had a more difficult time providing faith legitimacy, emotional legitimacy, or both, particularly in the southern Bible Belt states.

The Likelihood of Adoption

To recap, politicians will not legalize gambling without an impetus that lines up with their own views, but, quite often and, more importantly, with the social values and beliefs of the people. All the same, other sociocultural factors shape motives and lead people to accept or reject a proposal. Mobilization for or against legalization will ensue where the motives are strong enough, and the ability to influence political decisions will determine the outcome.

In line with Pinard's (1983a, 1983b) motivation model, I argued in Chapter 3 that individual motives to support or oppose proposals for legal gambling comprise an internal incentive (aspiration, deprivation, and/or moral obligation), a selective and/or collective incentive, and some expectancy the incentive will be delivered. Using this paradigm, we can see why legal lotteries emerged first in all three countries, followed by casinos and GMOCs. It was easier to establish legitimacy for lotteries. The early adopters of state-operated lotteries launched them during times of economic turmoil. When choosing whether to support a lottery, particularly through participation, each person's actions would be the outcome of a moral obligation, deprivation, or aspiration. Lotteries were often introduced during economic downturns, and most people who were economically deprived would aspire to improve their circumstances. The selective incentive of winning the lottery could have outweighed opposition based on moral or other grounds, and there would be some expectancy of individual success provided there was marginal hope of winning.

What about individuals who felt compelled to oppose lotteries based on moral obligations? This is where legitimation is key. Most state lotteries have been proposed under the auspices of providing for 'good causes.' Public goods can act as a strong collective incentive, dividing those opposed on moral grounds from those who are resisting for other reasons. Although the latter may still not like the idea, they may give in under the pretext that profit would go to worthy causes, or others may force them to accept it under social-norm pressures. Yet, if it were this simple, why did lotteries emerge unevenly across the three countries, and why did it take so long to introduce casinos or GMOCs?

There are several reasons why the Australian states were first to introduce lotteries. As noted above, they had the political power to adopt. The *Criminal Code* in Canada prevented some liberal provinces like Québec from establishing lotteries, and the American states experienced fraudulent practices and scandals that delegitimized lotteries and led to constitutional amendments prohibiting them. Conversely, Tattersall's and Queensland demonstrated lotteries could be operated without scandal, and Queensland allocated the proceeds to social welfare. Conservative religious and political beliefs also played a role. The regions that are most conservative with the highest levels of evangelical religious affiliations have tended to legalize lotteries last in each country; several American states have yet to do so. Ongoing involvement in the 'numbers rackets' by organized crime in the United States also reduced the ability to generate emotional legitimacy. Thus, states with few problems building faith and emotional legitimacy, through positive symbols or pointing to inevitability, stood a better chance for early adoption. As each state introduced lotteries, it paved the way for others to try.

The capacity to generate legitimacy has been more complicated with casinos and GMOCs. As with lotteries, legalization campaigns produced religious opposition in parts of Australia, Canada, and the United States, and success has varied with the ability of churches and opposition groups to mobilize local populations. However, creating legitimacy for these activities among both political elites and the public proved more difficult, wherever organized crime or social disorder were involved, since it reduced the opportunity for emotional legitimacy.

The settlement patterns of the United States gave rise to more favourable conditions for the manifestation of crime syndicates. The mafia, 'murder incorporated,' and other groups of gangsters controlled the numbers rackets, gambling, pinball machines, and the casinos in Nevada. Congressional hearings, media reports, and personal experiences all contributed to the perception that gambling was a criminal activity. The experience with organized crime in Australia and Canada does not appear as dramatic. Nevertheless, public inquiries in Australia increased concerns over criminal involvement in casinos and the New South Wales gaming-machine industry. The outcome was that criminal involvement in casinos and gaming machines became a concern for legislators, the police, and the public.

Another issue with casinos and GMOCs is that they are more closely linked to social disorder arising from excessive gambling. Thus, in all three countries, a collective incentive to *retain* prohibitions on casinos and gaming machines would have been higher than for lotteries. As a result, the state and capital were forced to take several additional steps to manufacture legitimacy for these activities. Casinos and gaming machines were repackaged as one more form of entertainment citizens could choose. The public was assured that organized crime would be squeezed out of the operation, and indeed most Canadian politicians made this a central plank in their arguments for introducing VLTs – albeit most did it after the fact. Many states also pledged funds for problem-gambling research and treatment. Lastly, proposals for casinos and GMOCs have often been linked to both individual incentives (e.g. increased jobs and lower taxation) and public goods (e.g. economic development and state welfare projects). This would appeal to both individual and collective aspirations. Compared with lotteries then, perceptions of problems associated with casinos and GMOCs made it more difficult to shift faith-based moral obligations or emotional-based potential deprivations using selective or collective incentives. Moreover, different local, regional, and even national cultures intervened, leading to diverse responses temporally and spatially.

Finally, sociocultural contexts feed back into the political-economic realm and the polity where the decisions to legalize gambling for profit are made. Sociocultural contexts produce different motivations to contribute toward collective action in support or opposition of the proposed gambling. Members of the polity will only be influenced by challengers where the latter can force their way in and affect the decision making process. This is where availability of industry and other resources, degree and type of organized resistance, and access to the polity come into play.

In short, the convergence of historically conditioned political, economic, social, and cultural conditions, combined with current contexts, influence the outcome of struggles among gambling opponents and proponents which lead to differences in gambling practices across time and space. This is an ongoing process, which is why gambling can oscillate between prohibition and legalization. It is also why we need a contingent model and reflexive approach that consider the interaction between political, economic, social, and cultural factors when accounting for the emergence of, and changes to, legal gambling in late modernity.

Notes

1. The Emergence of Gambling within a Historically Contingent Framework

1 The term late modernity refers to a form of capitalism where culture drives all spheres of political, economic, and social life (Jameson, 1984). Capital in modernity was organized around industrial production; in late modernity capital is disorganized, decentralized, and profits from the cultural sphere, specifically aesthetic and symbolic goods and services. Political interests have also fragmented as social identities moved from class-based to those centered upon taste, consumption, race, gender, and ethnicity (Lash and Urry, 1994).

2 The term corporatization refers to the deregulation of lotteries into quasi-government corporate organizations.

3 Neo-liberal states have increasingly deregulated their economies allowing private enterprise to provide public goods within a free market ideology. Citizens are also expected to act prudentially by self-regulating their behaviour in return for limited state involvement in their lives.

4 Binde (2005) and Pryor (2008) are exceptions. Binde (2005) examines indigenous gambling cross-culturally and provides several potential sociocultural predictors of gambling participation, and Pryor (2008) argues that gambling adoption cannot be understood using political-economic variables alone.

5 Similarly, political and corporate elites attempt to undermine potential challenges by protecting the legitimacy of existing gambling through responsible gambling discourse, funds to public goods, and expressed threats that organized crime will become involved (again) if the gambling activity is criminalized.

6 Weltanschauung is a German expression for a person's or group's outlook on life that shapes their conduct.

7 I have excluded legal wagering and internet gambling for several reasons. Wagering on horses, dogs, and sporting events is a large and significant feature of gambling, but has not had the same penetration among all western countries as lotteries and, more recently, casinos and GMOCs. Horse racing is also a fading industry in North America, which has led to attempts to introduce GMOCs at racetracks. I have not included internet gambling because, although it is growing, it remains illegal in many western countries. Nevertheless, each of these forms could have different enabling and constraining conditions.

8 Binde (2005) provides a wider set of sociocultural factors that might be used to predict where gambling occurs: the presence of money, social stratification, societal complexity, and intertribal relations; however, he uses these variables with indigenous gambling. Binde's analysis also implicitly suggests that historical contingency affects the emergence of gambling.

9 I have excluded some components and causal arrows to avoid complication.

10 Populist electoral practices could theoretically derail any attempts to introduce legal gambling, especially when combined with a required constitutional amendment through a popular vote. Some of the conditions could also enable *or* constrain the establishment of legal gambling. For example, organized crime involvement could lead to negative public reactions or could legitimize government involvement.

11 The Bretton Woods Agreement was a complex set of international financial monetary controls agreed to by most nations at Bretton Woods, New Hampshire in 1944. The agreement set controls on capital to prevent undermining welfare-state autonomy through financial speculation (for a more detailed description see Meier, 1971 and Helleiner, 1994).

12 The situation is a historical conjuncture that is not applicable across western countries, which is why I have excluded it as a general impetus in the framework.

13 Many also emphasize a particular region, which does not uncover variation even within individual states.

14 Habitus refers to a set of individual or collective predispositions that arise through the internalization of objective social and cultural conditions (Bourdieu, 1990).

15 I am not suggesting that attitudes toward all types of gambling have softened or opposition has disappeared. However, some forms of gambling (e.g. casinos or gaming machines outside of casinos) have sparked

more disapproval than others (e.g. lotteries). Attitudes also differ regionally depending on the configuration of enabling and constraining
conditions.

16 In some cases, the head of state overrules the wishes of elite groups and
the people by vetoing proposals.

17 The government of Nova Scotia in Canada legalized casino gambling in
1995 despite vocal resistance and an opinion poll showing that 56% of the
population was opposed (Nova Scotia Lottery Commission, 1993).

18 The government of New Brunswick in Canada committed to hold a referendum on video lottery terminals in 1999 amid increasingly vocal opposition McKenna (2008).

19 People who hold traditional social values are firmly committed to religious
faith, family, and male authority; they have little tolerance for abortion,
divorce, and different sexual orientation (see Chapter 4, 'Shared Social
Values and Legitimacy Building,' p. 112).

20 Those with self-expressive social values emphasize well-being and quality of life over materialism (see Chapter 4: 'Shared Social Values and
Legitimacy Building').

21 The development and success of collective action is complex and beyond
the scope here (see McCarthy & Zald, 1977; Oliver, 1993; and Kitts, 2006).

22 A coalition of religious groups, business interests, and politicians was
successful in mobilizing the electorate to defeat a lottery proposal in 1999
(Bobbitt, 2007, p. 91)

23 I am referring to political attitudes grounded in the ethics of moral propri-
ety of an action. Perceptions of gambling as morally offensive differ across
countries and regions.

24 Rychlak (1995) claims that little legal and no state-sponsored gambling
existed in the United States from the turn of the century until the mid-1960s.
Although Nevada was first to legalize casinos in 1931 (Schwartz, 2006,
p. 355) and Nevadan casinos were promoted throughout the United States,
it was not a 'national' industry. Indeed, Bolen and Boyd maintained in
1968 that Las Vegas was 'reserved for society's more affluent members' and
played a minor role in American gambling (1968, p. 618). The introduction
of casinos in New Jersey coincided with the first Australian casinos, but
several American states failed to introduce casinos in the decade that followed. The *pattern* overall has been for the Australian states to introduce
commercial casinos before a majority of American states or Canadian
provinces (see Eadington, 1998; McMillen, 1988b). Notwithstanding this,
Nevada is an anomaly; few jurisdictions in the world have the postmodern
spectacle of Las Vegas that draws millions of tourists each year.

2. Gambling for Profit in the Welfare Regimes

1 Familialism is an ideology or culture where the western family unit and the ideals associated with it are valued as a central social institution (see Leitner, 2003).
2 All western countries adopted variations of neo-liberal policies. However, as Habermas and Derrida (2003) point out, Europeans are largely sceptical about the power of the markets over state intervention.
3 GDP percentage change was averaged for each welfare regime category.
4 I am referring to the use of pastiche and spectacle to create an atmosphere of fantasy.
5 There are exceptions. The first casinos established in Australia and Canada were closer to the European model.
6 Gross Gaming Revenue is the amount wagered minus payouts to players and is calculated before payment of operating costs and taxes.
7 Per capita Mean Average USD = Liberal ($86); Liberal-Corporatist ($52); Corporatist ($39), Social Democratic ($11).
8 Several states have legalized GMOCs since 2005 increasing the overall number of machines and profit.
9 Per capita Mean Average USD = Liberal ($86); Liberal-Corporatist ($54); Corporatist ($62), Social Democratic ($91).
10 Per capita Mean Average USD = Liberal ($58); Liberal-Corporatist ($54); Corporatist ($63), Social Democratic ($106).
11 Australia obtains more overall revenue ($5.3 billion USD) than Canada ($2.5 billion USD) and the United States ($2.1 billion USD). See Chapter 3 and Chapter 4 for comparisons across the three countries.
12 Several Canadian provinces legitimized the introduction of GMOCs by claiming it was necessary to combat organized crime; however, they lean more toward risk governmentality than the Corporatist & Social Democratic states.
13 Per capita Mean Average USD = Liberal & Liberal-Corporatist ($226); Corporatist & Social Democratic ($146).
14 Per capita Mean Average USD = Liberal & Liberal-Corporatist ($105); Corporatist & Social Democratic ($43).
15 Cross-national research comparing rates of problem gambling while controlling for factors like access is required to determine whether corporatist and social democratic state approaches have been more successful.

3. Casinos in Australia, Canada, and the United States

1 For brevity, I deal solely with state-owned and land-based/riverboat commercial casinos here and I examine charitable and tribal casinos where

they have been influential of the other forms. I am specifically excluding card rooms with non-banked games (e.g. poker rooms) and gaming
machines outside of casinos (GMOC). Many racetracks in Canada and
the United States have slot machines or video lotteries, and these 'racinos' are often included in analyses of casinos. There are various types of
machine gambling in clubs, hotels, and liquor-licensed sites in all three
countries. I examine racinos and these other situations in Chapter 4.

2 Participation among Canadians in 2002 is from author's calculations taking
the average across the provinces.

3 The *Criminal Code* of Canada permitted some casino styled games (e.g.
'Wheel of Fortune') at agricultural fairs and exhibitions. The western
Canadian provinces also opened charitable casinos in the early to late 1970s.
However, the casinos were small, did not offer machine gambling and,
excepting Saskatchewan, did not become permanent until the early 1980s.

4 A Commonwealth referendum in 1986 cleared the way for a casino on
Christmas Island, and one eventually opened in 1993. The casino was
an immediate success, but a decline in market conditions, litigation, and
management problems forced its closure in 1998 (Australian Institute for
Gambling Research, 1999).

5 Personal Contact – Jesselyn Long, National Indian Gaming Commission,
12 December 2005.

6 The National Indian Gaming Commission provides a definition of
Class III Gaming as, 'games commonly played in casinos, such as slot
machines, blackjack, craps, and roulette, fall in the Class III category, as
well as wagering games and electronic facsimiles of any games of chance'
(National Indian Gaming Commission, n.d.).

7 Findlay maintains that residents of Las Vegas were uncomfortable with the
image and reputation of local casinos. Citizens went so far as to undertake
campaigns to 'reshape the city ... while insisting that it was not really any
different' (1986, pp. 193–4).

8 Voters in Arkansas defeated an initiative ballot in 1964 (59.6% to 40.4%)
that would have permitted casino gambling in Hot Springs (State of
Arkansas, n.d.).

9 For example, some states introduced lotteries to contend with illegal
numbers rackets, but it cannibalized horse racing profits, which in turn
increased pressures to allow slot machines at racetracks (Atkinson et al.,
2000).

10 Ritzer (1995) notes that cash-based economies limit consumption and the
state facilitated the credit card industry in appropriating workers' future
incomes. It is also interesting that household savings rates as a percentage
of disposable income declined during this period. For instance, Canadian

households in 2003 held an average $103 debt for every $100 of disposable income (Harchaoui & Tarkhani, 2004). Although household savings are tied to structural features such as old-age pensions and provision of health care, the new debt levels also reflects the push by capital and the state for workers to consume more.

11 The advent of dual-earner households fostered higher disposable incomes. The gross domestic product in all three countries is now heavily dependent on consumer spending.

12 Brian (2009) found no statistical evidence for state fiscal crises increasing the likelihood of adoption. I am not referring to the inability of states to generate revenue income to pay for services. States with fewer financial resources also have fewer opportunities to develop infrastructure and attract investment capital.

13 Québec sited a casino on the Ontario border several years after legalizing casinos.

14 A vertical fiscal imbalance (VFI) exists when the fiscal responsibilities of national and subnational governments are unequal to their revenue production. A horizontal fiscal imbalance (HFI) occurs where different regions provide higher levels of services, since they can raise higher revenue and/or the cost of providing services is lower. Both VFI and HFI typically lead to transfer payments from the federal government(s) with surpluses going to those with deficits (Bird & Tarasov, 2002).

15 When a central government relinquishes fiscal powers to subnational units, it reduces the ability for equalization transfer payments and increases the ability for some subnational units to outperform others.

16 To get around Canadian tariffs, American companies established manufacturing 'branch plants' in Ontario and Quebec in the early twentieth century; the plants could distribute the products without tariffs. The Free Trade Agreement between Canada and the United States made these plants redundant.

17 Canadians make up roughly 30% of visitors to the United States (United States Department of Commerce, Office of Travel and Tourism Industries–A, n.d) and Americans comprise the largest group of travellers to Canada (Statistics Canada–B, n.d.).

18 According to the Catechism of the Catholic Church, 'Games of chance (card games, etc.) or wagers are not in themselves contrary to justice. They become morally unacceptable when they deprive someone of what is necessary to provide for his needs and those of others. The passion for gambling risks becoming an enslavement. Unfair wagers and cheating at games constitute grave matter, unless the damage inflicted is so slight that the one who suffers it cannot reasonably consider it significant' (Catechism of The Catholic Church, n.d.).

19 We can divide Catholics into conservative and liberal groupings and conservative Catholics have been more opposed to casinos than liberal Catholics. Dombrink and Thompson (1990) observed that the Catholic Church came out against casino gambling in several casino legalization campaigns; Morton (2003) also noted some Catholic opposition to gambling in Canada. Ellison and Nybroten (1999) argue that conservative Protestants are more likely to oppose lotteries because they believe that lotteries encourage people to place their faith in luck and chance instead of god, promote greed and avarice, lead to unbridled self-interest, and violate scriptural rules concerning the stewardship of money. Still, Economopoulos (2006) has shown that religious commitment specifies support – the more committed display stronger opposition.

20 We can equate faith based legitimacy with deontology and emotional legitimacy with teleology (see Cabot & Thompson, 1996); the former is based in binding moral obligations whereas the latter considers whether the ends justify the means.

21 In 1960, 50.4% reported Protestant affiliation in Australia, and the United States had similar statistics in the mid-1960s: 62% in Australia (Australian Bureau of Statistics, 1994, 2005) and 67% in the United States (United States Census Bureau, 2001a, 2001b). By the mid-1990s, Protestant affiliation had decreased to 45.7% in Australia (Australian Bureau of Statistics, 1994, 2005) and 56% in the United States (United States Census Bureau, 2001a, 2001b). In Canada the number of Protestants had been declining since its peak at 56% in 1921; Protestants made up 44% of the population in 1991 (Statistics Canada, 2003); the number of Catholics peaked in 1971 at 46%.

22 Protests still erupted in the Australian Capital Territory, and the campaigns were successful in Victoria throughout the 1980s (Australian Institute for Gambling Research, 1999, p. 155).

23 O'Hara (1988, p. 242, fn 15) cites evidence that Anglicans were equally likely as Catholics to play poker machines.

24 I have adopted the classification scheme for evangelical denominations used by Jelen and Wilcox (1990). The mean percentages of people claiming a conservative Protestant religious affiliation are as follows: Australia (1991) – Tasmania and Northern Territory 12.2%, Western Australia, Southern Australia and Queensland 13.2%, Australian Capital Territory, New South Wales and Victoria 14.7% (Australian Bureau of Statistics, 1994); Canada (2001) Western Canada 6.9%, Ontario 7.4%, Quebec >1%, Atlantic Canada 17.0% (Statistics Canada, 2003); and, United States (1991) North East 13.8%, South 40.1%, Midwest 21.4% and West 25.3% (United States Census Bureau, 2001a, 2001b).

25 The presence of a casino or tribal compact was coded as a binomial variable and correlated with the percentages of religious affiliation (as categorized by Jelen & Wilcox, 1990) by state. However, the data does not coincide temporally to events and it is plausible a denomination could have increased or decreased during the period after adoption or signing of a compact and the data collection.

26 Not all Baptist denominations are conservative, but southern Baptists, predominant in the southern United States, are.

27 Satterthwaite (2005) examined failed referenda in Oklahoma and found Catholics had no impact, but the presence of evangelical religious groups was associated with the failure of gambling proposals. Boehmke and Witmer (2004) found a similar relationship with gaming compacts for tribal gambling on reserves. Using logistic regression, von Herrmann (2002) further demonstrated that religion is a strong negative predictor of casino adoption in the United States. Finally, Fairbanks (1977) argues that religious beliefs have an impact independent of economic and social factors, and religion has had the largest impact on gambling in states with large Protestant populations.

28 Based on testimony from Dr Andreas Schloenhardt, University of Queensland, who is also on record as stating that Australia is a 'marginal player in the world of organized crime' (Retrieved February 15, 2010 from University of Queensland, Research at UQ, Research Highlights, Crime Fighters: http://www.uq.edu.au/research/index.html?page=37177&pid=0).

29 Organized crime was heavily involved in illegal gambling in New South Wales.

30 A contribution could be as simple as casting a vote.

31 Lee and Back (2003) maintain that residents will support a casino development if they perceive positive benefits from it. Potential social problems typically engender resistance.

32 Dombrink and Thompson (1990) observed that previous experience with gambling was important to the success or failure of casino legalization campaigns in the United States between 1976 and 1988.

33 States with strong evangelical churches that can readily organize their constituents have been successful in stopping gambling proposals in the Bible Belt of the United States (Bobbitt, 2007).

34 As one moves from local to federal polities, barriers to admission increase and political actors become responsible for larger geographic areas with more divergent political variables to consider. This means that small business and citizens groups find it more difficult to enter the polity nationally than regionally. It also means national political elites must appease a more heterogeneous electorate than at the lower levels.

35 Facilitation into the polity is highest when citizens can vote directly on issues or initiate a ballot (initiative process).

36 Citizens are closest to and can provide more pressure on municipal governments. The distance increases as one goes to the state and then the federal levels.

37 There are studies of casino adoption (for example, see Dombrink & Thompson, 1990 for the United States; and Morton, 2003 for Canada), but they do not provide the same detail or are limited to specific states/ provinces and/or time periods.

38 Thirty-nine percent of Australians approved of casinos in their state in 1973 and approval had increased to 51% by 1981 (McMillen, 1993, p. 176).

39 South Dakota does not border Manitoba; however policy diffusion can spread across wide geographic areas. For example, Windsor, Ontario, is approximately 1,200 miles from Winnipeg, but the Ontario government learned lessons from the Manitoba government when planning its first casino (Klassen & Cosgrave, 2009).

40 ABSCAM was an FBI sting operation where agents posing as sheiks were offered cash to help them obtain a casino license in Atlantic City.

41 An Order in Council is a decision made by cabinet that precludes parliamentary debate. Accordingly, it precludes challengers and members outside the cabinet from the political decision-making process.

42 American companies established branch plants in Canada to avoid paying tariffs between the late nineteenth and early to mid-twentieth century. The American-Canadian Free Trade Agreement was enacted in 1988 removing trade barriers between the two countries, which eliminated the need for most American branch plants. This had a dramatic impact on the Ontario and Québec economies.

43 The province opened two casinos simultaneously. One in the capital city of Halifax, which has a vibrant economy and relatively large tourist base, and the second in Sydney, a remote and economically depressed city with a small tourist base. The rationale behind the Sydney casino is unknown, but it appears to have been an economically and socially questionable move.

44 The government of Newfoundland apparently dismissed a casino in 1994 because the premier and cabinet were concerned about the social impacts of such a move. The issue arose again in 1995 following introduction of a casino in Nova Scotia, but the premier was staunchly opposed (Canadian Press Newswire, October 2, 1995).

45 Organized crime was closely linked with the illegal machines.

46 From the turn of the century, American attitudes toward gambling shifted from viewing it as sin, to a vice and, most recently, to excessive gambling

as a disease (Preston, Bernhard, Hunter, & Bybee, 1998). The Public Gaming Research Institute (1980) attributed the lack of casino legalizations in the United States with the perceptions of crime and corruption with casinos, particularly in Nevada (Cited by Dombrink & Thompson, 1990, p. 19). Some forms of gambling in the United States were socially acceptable by the mid-1970s (see Kallick-Kaufman, 1979) but casino gambling was still suspect (Dombrink & Thompson, 1990, p. 19–24).

47 Proponents argued casinos would undermine organized crime in New Jersey in several ways. It would deprive crime syndicates of profits obtained through illegal gambling, free up resources to pursue organized crime more aggressively, and reduce corruption among public officials (Dombrink & Thompson, 1990).

48 New Jersey appears to have been largely successful in keeping organized crime outside of the Atlantic City casinos. However, problems with crime syndicates still exist (see *The Mob in Casinos*, Gambling Research Information & Education Foundation, April 2003).

49 Under their 'veto model' of approval, Dombrink and Thompson correctly posit that American states would not adopt casinos if at least one of the following conditions are absent: 1) a weak state economy and favourable experience with other forms of gambling; 2) 'political elites and active interests' or support from among political and business elites; 3) 'campaign sponsorship factors,' comprising strong credibility of, and financial commitment from, campaign sponsors; and, 4) 'campaign issue dominance' or the ability by casino advocates to shift debates away from crime and social problems to economic benefits (1990, p. 94–7).

50 Connecticut, Massachusetts, New Hampshire, New York, Pennsylvania, and Rhode Island all attempted to legalize casinos between 1977 and 1988 (Dombrink & Thompson, 1990).

51 Illegal casinos were rampant throughout the midwest as well as in some southern states, like Kentucky, Mississippi and Louisiana prior to the Second World War.

52 Indiana may have also been influenced by a failed attempt to establish casinos in Ohio in 1989 (Dombrink & Thompson, 1990).

53 For instance, Iowa has modified its riverboat regulations. Iowa initially restricted bets and required that the boats actually sail, but later removed betting limits and the boats are now permanently moored.

54 In 1987, a cruise ship began offering casino games during 'cruises to nowhere' in the Mississippi sound. The ship's operators argued the ship was in international waters, but the state disagreed and brought charges. The resulting arguments garnered the attention of Mississippi's legislators (Shepard III & Netz, 1999).

55 The plaintiff argued that casino games are identical to lotteries. However, the court ruled lottery games are 'games of chance' and casino *card* games involve skill. The ruling meant Missouri's riverboats could not offer casino games that did not involve skill, and slot machines and similar games required new legislation (Maxwell et al., 1999).

56 Tribal gaming is a very complex issue, which is beyond my scope here; Belanger (2006) provides an excellent expose for Canada, and Mason (2000) and Light and Rand (2005) offer a detailed analysis for the United States.

57 Indeed, clear acts of genocide occurred. For example, the British issued a proclamation in 1749 that a ten Guinea award would be given for every Mi'kmaq killed as evidenced by the body or their scalp (Paul, 2006). See also Markovich (2003) who finds that the historic treatment of aborigines in Australia constitutes a case of genocide.

58 No formal treaties were ever signed between the colonial governments and the aborigines (Council for Aboriginal Reconciliation, n.d.). A treaty was signed between John Batman and some indigenous leaders in 1835 that allowed Batman to purchase land, but it was immediately declared void by the governor who further proclaimed that the land in Australia belonged to the British crown (State Library of Victoria, n.d.).

59 The issue went to the Supreme Court of Canada where two First Nations Bands argued a constitutional right to self-government, including the right to economic independence and operation of gambling activities on reserves lands (Supreme Court of Canada Judgment, 1996). The court ruled aboriginal constitutional rights must be within historic context of other claimed rights, such as hunting and fishing. The court opined that gambling on reserves was never subject to aboriginal regulation nor was there evidence of historic involvement in high stakes gambling.

60 Personal Communication – Jon Altman, Australia National University, February 1, 2010.

61 Australian aboriginal communities have a history of social problems from alcohol abuse and gambling. Brady (2004) presents a case where an aboriginal community used gaming regulatory laws to prevent the introduction of Electronic Gaming Machines in a nearby hotel.

62 For instance, the United States broke away violently from Britain while Canada and Australia split on consensual terms. Early settlers to the United States were often seeking religious freedoms, whereas early immigrants to Canada were primarily French and British colonists, and many settlers to Australia were from Ireland and Britain (Ashkanasy, Trevor-Roberts, & Earnshaw, 2002, p. 31). Combined with unique geography, differences in trade, social, and cultural institutions arose.

63 Francophones in Canada are predominantly Catholic and one of two found-
ing populations, but they were geographically segmented and prevented by
the *Criminal Code* from legalizing their own gambling.
64 Motives among different political and business elites and the public may
be congruent or discordant.

4. Lotteries and Gaming Machines in Australia, Canada, and the United States

1 Cabot and Thompson (1996, p. 18) argue that societies that stress personal
rights and freedoms are more likely to tolerate gambling.
2 Criminals might be blamed for social disorder and individuals held
responsible for problems associated with excessive gambling.
3 It is important to note that the NASPL includes VLTs from some jurisdictions with traditional lotteries, which means these figures are over-inflated
for ticket lotteries.
4 Doughney (2005) argues the introduction of gambling can create demand,
and Marshall (2005) provides convincing evidence that the EGM market in one Australian region was producer and not consumer driven.
Nevertheless, there must be some acceptance of any activity before the
general population becomes involved.
5 Powerful groups and institutions can exert their influence to mould
cultural practices in a way that actors accept change without question.
However, existing cultural values may also clash with the new ones; this
is what we find with gambling and many fundamentalist Christians and
Muslims.
6 Ingelhart and Baker (2000) fail to define secular-rational societies; the
description here is derived from their lengthy discussion of it.
7 See Baer, Curtis, Grabb, and Johnston (1995) for a comparison of respect
for authority in the three countries; they found that Americans were the
most deferent to authority or at least equal to *English* Canadians.
8 Svallfors (2003) compared attitudes toward the welfare state in eight countries in 1996. His evidence suggests that Australians preferred government
intervention to provide employment, control inflation, and reduce the
income gap between the rich and the poor. Canadians looked to government to provide access to health care and care for seniors. Australians
and Canadians were close in attitudes on assisting the unemployed and
providing affordable housing. Americans scored the lowest across all indicators with the exception of providing financial assistance to university
students from low-income families.

9 Québec also prohibited alcohol but for a shorter duration than the other provinces (Québec–B, n.d.)

10 Public opinion statistics were unavailable. It is also important to note that the legalization of sex-trade work is a reaction to the 'globalisation of prostitution debates and policies' (Weitzer, 2009, p. 88) and pressures from sex-trade workers in the courts (CBC News Online, 2009, October 5).

11 With some exceptions (Australian Institute for Gambling Research, 1999; McMillen, 1993; Morton, 2003; O'Hara, 1988) national historical monographs of gambling are rare. National histories of gambling and particularly individual forms of gambling would prove invaluable to cross-national studies.

12 Sweepstakes and lotteries can be synonymous. However, at times, sweepstakes involve an event such as a horse race where preprinted tickets are sold with the outcome determined by the race.

13 Morton (2003) did not examine any other provinces beyond these five.

14 Irish Sweepstakes tickets were available across Canada, and $3 million dollars went to Ireland in 1938 from Toronto alone (Morton, 2003, p. 54).

15 Between 1790 and 1860, 24 of 33 states raised approximately $32 million dollars (United States Commission on the Review of the National Policy Toward Gambling, 1976, p. 145).

16 Monies from lottery companies created two of the largest banks in the United States – First National City Bank of New York (Citibank) and the Chase Manhattan Bank (Asbury, 1969).

17 Similar laws failed to curb Tattersall's in Australia.

18 Politicians in New York City and Massachusetts, New Jersey, Pennsylvania, Maryland, Louisiana, Illinois, Maine, New Hampshire, Connecticut, California, and Nebraska all proposed lotteries (Nibert, 2000)

19 I have made this comparison based on the adoption of lotteries by a majority of states in a geographic area between two periods.

20 A state is unlikely to lose revenue unless both sides of the border have populations of 25,000 people within 50 miles (Alm et al., 1993, p. 467). Nevertheless, pro-lottery supporters have used this assumption to their benefit. For example, Hansen (2004) describes an advertisement portraying a store clerk from Georgia thanking the Governor of South Carolina for opposing a lottery since South Carolinians would continue to spend money in Georgia.

21 This does not mean that corruption and fraud do not occur. For example, a major scandal erupted in Ontario over retailer fraud and the Ontario Lottery and Gaming Corporation's response to it (see Marin, March, 2007 for the Ontario Ombudsman's Report).

22 Much empirical evidence suggests that politicians often change the ratio of proceeds or shift the funds to another priority after earmarking lottery

profit for education (Hansen, 2004, Mikesell & Zorn, 1986; Miller & Pierce, 1997; Pulliam, 2003). In addition, although Novarro (2002) finds that lotteries increase spending on education, Pulliam (2003) maintains the funding is unstable. Binder, Ganderton, and Hutchens (2001) further argue that the increased resources primarily benefit the middle class, and French and Stanley (n.d.) claim that presence of an 'education' lottery does not increase enrolment.

23 Alaska borders the Yukon Territory, which has a lottery, but the population density and distances are not conducive to cross-border sales.

24 A number of bills have been tabled in the Hawaiian congress in 2009 and 2010 including proposals for an education lottery and casinos (see http://www.hcalg.org/Congressional_Bills_Fall_2009.pdf, http://www.hcalg.org/2010_Gambling_Bills_2-1-2010-3.pdf, Retrieved March 17, 2010 from the Hawaiian Coalition Against Legalised Gambling: http://www.hcalg.org/).

25 Idaho also had 51% support, but this was the second referendum. Sixty per cent supported the first referendum but the Idaho Supreme Court ruled it unconstitutional.

26 Local-option referenda made slot machines legal in four counties in 1948–9 (Janis, 2004). The campaign to prohibit the machines would have allowed lottery proponents to identify key issues, groups, and geographic areas where they could dedicate their resources. Additionally, those who were opposed to prohibition may have welcomed the lottery, and those in favour of prohibiting slot machines may have seen it as a compromise solution.

27 For example, machine manufacturers introduced automated dice and roulette machines in the early 1890s (Fey, 1983). The roulette machine still appears to be in existence (Moody, 1995).

28 Although some states prohibited the manufacture of slot machines, most companies acted with impunity (Anonymous, 1950). In fact, it was generally legal to manufacture and sell gaming machines; it was illegal to operate one and to transport them into states that prohibited them after 1951. This incongruity between the prohibition of gaming machines and alcohol in the United States points to the strength of the machine manufacturers and political interests over the reformers of the period.

29 Schull (2005, p. 66) observes that at least one 'gaming industry analyst' advocates the use of scientific management to 'compress a greater number of spending gestures into smaller units of time,' thereby increasing duration of play and expenditures.

30 An American company has introduced electronic poker tables that eliminate poker chips, cards and dealers; the company estimates that the number

of 'Texas Hold 'em' hands increases 50% over a poker table with a dealer, raising the house 'rake' and eliminating the dealer's salary (Whitmire, 2006).

31 Gephart Jr. (2001, p. 144) argues that corporate institutions create 'safe risks' or simulated risks infused with spectacle for mass consumption. Consumers voluntarily enter into these situations with the expectation they will exit unharmed. However, commercial gambling disguises the real risks by de-monetizing the gambling transaction, providing inducements to play, and hyper-symbolizing the winning experience through visual and auditory stimulation. Although Gephart Jr. is specifically referring to casino gambling, gaming machines easily accomplish these tasks in what we might call hyper-gambling.

32 Regulators could test the computer chip for integrity, which expanded regulatory control.

33 Ashley (1990) suggests that language used in gambling is crucial in constructing the gamblers' world and experiences within it. It is interesting that gamblers in Las Vegas (Schull, 2005, p. 73) and Victoria, Australia (Livingstone, 2005, p. 528) refer to the dissociative state experienced while playing gaming machines as 'the zone.' VLT players in Nova Scotia, Canada, use the same term. This is an indication of the globalization of an informal gambling lexicon suggesting that at least some gaming-machine players have the same experiences across time and space.

34 Cosgrave and Klassen (2001) assert that the state entered the cultural realm through the legalization and legitimation of gambling to generate profit.

35 The altering of machine aesthetics glossed over the gambling features of gaming machines (see Gephart Jr., 2001), providing a platform for the industry and other proponents to attempt to legitimize gaming machines as a form of entertainment.

36 Ambient or convenient gambling refers to lower time-space barriers to gambling opportunities. Marshall (2005) argues from a 'time-geography' perspective that fewer barriers can increase gambling consumption.

37 Opposition over the adoption or expansion of GMOCs in Canada and the United States have forced some provinces and states to propose situating the machines at racetracks. The Australian states have not followed this model. Although the legislation in most states would allow GMOCs at racetracks, they would not have the advantage of exclusivity present in North America (Personal communication – Mary Capuano, Australian Racing Board Limited, 9 March 2007).

38 In 2004–5, 2,416 clubs held 116,786 machines compared with 3,455 hotels with 71,110 machines (Australian Gaming Council, 2007). Nevertheless,

hotels operated approximately 90% in South Australia and Tasmania, and about 50% in Queensland and Victoria (p. 8).

39 Table 4.7 shows the adoption of poker machines in Australia and does not include cashless 'approved amusement devices' (AADs) that often pay out goods and are considered differently than poker machines.

40 The NSW Supreme Court drew a distinction between slot machines and fruit machines and ruled clubs could retain the latter provided the profits solely benefited the club's members or the larger community. The *Royal Commission on Greyhound Racing and Fruit Machines* declared the machines illegal in 1932. However, the machines remained in clubs because of uncertainty as to how to reconcile the 1921 ruling with the 1932 decision (O'Hara, 1988; Wilcox, 1983).

41 Returning Servicemen League (RSL) clubs, similar to Veterans' associations and Canadian Legions, were established at the end of the First World War.

42 The Australian Club Development Association, which was a lobby group comprised of licensed clubs and apparently financed by the gaming-machine industry, purportedly lobbied all three governments to legalize machines between 1982 and 1987 (Wilcox, 1983).

43 An alliance of church groups had successfully opposed the introduction of casinos into Victoria by using socially pragmatic arguments as opposed to theological and moral reasons. They pursued the same approach with the *Wilcox Inquiry* and claimed victory when the proposal did not move forward (Reid, 1985).

44 There was a substantial increase in poker machines and problem gambling throughout the state by 1997 as hotels and clubs scrambled to increase their profits (Queensland Office of Gaming Regulation, 1999). By 1999 the Queensland government felt the need to conduct a ministerial review to provide a 'more balanced and responsible approach' to gaming in Queensland (p. 1).

45 This ploy apparently did not persuade the South Australian public as evidenced by an *Adelaide Advertiser* poll in 1992 that showed 60% of the public opposed the introduction of poker machines (cited in Costello & Millar, 2000, p. 145). This finding raises an interesting point. South Australia legalized lotteries in 1967 following a referendum, yet it did not use a populist mechanism to decide poker machines, possibly out of fear of defeat.

46 The poker machine issue has also not been resolved in South Australia. In 1997, an independent candidate was elected on the platform of 'No Pokies,' and a second independent was elected under the same banner in 2006.

47 A recent indirect measure indicates that opposition may be mixed. The Charles Darwin School for Social Policy Research found opinions divided

in 2006 over the number of poker machines in the state. The researchers speculate that the 'rapid increase in the number of gaming machines ... has perhaps created a shift toward attitudes of tolerance for this form of gambling' (Charles Darwin School for Social Policy Research, 2006, p. 23).

48 McMillen and Togni (2000) assert that the central premise behind the legalization of poker machines in ambient settings was to provide revenue that could benefit the wider community.

49 Initially there were structural differences between a video lottery terminal (VLT) and a slot machine. VLTs offered a variety of computerized games whereas slot machines typically provided reel games. In addition, VLTs rewarded players with credits redeemed for cash, and slot machines provided redeemable tokens or cash. Still, provincial governments draw a legal distinction between the two. VLTs in Canada are in liquor-licensed venues and slot machines are situated in casinos and racinos. Provinces that have capped the number of VLTs have not placed a limit on the number of slot machines.

50 Alberta introduced the *Slot Machine Act* in 1924, prohibiting slot machines (Robinson, 1983, p. 113).

51 Morton (2003, p. 50) remarks that gaming machines during this period were very popular. For example, in 1936 an estimated 3,000 to 5,000 machines were situated in the city of Vancouver.

52 For example, one justice of the Alberta Court of Appeal complained that while the *Criminal Code* prohibited gaming machines, it had not made it an 'offence to keep and use them' (cited in Ford, 1936, p. 317). Porter, Curtis, Robinette, Claxton, and Cronkite (1936) diverge from this interpretation while reviewing the *Criminal Code,* but they note that although the machines were illegal the legislation had apparently not provided a penalty for keeping or operating them. Read (1935, p. 259) also found that the wide availability of slot machines led Manitoba to consider 'special legislation to deal with the matter.'

53 The *Canadian Bill of Rights* was passed in 1960, and one clause set out that the law could not violate the rights or freedoms of Canadians such that it amounted to an instance of 'cruel and unusual punishment.' Several people who had slot machines confiscated attempted to argue the seizure amounted to cruel and unusual punishment, since they would face heavy financial losses. The presiding judge ruled against them (Bowles, 1962–5, p. 72).

54 An Order in Council (OIC) gives notice of an administrative decision by the Governor General of Canada or the Lieutenant Governor of a Province. The orders most often originate within the federal or provincial cabinet and are approved by the Governor General or Lieutenant

Governor. Although many are simply proclamation of appointments, others are regulations or legislative orders related to, or authorized by, existing legislative acts. Alberta, Alberta Gaming and Liquor Commission (2001, Vol 1 3–6; Vol 2 A2–12); Manitoba (1991), *Video Lottery Regulation 245/91* (1991); New Brunswick, *New Brunswick Regulation 90-142, Video Lottery Scheme Regulation – Lotteries Act* (1990); Newfoundland and Labrador, *Statutes of Newfoundland, 1991, Chapter 53* (1991); Nova Scotia, Nova Scotia Gaming Control Commission (1996: 14); Prince Edward Island, *Lotteries Commission Act, Video Lottery Scheme Regulation* (n.d.); Québec, *An Act respecting the Société des loteries du Québec* (R.S.Q., c. S-13.1, s. 13) (n.d.); Saskatchewan, Personal contact – Tim Prince, Saskatchewan Legislative Library, 2007.

55 British Columbia and Ontario faced heated opposition to the introduction of GMOCs and held public hearings. For example, Ontario outlined its proposed Video Lottery Program in May 1996, and then held three weeks of hearings in Toronto, Thunder Bay, Kenora, Fort Erie, Sarnia, Ottawa, and Sudbury. Not surprisingly, those who stood to benefit from the machines (the hospitality and horse race industries) were in favour, and the political opposition, charitable organizations, church groups, and addictions professionals were opposed.

56 Azmier (2001) maintains the actual number of illegal machines was unknown and, as noted above, illegal slot machines were in Canada for a very long time. New Brunswick, Nova Scotia, and Prince Edward Island all chose to situate VLTs in non-age-restricted locations, which also undermines claims of stricter control. Finally, many businesses chosen as site holders operated GMOCs prior to legalization making them active participants in the illegal market; in this sense, some provinces rewarded businesses and individuals involved in unlawful activities.

57 The difficulty in enforcing the law can be seen in the Supreme Court of Canada Judgment, R. *v.* Kent, [1994] 3 S.C.R. 133, where the court upheld an acquittal of a Nova Scotia store owner accused of operating a gaming house. The accused had several machines people played for credits and then allegedly traded for cash. However, the court ruled the crown could not prove its case in that playing a machine for credits was not against the law.

58 Within two years the dedicated revenue was reduced to an annual sum of $10 million (CAD) with the remainder going to the consolidated fund (New Brunswick *Video Lottery Program Review*, n.d.).

59 Hyson (2002) makes a case that the government affected the results through improper administration of the referendum: the process lacked

transparency and was generally unfair and biased toward the pro-VLT campaign.

60 Some debate exists as to the rationale for legalization in Newfoundland. The Canadian Gaming Association (2006) claims they were economic, while Wangersky (2006) cites illegal gaming machines.

61 For example, Newfoundland's Auditor General noted in March, 2004 that it was the sole Canadian province that had not conducted a problem gambling prevalence study (Newfoundland and Labrador Auditor General, 2004, p. 380). Eight months later the Premier refused to entertain the possibility of a provincial referendum on the subject, and called for 'some empirical data ... to see exactly what the affliction is' (Newfoundland and Labrador Legislative Assembly, 2004, December 6).

62 See the Kimball Report (Nova Scotia, 1993); the Morris Report (Nova Scotia Lottery Commission, 1993); and the Fogarty Report (Nova Scotia, 1994).

63 For example, in 2004, the head of 'Video Online Terminators Society' launched a personal lawsuit against the Nova Scotia government claiming the province failed to provide due diligence by assessing the potential impacts of VLTs before introducing them in the province (see Appendix C of Gaming Law Review (2005b) 9,2: pp. 131–3). In 2005, a report also showed just 25% of Nova Scotians approved of VLTs (Omnifacts Research, 2005).

64 A provincial inquiry was held in 1993 and made recommendations aimed at reducing opposition, which the government largely ignored. The number of VLTs was also capped in 1996, but the government refused to remove them from non-age-restricted venues, undoubtedly over fear of a lawsuit from retail operators (Supreme Court of Prince Edward Island, 2005).

65 Plebiscites in Canada are a non-binding electoral process. As a rule, provincial governments enact legislation following plebiscites, but are not required to do so.

66 Racinos in the Canadian provinces have largely been a response to lobbying from the horse race industry after attendance declined dramatically with the introduction of casinos and VLTs.

67 Although the profits were slated for rural economic development (Manitoba, 1993), when the revenue-sharing formula was set, 65% was allocated to the general fund, 25% went to rural economic development, and 10% was given to municipalities where the VLTs were located (Manitoba Gaming Control Commission, 1998, p. 20).

68 The freeze did not prevent the government from introducing VLT-style gaming machines at Assiniboia Downs making it Canada's first racino, nor did it prevent the government from negotiating 20 agreements with the provinces' First Nations bands.

69 One VLT site holder in Winkler sued and took the case to the Supreme Court of Canada, which ruled in favour of the town (see Supreme Court of Canada Judgment 2003).

70 Even though Loto-Québec did not actually launch GMOCs for several years, it seems Québec was disregarding the *Criminal Code* (as it did with lotteries in the first two decades of the twentieth century).

71 In fact, the government may have used the collapse of the video poker amusement machine industry as an opportunity to take control of a highly profitable revenue generator found in several other provinces (Personal Communication – Jean Marc Laniel, July 17, 2007).

72 See Québec – B, (n.d.) *An act respecting the Régie des alcools, des courses et des jeux* (June 1993) which amended Québec – A, (n.d.), *An Act respecting lotteries, publicity contests and amusement machines.*

73 The Société des loteries vidéo du Québec (SLVQ) also began placing VLTs at racetracks in the 1990s.

74 The announcement came just over two weeks after voters in New Brunswick narrowly supported keeping VLTs in that province, an event that could not have been lost on the Québec government.

75 The corporation suggested a 31% reduction in VLT sites and the existing VLTs be moved to five 'gaming centres' bordering high-density population or tourism areas (Loto-Québec, 2004: 25–9). It also recommended removing VLTs from areas where the average household income was below $50,000, and the number of machines was above 2 per 1000 residents. Lastly, it called for the establishment of a separate non-profit organization independent of government to deal with issues surrounding problem gambling (p. 27).

76 Gilliland and Ross (2005) examined the spatial distribution of VLTs in Montreal and Laval in 2002 and concluded the adoption of VLTs in poor neighbourhoods was higher than in affluent ones.

77 As noted in Chapter 3, the courts forced the provincial government to recognize the municipal by-laws. Other provinces, such as Saskatchewan, argued that gambling fell under provincial jurisdiction and municipalities had to accept provincial decisions. It is interesting that critics of VLTs in the other provinces have not challenged the governments' jurisdiction in the courts.

78 For example, North Saanich turned down a zoning application for slot machines in 2006, eliminating live horse racing that had existed there for 150 years. The title of *Bill 75* was an effort to gain support: '*An Act to regulate alcohol and gaming in the public interest, to fund charities through the responsible management of video lotteries and to amend certain statutes related to*

liquor and gaming' (Ontario Legislative Assembly, 1996, October 10) or the Ontario Legislative Assembly, 1996.

79 Surprisingly, the Ontario Addictions Research Foundation was not unequivocally opposed and suggested the government first provide a comprehensive plan that would include research, treatment, and public awareness campaigns; all other addictions organizations and experts were firmly opposed (McNaught & Poelking, 1996).

80 Charitable groups, the police, and a government scandal did not help its position. Many charities demanded an impact assessment on their fundraising activities even though the government was offering them 10% of VLT profits. In addition, some police agencies maintained legal VLTs would not eliminate the illegal market and could in fact exacerbate enforcement (Ontario Legislative Assembly, 1996, October 10). The Solicitor General was also forced to admit that the caucus held back a secret Ontario Provincial Police report linking organized crime to gambling for months.

81 This observation is based on secondary sources. For example, Anonymous (1950) and the *Yale Law Journal* (1951, p. 1403, fn. 46) maintained in the early 1950s that slot machines had never been an 'underground activity,' and were openly manufactured and widely advertised in trade journals. Anonymous (1950) further estimated the gross wager on slot machines at 1 billion dollars and the *Yale Law Journal* (1951, 14) reported that 200,000 machines could be found across the United State in 1951. The *Iowa Law Journal* (1949) also observed that contributions to federal revenue under a 1941 gaming-machine tax law were highest in some states that expressly prohibited slot machines. See also Anonymous (1950), Dombrink (1988), Drzazga (1963), Lindberg, Petrenko, Gladden, & Johnson (1998), Nuwer (n.d.), Peterson (1949), and Roberts (1969), in addition to the *Kefauver Inquiry*, U.S. Senate Special Committee to Investigate Organised Crime in Interstate Commerce (1951) for commentary concerning the proliferation of gaming machines and references to organized crime. Numerous current articles also exist in the popular press about court cases regarding illegal machines and corruption across the United States (e.g., Schneider, 2004, December 12; United States of America v. Calabrese et al. (2006, August)). Further historical research for Australia and Canada may reveal fewer differences among the three countries in terms of the presence of illegal machines, corruption, and control by organized crime.

82 Speakeasies were not the only locations with slot machines. Chafetz (1960) claims eastern and midwestern spas routinely used slot machines to attract patrons.

83 Dombrink (1988: 201) reports that 'video gambling machine purveyors' bribed numerous police officers in Philadelphia including the 'second-in-command of the entire city.' Lindberg et al. (1998) discuss organized crime involvement with the video poker business and cites a case in 1992 where several Louisiana Senators accepted bribes from a video gaming company with reputed organized crime links. In 2007, the former North Carolina state House Speaker, Jim Black, was sent to prison for bribery and obstructing justice; it was revealed in his trial that he had accepted illegal campaign donations from a lobbyist whose clients included video poker interests that Black had apparently protected for years (Kane & Curliss, 2006, May 18, Modified May 20; Beckwith & Kane, 2007, July 11).

84 During the Kefauver inquiry into organized crime in 1951, the U.S. Assistant Attorney General observed, 'The slot machine and pinball gambling machine industry remains one of the mainstays of organised crime ... [and criminals prefer pinball gambling over slot machines because they are more profitable]' (As cited in King, 1964, p. 205).

85 Nevada legalized slot machines in 1903 and prohibited them in 1910. They were again legalized in 1913 under the stipulation that prizes be limited to cigars, drinks, or sums of less than two dollars (Fey, 1983; Personal Contact – David Schwartz, University of Las Vegas, 2006).

86 It is unclear whether slot machines were actually legal or not. The *Iowa Law Journal* (1949) claims that Montana's law authorized non-profit clubs to obtain licences for gaming machines but prohibited their use. On the other hand, Peterson (1949) and the *Yale Law Journal* (1951) maintain that Montana permitted slot machines in private clubs. Overall the evidence suggests that slot machines were legal.

87 *Time* (1953: March 2) estimated that in 1952, Idaho's 3,438 legal machines provided $486,262 (US) to the state and considerable revenue for smaller communities.

88 There is some debate as to the rationale behind the act: Anonymous (1950) maintains it was strictly a cash grab by the federal government, whereas Frey (1998) views it as more of a strategy to deal with illegal gambling.

89 To get around the law, manufacturers began replacing the reels and drums of mechanical machines with electrical consoles. In addition, many states had ruled that pinball gambling machines did not deliver 'articles of value' and they effectively remained outside the law. The federal government had also not prohibited slot machines; it simply forbade shipment across state lines, and clubs stockpiled machines in anticipation of the act (*Yale Law Journal*, 1951).

90 In 1943, 85,987 premises were paying the federal stamp tax for gaming machines, a number that dropped to 69,786 in 1949 (Anonymous, 1950, p. 67) and 31,827 in 1962–3 (King, 1964, p. 207).

91 For example, slot machine proponents in Washington put forward an initiative (I-892) in 2004 that would have paved the way for gaming machines in neighbourhood settings to reduce property taxes. The initiative was soundly defeated 61% to 39% (Washington Secretary of State, n.d.), yet other states like Pennsylvania managed to legalize slots by placing them at racetracks and in betting parlours.

92 The public was staunchly opposed to gaming machines in 1950, but less so in 1985, and religious groups have failed to initiate referendums on any form of gambling. Furthermore, Montana is sparsely populated, with less than a million people; yet in 2002, the state-wide wager was $761.4 million (US), and 93% came from gaming machines (Montana Department of Justice Gambling Control Division, 2002).

93 In 1985, Nebraska allowed its Lottery Corporation to test a video lottery not linked to a central system but the trial was terminated in the same year (Rhode Island Lottery, 2006).

94 The electorate has voted on proposed constitutional amendments and initiatives concerning VLTs in 1992, 1994, 2000 and 2006. The results have ranged from 53% – 47% in 1994 to 63% – 37% in 2006. The text accompanying the ballots may have played a role since the highest levels of approval came when revenue for the state was mentioned in the question. In 2006, the Secretary of State distributed a pamphlet explaining Initiative 7 with the following: 'The State operates video lottery as authorized by State law. During the last year, the State received approximately one hundred twelve million dollars ($112,000,000.00) from video lottery [sic] which is 11% of the state general fund budget. The proposed law would repeal video lottery and eliminate this source of revenue' (South Dakota Secretary of State, 2006).

95 For example, South Dakota (1998) passed bill SB147, *An Act to Study the Effects of Gaming in South Dakota,* in 1998. Most recently, the state began contributing $200,000 to the South Dakota Department of Human Services to address problem gambling.

96 Donnis (2003) also highlights a scandal involving bribes to ensure the number of VLTs at one of the tracks was approved.

97 Oklahoma's legislation allows for electronic bonanza-style bingo games, electronic instant bingo games, and electronic amusement games at horse racing tracks (Oklahoma State Senate Legislative Brief, 2004) and will not be dealt with here.

98 Casinos catering to the middle and upper classes, and working-class 'hells,' were in existence long before gaming machines. However, they were not as abundant as gaming machines, nor would the games appeal to as wide a range of clientele as gaming machines that required little skill to play.

99 Although Morton (2003, p. 48) notes that a club in Vancouver in the early 1930s had 12,000 members, Caldwell (1972) maintains that the social institution of the club as found in Australia did not exist in either Canada or the United States in 1972.

100 This argument is still used to counter arguments that GMOCs should be prohibited.

Glossary

Bretton Woods Agreement. A complex agreement of international financial monetary controls signed at Bretton Woods, New Hampshire in 1944. One aspect of the agreement was the setting of controls on capital to prevent undermining welfare-state autonomy through financial speculation.

Class III Gaming. Tribal gaming in the United States that includes electronic gaming machines, table games and wagering.

Collective Action. The collective behaviours of a group in response to shared goals or to address shared problems.

Collective Good. A good all citizens have access to that cannot be divided among individuals; for example, public education.

Corporatization. Deregulation of a government service and institution of a quasi-governmental corporate organization overseen by the state.

Corporatism. A political-economic system of governance where control over social and economic life is exercised, under state direction, through unelected corporate bodies that represent economic, social, cultural and professional groups.

Devolution. The transfer of political, economic, and social responsibilities or revenue from central governments to lower level polities.

Ètatism or Statism. An economic system where the state has central control over economic planning and industry.

Familialism. An ideology or culture that values the Western family as a central social institution and the ideals associated with it.

Fordism. A capitalist system of production characterized by mass assembly-line production and semi-skilled workers.

Glocalization. The manner through which local cultures interpret and act within processes of globalization, creating different outcomes in political-economic and sociocultural spheres.

Governmentality. Actions undertaken by political, economic, and/or social groups to shape worldviews and practices of individuals; actors internalize these practices within conflict and compromise, and shape and modify themselves to the degree they agree with them.

Habitus. The influence of routine practices in an actor's environment that instill a set of dispositions, perceptions, and practices they are unaware of and take for granted.

Horizontal Fiscal Balance. A horizontal fiscal balance is where differences exist among subnational units in the provision of services, the result of greater revenue generating capabilities in one or more regions. *See also Vertical Fiscal Imbalance.*

Hypercommodification. A process where the use value of commodities disappear and is replaced by signification value, which designates a status embodied in the commodity but is meaningless outside of it. Hypercommodities are distributed and consumed as lifestyle choices.

Late Modernity. A period characterized by a cultural as opposed to industrial based economy where capital is disorganized, decentralized, and focused on obtaining profit from aesthetic and symbolic goods and services. Political interests are fragmented along religious, gender, environmental and other lines as opposed to class-based.

Legitimacy. The willingness to comply with a set of rules or demands based on normative or legal grounds.

Neo-liberalism. A set of policies or ideologies that minimizes state intervention in the markets and citizens lives, asserting that social benefits are best generated by minimal government interference and free market forces, thereby shifting risks from governments and corporations on to individuals.

Order in Council. An Order in Council or OIC is a proclamation by the Canadian Governor General or Provincial Lieutenant Governor of an administrative decision often based in pre-existing laws. However, OICs are most often initiated by government Cabinets and approved by the Queen's representative.

Polity. A government/political body and/or arena where governmental decisions are influenced by political, economic, and social groups.

Prudentialism. A set of principles that advocate individual responsibility to reduce or eliminate social risks.

Québec's Quiet Revolution. A period during the 1960s characterized by a radical shift to secularism, increased welfare-state building, and emergence of a political movement dedicated to separation from Canada.

Vertical Fiscal Imbalance. A vertical fiscal imbalance (VFI) exists when there is unequal revenue generating capabilities among national and subnational units within a federation. *See also Horizontal Fiscal Imbalance.*

Weltanschauung. The German term for an individual or group's worldview that shapes their conduct.

References

Abt, V., Smith, J.F., & Christiansen, E.M. (1985). *The business of risk: Commercial gambling in mainstream America.* Lawrence: University of Kansas Press.

Ackerman, W.V. (1996). Financing historic preservation in rural communities: A case of legalized gaming, *CRM Cultural Resource Management 19*(4), 27–32.

ACT Gambling and Racing Commission. (2002). Review of the gaming machine act 1987, policy paper. *ACT Gambling and Racing Commission,* Canberra. Retrieved December 22, 2009, from http://www.gamblingandracing.act.gov. au/Documents/Policy%20Paper%20Gaming%20Machine%20Act.pdf

ACT Gambling and Racing Commission. (2003). *Annual report 2002–2003.* Australian Capital Territory, Canberra. Publication No 3/1159. Retrieved December 15, 2009, from http://www.gamblingandracing.act.gov.au/ Documents/Annual%20Report%202002%20to%202003.pdf

Adams, M. (2003). *Fire and ice: The United States, Canada and the myth of converging values.* Toronto: Penguin Canada.

Advertiser Sunday Mail (2007, April 21). *Alarm bells are ringing over pokies.* Retrieved November 30, 2009, from http://www.news.com.au/adelaidenow/ story/0,22606,21597184-5006336,00.html

Alberta Gaming and Liquor Commission. (2001). *Gaming licensing policy review: Achieving a balance, Vol 1.* St. Albert, AB. Retrieved December 2, 2009, from http://www.aglc.ca/pdf/lpr/LPR_Report-Complete.pdf

Alberta Legislative Assembly. *Legislative debates* (Hansard). 22 Legislature. 3rd Session. May 23, 1991, 1347–74. Retrieved December 17, 2009, from http://www.assembly.ab.ca/Documents/isysquery/bc647353-f0a0-4e09-9346-2ba572733664/1/doc/

Alberta Lotteries Review Committee. (1995). *New directions for lotteries and gaming: Report and recommendations of the Lotteries Review Committee.* Retrieved December 12, 2009, from Dspace at University of Calgary, Alberta Gaming Research Institute, Gambling Literature. http://hdl.handle.net/1880/127

Allen Consulting Group. (2009). *Casinos and the Australian Economy*. Report to the Australasian Casino Association, April 2009. Retrieved January 15, 2010, from http://www.auscasinos.com/pdf/media/CasinosandtheAus Economy.pdf

Alm, J., McKee, M., & Skidmore, M. (1993). Fiscal pressure, tax competition, and the introduction of state lotteries. *National Tax Journal, 46*(4), 463–76.

American Gaming Association. (2006). *Industry information, state information: Statistics*. Retrieved August 30, 2007, from http://www.americangaming. org/Industry/state/statistics.cfm?stateid=9999

American Gaming Association. (2009). *State of the States: The AGA survey of casino entertainment*. Retrieved January 15, 2010, from http://www.american gaming.org/assets/files/aga-sos2009web.pdf

Angus Reid. (2007, June 5). Americans discuss morally acceptable issues. *Angus Reid Global Monitor*. Retrieved January 15, 2010, from http://www. angus-reid.com/polls/view/15993/

Angus Reid. (2007, December 25). Canadians review what is morally acceptable. *Angus Reid Global Monitor*. Retrieved January 15, 2010, from http:// www.angus-reid.com/polls/view/29454/

Anonymous. (1950). Slot machines and pinball games. *Annals of the American Academy of Political and Social Science, 269*(May), 62–70.

Agrusa, J.F. (1998). Perceptions and attitudes toward the legislation of gaming in Hawaii by Japanese-speaking tourists and English-speaking tourists. *Asia Pacific Journal of Tourism Research, 2*(2), 57–64. Retrieved January 6, 2010, from http://dx.doi.org/10.1080/10941669808721997

Agrusa, J.F. (2000). Legalization of gambling in Hawaii and its potential effects on Japanese intention to visit: A philosophical inquiry. *Journal of Travel & Tourism Marketing, 9*(1), 211–217. Retrieved January 6, 2010, from http://dx.doi.org/10.1300/J073v09n01_13

Arano, K.G., & Blair, B.F. (2008). Modeling religious behaviour and economic outcome: Is the relationship bicausal? Evidence from a survey of Mississippi households. *The Journal of Socio-Economics, 37*, 2043–53. Retrieved April 5, 2010, from Elsevier Doi:10.1016/j.socec.2007.06.006

Asbury, H. (1969). *Sucker's progress: An informal history of gambling in America from the colonies to Canfield*. Montclair: Patterson Smith.

Ashkanasy, N.M., Trevor-Roberts, E., & Earnshaw, L. (2002). The anglo cluster: The legacy of the British empire. *Journal of World Business, 37*, 28–39. Retrieved January 5, 2010, from http://www.thunderbird.edu/wwwfiles/ms/ globe/Links/jwb_anglo_%20cluster.pdf

Ashley, L.R.N. (1990). The words of my mouth, and the meditation of my heart: The mindset of gamblers revealed in their language, *Journal of Gambling Studies, 6*(3), 241–61.

Atkinson, G., Nichols, M., & Oleson T. (2000). The menace of competition and gambling deregulation, *Journal of Economic Issues, 34*(3), 621–34.

Australian Bureau of Statistics. (1994). *Australian Social Trends Catologue No. 4102.0, Special feature: Trends in religious affiliation,* ABS, Canberra. Retrieved January 22, 2010, from http://www.abs.gov.au/ausstats/abs@.nsf/2f762f95845 417aeca25706c00834efa/10072ec3ffc4f7b4ca2570ec00787c40!OpenDocument

Australian Bureau of Statistics. (2001a). Taxation during the first 100 years of federation. *Year Book Australia, 2001, Catalogue No. 1301.0,* ABS, Canberra. Retrieved February 12, 2010, from http://www.abs.gov.au/AUSSTATS/abs@. nsf/Previousproducts/1301.0Feature%20Article472001?opendocument&tab name=Summary&prodno=1301.0&issue=2001&num=&view=

Australian Bureau of Statistics. (2001b). *Year Book Australia, 2001,* Canberra.

Australian Bureau of Statistics. (2005). *Year Book Australia, 2005, Catalogue No. 1301.0, Culture and Recreation; Religious Affiliation.* ABS, Canberra. Retrieved January 12, 2010, from http://www.abs.gov.au/Ausstats/abs@.nsf/0/E4F6E98 AA14943F3CA256F7200832F71?Open

Australian Bureau of Statistics. (2006). *Australian historical population statistics, 2006, Catalogue No. 3105.0.65.001,* ABS, Canberra. Retrieved January 25, 2010, from http://www.abs.gov.au/AUSSTATS/abs@.nsf/DetailsPage/3105.0.65. 0012006?OpenDocument

Australian Department of Foreign Affairs and Trade. (n.d.). *About Australia - indigenous peoples: An overview.* Retrieved February 1, 2010, from http:// www.dfat.gov.au/facts/Indigenous_peoples.html

Australian Gaming Council. (2007, January). *A Database on Australia's Gambling Industry.* Victoria: Australian Gaming Council.

Australian Government Productivity Commission. (2009). *Gambling. Overview including key points.* Retrieved March 29, 2010, from http://www.pc.gov.au/__ data/assets/pdf_file/0003/91884/02-overview.pdf

Australian Institute for Gambling Research. (1999). *Australian gambling comparative history and analysis, October 1999.* Sydney, New South Wales.

Australian Institute of Primary Care. (2006). *The electronic gaming machine (EGM) industry and technology final report.* Prepared for the (former) Victorian Gambling Research Panel. Melbourne: La Trobe University

Azmier, J.J. (2000). *Canadian gambling behaviour and attitudes: Main report.* Calgary: Canada West Foundation.

Azmier, J.J. (2001). *Gambling in Canada special report: Video lottery terminals in New Brunswick.* Retrieved December 15, 2009, from http://www.cwf.ca/V2/ files/200103.pdf

Azmier, J.J., Jepson, V., & Patton, S. (1999). *Canada's gambling regulatory patchwork: A handbook.* Retrieved January 11, 2010, http://www.cwf.ca/V2/ files/199915.pdf

Baer, D., Curtis, J., Grabb, E., & Johnston, W. (1995). Respect for authority in Canada, the United States, Great Britain and Australia. *Sociological Focus, 28*(2), 177–95.

Bakken, I.J., Øren, A., & Götestam, K.G. (n.d.). *Norway: The slot machine and problem gambling: A study commissioned by the Norwegian gaming and foundation authority.* Retrieved March 31, 2010, from http://www.easg.org/media/file/conferences/novagorica2008/wednesday/1400-ses2/bakken_inger.pdf

Baldwin, J.R., Brown, M., Maynard, J.P., & Zietsma, D. (2004). *Catching up and falling behind: The performance of provincial GDP from 1990 to 2003.* Statistics Canada: Micro-Economic Analysis Division. Retrieved January 10, 2010, from http://www.statcan.ca/english/research/11F0027MIE/11F0027 MIE2004024.pdf

Barker, T., & Britz, M. (2000). *Jokers wild: Legalized gambling in the twenty-first century.* Westport: Praeger.

Barnes, T. (2005, January 2). Close-up 2004: Slots are key to 'new Pennsylvania': Rendell betting $1 billion in new revenue will give residents break on property tax.' *Post-Gazette Harrisburg Bureau.* Retrieved January 12, 2010, from http://www.post-gazette.com/pg/05002/435951.stm

Baró Diaz, M. (2005, March 10). Miami-Dade Hispanics took major role in rejecting slots proposal: Governor's appeals helped sway voters. *Sun Sentinel.* Retrieved January 14, 2010, from http://www.sun-sentinel.com/news/nationworld/sfl-dmiamislots10mar10,0,3624464.story

Bean, M.E. (2004). *Analysis of ballot proposal 04-1: Voter approval for gambling expansion, November 2004 general election.* Retrieved April 5, 2010, from http://house.michigan.gov/hfa/PDFs/ballot.pdf

Beare, M.E., & Naylor, R.T. (1999). *Major issues relating to organized crime: Within the context of economic relationships.* Nathanson Centre for the study of organized crime and corruption report to the Law Commission of Canada. Retrieved February 14, 2010, from http://www.ncjrs.gov/nathanson/organized.html

Beckwith, R.T., & Kane, D. (2007, July 11). [Former NC House Speaker Jim] Black sentenced to 63 months in prison. *Raleigh News and Observer* via Free Republic. Retrieved January 26, 2010, from http://www.freerepublic.com/focus/f-news/1864267/posts

Belanger, Y. (2006). *Gambling with the future: The evolution of Aboriginal gaming in Canada.* Saskatoon: Purich Publishing Ltd.

Bellhouse, D.R. (1991). The Genoese lottery. *Statistical Science, 6*(2), 141–8. Retrieved December 15, 2010, from http://projecteuclid.org/DPubS/Repository/1.0/Disseminate?view=body&id=pdf_1&handle=euclid.ss/1177011819

Berger, D.E., Snortum, J.S.R., Homel, R.J., Hauge, R., & Loxley, W. (1990). Deterrence and prevention of alcohol-impaired driving in Australia, the United States, and Norway, *Justice Quarterly, 7*(3), 453–65. Retrieved February 2, 2010, from http://www.informaworld.com/smpp/content~content=a718864588~db=all

Bernd Spahn, P., & Shah, A. (1995). Intergovernmental fiscal relations in Australia. In J. Roy (Ed.) *Macroeconomic management and fiscal decentralization* (pp. 49–72). Washington: World Bank.

Berry, F.S., & Berry, W. (1990). State lottery adoptions as policy innovations: An event history analysis. *American Political Science Review, 84*(2), 395–415.

Binde, P. (2005). Gambling across cultures: Mapping worldwide occurrence and learning from ethnographic comparison. *International Gambling Studies, 5*(1), 1–27.

Binder, M., Ganderton, P.T., & Hutchens, K. (2001) *Who benefits from a lottery-funded college subsidy? Evidence from the New Mexico success scholarship.* Retrieved December 20, 2009, from http://gandini.unm.edu/research/Papers/Lottery.pdf

Bird, R.M., & Tarasov, A.V. (2002). Closing the gap: Fiscal imbalances and intergovernmental transfers in developed federations. *Georgia State University International Studies Program Working Papers Series Number 02 –2.* Retrieved January 6, 2010, from http://aysps.gsu.edu/isp/files/ispwp0202.pdf

Black, E. (2008). Gambling mania: Lessons from the Manitoba experience. *Canadian Public Administration, 39*(1), 49–61.

Blanche, E. (1950). Lotteries yesterday, today, and tomorrow. *Annals of the American Academy of Political and Social Science, 269,* 71–6.

Blevins, J., & Jensen, K. (1998). Gambling as a community development quick fix. *The Annals of the American Academy of Political and Social Science, 556,* 109–123.

Bobbitt, R. (2007). *Lottery wars: Case studies in Bible Belt politics, 1986–2005.* New York, NY: Lexington.

Boehmke, F.J., & Witmer, R. (2004). Disentangling diffusion: The effects of social learning and economic competition on state policy innovation and expansion. *Political Research Quarterly, 57*(1), 39–51.

Bolen, D.W., & Boyd, W.H. (1968). Gambling and the gambler: A review and preliminary findings. *Archives of General Psychiatry, 18*(5), 617–30.

Bourdieu, P. (1990). Structures, habitus, practices. In P. Bourdieu, *The logic of practice* (pp. 52–65). Cambridge: Polity Press.

Bourgeois, D. (2001). *The potential economic, social and image impacts of a casino in Moncton.* Report presented to Moncton City Council by the Citizens' Committee on Destination Gaming. Retrieved April 3, 2010, from http://

www.moncton.ca/Assets/Government+English/Publications+English/Poten
tial+Impact+of+a+Casino+in+Moncton.pdf

Bowles, R.S. (1962). Our courts and our Parliament view – The Canadian Bill of Rights. *Manitoba Law School Journal, 1962–1965,* 55–88. Retrieved April 20, 2010, from http://heinonline.org/

Bradfield, S. (2006). Separatism or status-quo? Indigenous affairs from the birth of land rights to the death of ATSIC. *Australian Journal of Politics and History,* 52(1), 80–97. Retrieved February 2, 2010, from Wiley Interscience: doi: 10.1111/j.1467-8497.2006.00409a.x

Brady, M. (2004). Regulating social problems: The pokies, the productivity commission and an Aboriginal community. CAEPR Working Paper No. 269/2004. *Centre for Aboriginal Economic Policy Research. Australian National University.* Retrieved February 2, 2010, from http://www.anu.edu.au/caepr/system/files/Publications/DP/2004_DP269.pdf

Braidfoot, L. (1988). Legalization of lotteries in the 1980s. *The Journal of Gambling Behavior,* 4(4), 282–90.

Brand, J., & Egan, J. (n.d.). *Update of racino legislation in the United States from 2004–2006.* Retrieved November 30, 2009, from http://ag.arizona.edu/rtip/students/research/06_student_research/racino_legislation_update_final.pdf

Braunlich, C.G. (1999) Indiana. In A.N. Cabot, W.N. Thompson, A. Tottenham, & C.G. Braunlich (Eds.), *International casino law* (pp. 33–8). Las Vegas: Institute for the Study of Gambling and Commercial Gaming.

Breton, A., & Fraschini, A. (2003). Vertical competition in unitary states: The case of Italy. *Public Choice,* 114(1–2), 57–77. Retrieved January 18 2010, from ABI/INFORM Global database. Document ID: 330927681

Brian, R. (2009). Diffusion of an economic development policy innovation: Explaining the international spread of casino gambling. *Journal of Gambling Studies.* Retrieved February 5, 2010, from www.springerlink.com doi: 10.1007/s10899-009-9166-4

British Columbia Association for Charitable Gaming. (n.d.). *British Columbia association for charitable gaming history. Question: What has BCACG done for charities?* Retrieved January 22, 2010, from http://www.bcacg.com/History.php

British Columbia Legislative Assembly. (1992). *Legislative debates (Hansard).* 35th Parl., 1st Session. (9 June 1992). Retrieved January 20, 2010, from http://www.leg.bc.ca/hansard/35th1st/h0609pm.htm#2394

British Columbia Legislative Assembly. (1997). *Legislative debates* (Hansard). 36th Parl., 2nd Session. (23 April 1997, afternoon, 4-4: 7146). Retrieved January 20, 2010, from http://www.leg.bc.ca/hansard/36th3rd/h0423pm.htm

British Columbia Legislative Assembly. (1999). *Legislative debates* (Hansard) 36th Parl., 3rd Session. (16 June 1999, afternoon, 16-4: 13765 - 13771).

Casinos. Retrieved February 2, 2010, from http://www.leg.bc.ca/hansard/
36th3rd/h0616p9.htm

British Columbia Lottery Corporation. (2001). *BCLC Annual Report 2000/01.*
Retrieved April 3, 2010, from http://www.bclc.com/documents/annual
reports/BCLCAnnualReport0001.pdf

Broadway, R., & Watts, R.L. (2004). Fiscal federalism in Canada, the USA, and
Germany. *Working Paper 2004 (6) Prepared for the Consortium for Economic
Policy Research and Advice (CEPRA).* Retrieved February 9, 2010, from http://
www.queensu.ca/iigr/working/watts/wattsboadway.pdf

Broomhill, R. (2001). Neoliberal globalism and the local state: A regulation
approach. *Journal of Australian Political Economy, 48,* 115–40.

Brown, D.J., Kaldenburg, D.O., & Browne, B. (1992). Socio-economic status
and playing the lotteries. *Sociology and Social Research, 76*(3), 161–7.

Brown, D.O, Roseman, M.G., & Ham, S. (2003). Perceptions of a Bible Belt
State's proposed casino gaming legislation by religious affiliation: The case
of Kentucky residents. *UNLV Gaming Review and Research Journal, 7*(1), 49–58.

Buchler, H.A., Jr., Buchler, C.A., Credo, W.C. III, & Raymond, R.L. (1999)
Louisiana. In A.N. Cabot, W.N. Thompson, A. Tottenham, & C.G. Braunlich
(Eds.), *International casino law* (pp. 42–63). Las Vegas: Trace Publications.

Cabot, A.N., & Thompson, W.N. (1996). Gambling and public policy. *Casino
gaming: Policy, economics, and regulation* (pp. 18–70). Las Vegas: Institute for
the Study of Gambling and Commercial Gaming.

Cabot, A.N., Thompson, W.N., Tottenham, A., & Braunlich, C.G. (Eds.) (1999).
International casino law. Las Vegas: Institute for the Study of Gambling and
Commercial Gaming.

Caldwell, G.T. (1972). *Leisure co-operatives: The institutionalization of gambling
and the growth of large leisure organizations in New South Wales.* Unpublished
PhD Thesis, Australian National University.

Campbell, C.S. (1991). Gambling in Canada. In M. Jackson, & C. Griffiths
(Eds.), *Perspectives on crime and criminality* (pp. 153–165). Toronto: Harcourt
Press Jovanovich.

Campbell, C.S. (1994). *Canadian gambling legislation: The social origins of legalization.* Unpublished PhD Thesis, Simon Fraser University.

Campbell, C.S. (2000). *Non-profits and gambling expansion: The British Columbia
experience* (Gambling in Canada Research Report No. 9, Canada West
Foundation). Retrieved April 3, 2010, from http://dspace.ucalgary.ca/bit-
stream/1880/315/2/Non_Profits_and_Gambling_Expansion.pdf

Campbell, C.S., Hartnagel, T.F., & Smith, G.J. (2005). The legalization of gambling in Canada. *Law Commission of Canada.* Retrieved February 21, 2010,
from Dalhousie University e-Library http://site.ebrary.com.ezproxy.library.
dal.ca/lib/dal/docDetail.action?docID=10145851

Campbell, C.S., & Ponting, J.R. (1984). The evolution of casino gambling in Alberta. *Canadian Public Policy*. Retrieved February 14, 2010, from http://www.jstor.org/stable/3550938

Campbell, C.S., & Smith, G.S. (2003). Gambling in Canada – from vice to disease to responsibility: A negotiated history. *Canadian Bulletin of Medical History*, 20(1), 121–49.

Canada Council. (1981). *Lotteries and the arts: The Canadian experience 1970 to 1980*. Ottawa: Canada Council Research and Evaluation.

Canada in the Making. (n.d.). *Aboriginals treaties and relations*. Retrieved February 2, 2010, from http://www.canadiana.org/citm/themes/aboriginals_e.html

Canada Newswire. (2005, December 8). *Florida legislature passes slot machine legislation for Broward County pari-mutuel facilities*. Retrieved February 1, 2010, from http://phx.corporate-ir.net/phoenix.zhtml?c=98631&p=irol-newsArticle&ID=794371&highlight=

Canadian Gaming Association. (2006). *VLT gaming in Canada*. Retrieved December 12, 2009, from http://www.canadiangaming.ca/media_uploads/pdf/98.pdf

Canadian Partnership for Responsible Gambling. (2005). *Canadian Gambling Digest 2004–2005*. Retrieved January 30, 2010, from http://www.cprg.ca/articles/canadian_gambling_digest_2004_2005.pdf

Canadian Partnership for Responsible Gambling. (2007). *Organization and Management of Gambling in Canada*. Retrieved April 3, 2010, from http://www.cprg.ca/articles/Organization_Booklet_2007.pdf

Canadian Partnership for Responsible Gambling. (2009). *Canadian Gambling Digest*. Retrieved January 15, 2010, from http://www.cprg.ca/articles/Canadian_Gambling_Digest_2007_2008.pdf

Canadian Press Newswire. (1995, March 1). *Government accused of taking police report out of context (to show Coordinated Law Enforcement Unit supports video lottery terminals)*. Retrieved January 21, 2010, from ABI/INFORM Global database. Document ID: 440974061

Canadian Press Newswire. (1995, October 2). *Newfoundland must reconsider casinos: Industry minister*. Retrieved January 21, 2010, from ABI/INFORM Global database. Document ID: 419282231

Canadian Press Newswire. (2002, May 6). *Judge approves trial against Loto-Quebec over ill-effects of VLT gambling*. Retrieved January 20, 2010, from ABI/INFORM Global database. Document ID: 348292001

Canfield, C. (2006, November 6). Hollywood slots marks its first year. *Morning Sentinel*. Retrieved February 14, 2009, from http://morningsentinel.mainetoday.com/news/local/3297906.html

Caplow, T., Hicks, L., & Wattenburg, B.J. (2001). *The first measured century: An illustrated guide to trends in American 1900–2000*. Washington: AEI PRESS.

Castles, F.G. (2003). The future of the welfare state: Crisis myths and crisis realities. In R. Breton & J.G. Reitz (Eds.), *Globalization and society: Processes of differentiation examined* (pp. 283–98). Westport: Greenwood Press.

Catechism of the Catholic Church. (n.d.). *Part three: Life in Christ, Section Two: The Ten Commandments: Chapter Two: 'You Shall Love Your Neighbour as Yourself,' Article 7: The Seventh Commandment, Number II: Respect for Persons and their Goods – Respect for the Goods of Others: Article 2413 Games of Chance*. Retrieved December 17, 2009, from http://www.vatican.va/archive/ccc_css/archive/catechism/p3s2c2a7.htm

CBC News Online. (2001, May 31). Quebec withdrawing 1,000 video lottery terminals. Retrieved January 10, 2010, from http://www.cbc.ca/storyview/CBC/2001/05/30/quebec_vlt010530

CBC News Online. (2007, November 8). N.B. wagers on establishing a casino. Retrieved January 31, 2010, from http://www.cbc.ca/canada/new-brunswick/story/2007/11/08/gambling-policy.html

CBC News Online. (2009, October 5). Sex-trade workers to fight Canada's prostitution laws. Retrieved March 15, 2010, from http://www.cbc.ca/canada/toronto/story/2009/10/05/prostitution-law005.html

Center for Policy Analysis, University of Massachusetts. (2007). *Taking the gamble VI: What's happening in Maine? Polling & Program Evaluation Research Series No. 56*. Retrieved December 15, 2010, from http://www.umassd.edu/cfpa/docs/taking_the_gamble_6.pdf

Central Intelligence Agency. (n.d.). *The world factbook*. Retrieved May 6, 2010, from https://www.cia.gov/library/publications/the-world-factbook/index.html

Chafetz, H. (1960). *Play the devil: A history of gambling in the United States from 1492 to 1955*. New York: Clarkson N. Potter.

Charles Darwin School for Social and Policy Research. (2006). *An overview of gambling in the Northern Territory: Integrated summary and future directions of the Charles Darwin University Gambling Research Program 2005–06*. Retrieved January 10, 2010, from http://www.cdu.edu.au/sspr/documents/Gamblingoverview.pdf

Christiansen, E.M. (2005). The impacts of gaming taxation in the United States. *AGA Research 10th Anniversary Research Series*. Retrieved November 22, 2009, from http://www.americangaming.org/assets/files/studies/The_Impacts_of_Gaming_Taxation.pdf

Christiansen Capital Advisors (2003). *2003 gross gambling revenues by industry and change from 2002*. Retrieved November 15, 2009, from http://grossannual

wager.com/Primary%20Navigation/Online%20Data%20Store/Free%20
Research/2003%20Revenue%20by%20Industry.pdf

Clotfelter, C.T., & Cook, P.J. (1987). Implicit taxation in lottery finance. *National Tax Journal, 40*(4). 533–46. Retrieved December 21, 2010, from ABI/INFORM Global database. Document ID: 618325261.

Club Association of West Virginia, Inc. v. Wise, 156 F. Supp 2d 599 (S.D.W.Va. 2001). Retrieved January 29, 2010, from http://caselaw.lp.findlaw.com/scripts/printer_friendly.pl?page=4th/012154p.html

Cogar, S.W. (2001). 2001 West Virginia legislative update: Laws passed that affect law enforcement. *Report from the West Virginia Police.* Retrieved January 29, 2010, from http://www.wvstatepolice.com/legal/2001_update.htm

Comaroff, J., & Comaroff, J. (2000). Millennial capitalism: First thoughts on a second coming. *Public Culture, 12*(2), 291–343.

Commission fédéral des maisons de jeu. (2003). *Rapport Annuel.* Retrieved January 29, 2010, from http://www.esbk.admin.ch/etc/medialib/data/esbk/geschaeftsberichte.Par.0012.File.tmp/jahresbericht_2003-f.pdf

Commonwealth of Pennsylvania. (n.d.). Governor Rendell again says time is now for Pennsylvania Legislature to adopt school property tax relief for homeowners. Retrieved February 18, 2008, from http://www.portal.state.pa.us/portal/server.pt/gateway/ptargs_0_2_667806_0_0_18/governor%20rendell%20again%20says%20time%20is%20now%20for%20pennsylvania%20legislature%20to%20adopt%20school%20property%20tax%20relief%20for%20homeowners.pdf

Congleton, R.D., Kyriacou, A., & Bacaria, J. (2003). A theory of menu federalism: Decentralization by political agreement. *Constitutional Political Economy, 14*(3), 167–90. Retrieved February 5, 2010, from ABI/INFORM Global database. Document ID: 424426851

Cosgrave, J.F. (2009). Governing the gambling citizen: The state, consumption, and risk. In J.F. Cosgrave, & T.R. Klassen (Eds.), *Casino state: Legalized gambling in Canada* (pp. 46–66). Toronto: University of Toronto Press.

Cosgrave, J.F., & Klassen, T.R. (2001). Gambling against the state: The state and the legitimation of gambling. *Current Sociology, 49*(5), 1–15.

Costello, T., & Millar, R. (2000). *Wanna bet?Winners and losers in gambling's luck myth.* St. Leonard's: Allen and Unwin.

Council for Aboriginal Reconciliation. (n.d.). *Documents of reconciliation: Terra nullius and sovereignty.* Retrieved February 4, 2010, from http://www.austlii.edu.au/au/orgs/car/docrec/policy/brief/terran.htm

Criminal Intelligence Service Association. (n.d.). *Annual Report 2004 Traditional (Italian based) organized crime (TOC).* Retrieved February 15, 2010, from http://www.cisc.gc.ca/annual_reports/annual_report_2004/traditional_2004_e.html

Dalton et al. v. Pataki. (2005). *Joseph Dalton et al. v. George Pataki, as Governor of the State of New York et al.* Retrieved January 30, 2010, from http://www.law.cornell.edu/nyctap/I05_0062.htm

Delaware State Lottery Office Video Lottery Regulations. (2005). *Definitions.* Retrieved January 12, 2010, from http://lottery.state.de.us/pdf/Video_Lottery_Regulations.pdf

Dixon, D. (1996). Illegal betting in Britain and Australia: Contrast in control strategies and cultures. In J. McMillen (Ed.), *Gambling cultures: Studies in history and interpretation* (pp. 86–100). New York: Routledge.

Dollery, B. (2002). A century of vertical fiscal imbalance in Australia Federalism. *History of Economics,* Summer, 26–43. Retrieved April 20, 2010, from http://www.hetsa.org.au/pdf/36-A-03.pdf

Dombrink, J. (1988). The touchables: Vice and police corruption in the 1980's. *Law and Contemporary Problems, 51*(1 Winter), 201–32.

Dombrink, J., & Thompson, W.N. (1990). *The last resort: Success and failure in campaigns for casinos.* Reno: University of Nevada Press.

Donnis, I. (2003, September 19–25). Gone to the dogs: The Lincoln Park case marks another embarrassment for former speaker Harwood. *The Providence Phoenix Online.* Retrieved February 4, 2010, from http: www.providence phoenix.com/features/top/documents/03167407.asp

Doughney, J. (2002). Socioeconomic banditry: Poker machines and income redistribution in Victoria. In T. Eardley, & B. Bradbury (Eds.). *Competing visions: Refereed proceedings of the National Social Policy Conference 2001, SPRC Report 1/02,* 136–54. Social Policy Research Centre, University of New South Wales.

Doughney, J. (2005). *An unconscionable business. The ugly reality of electronic gambling: A selection of critical essays on gambling research, ethics and economics.* Australasian Gaming Council. Retrieved January 21, 2010, from http://www.austgamingcouncil.org.au/images/pdf/eLibrary/2894.pdf

Driver, R. (1999, April 30). To expand gambling, just ignore the voters. *Providence Journal.* Retrieved January 15, 2010, from http://www.roddriver.com/gambling_990430.html

Drzazga, J. (1952). Gambling and the law – slot machines. *Journal of Criminal Law, Criminology and Police Science, 43*(1), 114–23.

Drzazga, J. (1963). *Wheels of fortune.* Springfield: Charles C. Thomas.

Dupré, R. (2004). *The prohibition of alcohol revisited: The US case in international perspective.* Paper presented at 2004 International Society for New Institutional Economics Conference, Tucson, Arizona, 30 September–3 October 2004. Retrieved February 10, 2010, from http://www.isnie.org/ISNIE04/Papers/dupre.pdf

Eadington, W.R. (1996). Ethics and policy considerations in the spread of commercial gambling. In J. McMillen (Ed.). *Gambling cultures: Studies in history and interpretation* (pp. 243–62). New York: Routledge.

Eadington, W.R. (1998). Contributions of casino-style gambling to local economies. *The Annals of the American Academy of Political and Social Science, 556,* 53–65.

Eadington, W.R. (1999). The economics of casino gambling. *Journal of Economic Perspectives, 13*(3), 173–92.

Economopoulos, A. (2006). Opposing the lottery in the United States: Forces behind individual attitudes towards Legislation in 1975. *International Gambling Studies, 6*(2), 267–91.

Edwards, B., & McCarthy, J.D. (2004). Resources and social movement mobilization. In D.A. Snow, S.A. Soule, & H. Kriesi (Eds.). *The Blackwell Companion to Social Movements* (pp. 116–52). Oxford: Blackwell.

Ellison, C.G., & Nybroten, K.A. (1999). Conservative Protestantism and opposition to state-sponsored lotteries: Evidence from the 1997 Texas poll. *Social Science Quarterly, 80*(2), 356–69.

Engler, L.A. (2004). Slot machines one-armed bandits or just plain fun? *Antiques and Collecting Magazine, 109*(7), 27–33.

Erekson, O.H., Platt, G., Whistler, C., & Ziegert, A.L. (1999). Factors influencing the adoption of state lotteries. *Applied Economics, 31,* 875–84.

Esping–Andersen, G. (1990). *The three worlds of welfare capitalism.* Princeton: Princeton University Press.

Esping–Andersen, G. (1999). *Social foundations of postindustrial economies.* New York: Oxford University Press.

Fairbanks, D. (1977). Religious forces and 'morality' policies in the American States. *The Western Political Quarterly, 30*(3), 411–417.

Falkiner, T., & Horbay, R. (2006). Unbalanced reel gaming machines. Retrieved January 18, 2010, from http://www.casinofreepa.org/images/documents/falkiner_horbay_09_09_06.pdf

Feather, N.T. (1998). Attitudes toward high achievers, self-esteem, and value priorities for Australian, American, and Canadian Students. *Journal of Cross-Cultural Psychology, 29*(6), 749–59. Retrieved February 12, 2010, from Sage ONLINE doi: 10.1177/0022022198296005

Fey, M. (1983). *Slot machines: An illustrated history of America's most popular coin-operated gaming device.* Las Vegas: Stanley Paher – Nevada Publications.

Findlay, J.M. (1986). *People of chance: Gambling in American society from Jamestown to Las Vegas.* Oxford: Oxford University Press.

Firestone, D. (1999, October 15). South Carolina High Court derails video poker games. *New York Times.* Retrieved January 22, 2010, from http://www.nytimes.com/1999/10/15/us/south-carolina-high-court-derails-video-poker-games.html

Fiske, J., Hodge, B., & Turner, G. (1988). *Myths of Oz: Reading Australian popular culture.* Boston: Allen and Unwin.

Florida Committee on Regulated Industries. (2004). *Legalized gambling in Florida – the competition in the marketplace: Report Number 2005 – 155.* Prepared for the Florida Senate. Retrieved January 16, 2010, from http://www.flsenate.gov/data/Publications/2005/Senate/reports/interim_reports/pdf/2005-155rilong.pdf

Ford, H.M. (1936). Slot machine legislation in the Prairie Provinces. *Alberta Law Quarterly, 1*(8) (1934–1936), 311–319. Retrieved January 29, 2007, from http://heinonline.org.

Francis, P.E., & Keilin, E.J. (2004). *Gambling revenues: A working paper prepared as support for 'Can New York Get an A in School Finance Reform?'* A Report by the Citizens Budget Commission. Retrieved January 29, 2010, from http://www.cbcny.org/CBC_WorkingPaper-Gambling_11-04.pdf

French, P.E., & Stanley, R.E. (n.d.) *Enrollment levels in institutions of higher education: Are state lotteries making a difference in the American States.* Retrieved January 22, 2010, from http://www.angelfire.com/tn3/rstanley/Statelotteries.PDF

Frey, J.H. (1998). Federal involvement in U.S. Gaming Regulation. *Annals of the American Academy of Political and Social Sciences, 556,* 138–51.

Frontier Centre for Public Policy. (2002). The west's biggest provincial government: Manitoba. Retrieved February 21, 2010, from http://www.fcpp.org/pdf/FC009.pdf

Furlong, E.J. (1998). A logistic regression model explaining recent state casino gaming adoptions. *Policy Studies Journal, 26*(3), 371–83.

Gambling Research Information and Education. (2003). *The Mob in casinos.* Retrieved April 5, 2010, from http://www.casinowatch.org/crime/mob.html

Gaming Law Review. (2005a). *In re advisory to opinion to the House of Representatives (Casino II), 9*(5), 552–66. Retrieved December 14, 2010, from Mary Anne Liebert, Inc. doi:10.1089/glr.2005.9.552

Gaming Law Review. (2005b). *Supreme Court of Nova Scotia Walsh v. Atlantic Lottery Corporation, Appendix C, 9*(2), 131–3. Retrieved December 14, 2010, from Mary Ann Liebert, Inc. doi: 10.1089/glr.2005.9.131

Garrett, T.A., & Wagner, G.A. (2004). State Government finances: World War II to the current crises, *Review,* Federal Reserve Bank of St. Louis, *86*(2), March/April, 9–26.

Gephart, R.P., Jr., (2001). Safe risk in Las Vegas. *M@n@gement, 4*(3), 141–58.

Gilliland, J.A., & Ross, N.A. (2005). Opportunities for video lottery terminal gambling in Montréal. *Canadian Journal of Public Health, 55* (January–February), 55–9.

Goddard, L. (2000). S.C. video poker ban energizes gaming friends, foe. *Stateline.org: State Policy and Politics.* Retrieved, February 19, 2010, from http://www.stateline.org/live/ViewPage.action?siteNodeId=136&languageId =1&contentId=14114

Government of Saskatchewan. (1995, January 27). *Government addresses VLT concerns.* Retrieved January 11, 2010, from http://www.gov.sk.ca/news? newsId=98ca1336-fa2d-43e9-991d-b1ed9bb997a9

Government of Saskatchewan. (2002, March 22). *Hospitality industry receives more VLTs.* Retrieved January 11, 2010, from http://www.gov.sk.ca/news? newsId=41bbff87-8053-450c-8875-0d8cb056fdae

Government of Saskatchewan. (2007, March 16). *Government releases gaming report.* Retrieved January 11, 2010, from http://www.gov.sk.ca/news?news Id=0c29fd76-8de5-47ee-8f8a-98efcfa25f78

Greenbrier County Coalition against Gambling Expansion, et al., Petitioners. (2003). Retrieved December 29, 2009, from http://www.state.wv.us/wvsca/ docs/fall03/31540.pdf

Griffiths, M., & Wood, R.T.A. (n.d.). Lottery gambling and addiction: An overview of European research. Retrieved January 18, 2010, from https://www. european-lotteries.org/data/info_130/Wood.pdf

Gromer, D.E., & Cabot, A.N. (1993). *South Dakota.* In A.N. Cabot, et al. (Eds.). *International Casino Law,* 2nd Edition (134–50). Las Vegas: Institute for the Study of Gambling and Commercial Gaming.

Gross, M. (1998). Legal gambling as a strategy for economic development. *Economic Development Quarterly, 12*(3). 203–13.

Habermas, J. (1975). *Legitimation crisis.* Translated by Thomas McCarthy. Boston: Beacon Press.

Habermas, J., & Derrida, J. (2003). February 15, or What binds Europeans together: A plea for a common foreign policy, beginning in a core of Europe. *Constellations, 10*(3), 291–7.

Haig, B. (1985). Legal gambling since 1920/21 in G. Caldwell, B. Haig, M. Dickerson, & L. Sylvan (Eds.). *Gambling in Australia.* (pp. 28–44). Sydney: Croom Helm.

Hallifax, J. (2004, November 5). South Florida OKs slot machines proposal. *Associated Press.* Retrieved January 10, 2009, from http://newsmine.org/ content.php?ol=cabal-elite/election-fraud/electronic/2004-general/south-florida-oks-slot-machines.txt

Ham, S., Brown, D.O., & Jang, S. (2004). Proponents or opponents of casino gaming: A qualitative choice model approach. *Journal of Hospitality & Tourism Research, 28*(4), 391–407. Retrieved April 5, 2010, from International Council on Hotel, Restaurant and Institutional Education. doi: 10.1177/1096348004270105

Hansen, A. (2004). Lotteries and State Fiscal Policy. *Background Paper.* Washington D.C. Tax Foundation. Retrieved January 26, 2010, from http://www.taxfoundation.org/files/0817c13300e7a380682288694149aebd.pdf

Hansen, M., & Rossow, I. (2010). Limited cash flow on slot machines: Effects of prohibition of note acceptors on adolescent gambling behaviour. *International Journal of Mental Health and Addiction,* 8: 70–81 Retrieved March 30, 2010, from 10.1007/s11469-009-9196-2

Harchaoui, T.M., & Tarkhani, F. (2004). Shifts in consumer spending. *Statistics Canada Perspectives on Labour and Income, Statistics Canada Catalogue. No. 75-001-XIE Ottawa,* 5(6), 17–21. Retrieved June 15, 2006, from http://www.statcan.ca/english/freepub/75-001-XIE/10604/art-2.pdf

Harvey, D. (2000). *Spaces of hope.* Berkeley: University of California Press.

Hattori, A. (1994, September 6) Ruling drives S.D. Governor to rescind budget cuts. *Bond Buyer, 308* (29479), 5.

Helleiner, E. (1994). *Reemergence of global finance: From Bretton Woods to the 1990s.* Ithaca: Cornell University Press.

Hing, N. (2000). *Changing fortunes: Past, present and future perspectives on the management of problem gambling by New South Wales registered clubs.* Unpublished doctoral dissertation, University of Western Sydney – Macarthur.

Hing, N. (2006). A history of machine gambling in the NSW club industry: From community benefit to commercialization. *International Journal of Hospitality & Tourism Administration,* 7(2–3), 83–107.

Hing, N., & Breen, H. (2002). A profile of gaming machine players in clubs in Sydney, Australia. *Southern Cross University School of Tourism and Hospitality Management Papers.* Retrieved March 17, 2010, from http://epubs.scu.edu.au/cgi/viewcontent.cgi?article=1021&context=tourism_pubs

HLT Advisory. (2006). *VLT gaming in Canada.* Report prepared for Canadian Gaming Association. Retrieved February 15, 2010, from http://www.canadiangaming.ca/media_uploads/pdf/8.pdf

Hood, C., Rothstein, H., Baldwin, R., Rees, J., & Spackman, M. (1999). Where risk society meets the regulatory state: Exploring variations in risk regulation regimes. *Risk Management: An International Journal,* 1(1), 21–34.

Horne, C. (2009). A social norms approach to legitimacy. *American Behavioral Scientist,* 53(3), 400–15. Retrieved January 18, 2010, from doi: 10.1177/0002764209338799

Huebusch, K. (1997). Taking chances on casinos. *American Demographics,* 19(5), 34–40.

Hunt, J.D. (1925). Review of Legislation, 1923. II. North America. I. Dominion of Canada. 2. Alberta. Slot-machine Tax. *Journal of Comparative Legislation and International Law, Third Series, VII,* 36–7. Retrieved May 31, 2007, from http://heinonline.org

Hyson, S. (2002). *Was this the way to conduct a referendum? New Brunswick's gamble on VLTs (Video Lottery Terminals)*. Retrieved June 14, 2007, from ABI/ INFORM Global database. Document ID: 357980611

Indiana Historical Bureau. (1995). *Indiana close up essay – Gambling: Lottery and riverboats*. Retrieved January 22, 2010, from http://www.in.gov/history/files/ lotterygambling.pdf

Inglehart, R., & Baker, W.E. (2000). Modernization, cultural change, and the persistence of traditional values. *American Sociological Review, 65*(1), 19–51. Retrieved February 15, 2010, from JSTOR. doi: 10.2307/ 2657288

Iowa Law Journal. (1949). *Statutory trends toward legalization of gambling – notes and legislation*. Retrieved August 12, 2007, from http://heinonline. org.

Jackson, P., & Penrose, P. (Eds.) (1994). *Constructions of race, place and nation*. Minneapolis: University of Minneapolis Press.

Jameson, F. (1984). Postmodernism, or the cultural logic of late capitalism. *New Left Review, 146*, 53–92.

Janis, S. (2004, January 12). Little Vegas: What can Maryland's troubled history with slot machines tell us about the odds for the future. *Baltimore City Paper*. Retrieved December 21, 2009, from http://www.citypaper.com/news/ story.asp?id=9408

Jelen, T.G., & Wilcox, C. (1990). Denominational preference and the dimensions of political tolerance. *Sociological Analysis, 51*(1), 69–81.

Jenkins J.C. (1983). Resource Mobilization Theory and the Study of Social Movements. *Annual Review of Sociology, 9*, 527–53.

Jensen, J.L. (2003). Policy diffusion through institutional legitimation: State lotteries. *Journal of Public Administration Research and Theory, 13*(4), 521–41.

Kallick-Kaufman, M. (1979). The micro and macro dimensions of gambling in the United States. *Journal of Social Issues, 35*, 7–26.

Kane, D., & Curliss, J.A. (2006, May 18; Modified May 20). Black hands over new lottery data. *The News & Observer.com*. Retrieved February 10 2010, from http://www.newsobserver.com/news/crime_safety/story/35096. html?storylink=mirelated

Kappler, C.J. (1904). *Treaty with the Delawares September 1778; 7 Statute 13*. Retrieved January 31, 2010, from http://digital.library.okstate.edu/kappler/ Vol2/treaties/del0003.htm#mn3

Kelly, J., Marfels, C., & Nevries, H. (1999). Germany. In A.N. Cabot, et al. (Eds.). *International Casino Law* (pp. 371–80). Las Vegas, Nevada: Institute for the Study of Gambling and Commercial Gaming.

Koutantou, A (2011, January 26). *FACTBOX-Key facts on Greek gaming market*. Retrieved February 8, 2011, from http://www.lse.co.uk/FinanceNews. asp?ArticleCode=hmam0c9vgmymc13&ArticleHeadline=FACTBOX Key_facts_on_Greek_gaming_market

King, R. (1964). The rise and decline of coin-machine gambling. *The Journal of Criminal Law, Criminology and Police Science, 55*(2), 199–207.

King, R. (1969). *Gambling and Organized Crime*. Washington: Public Affairs Press.

Kingma, S. (1996). A sign of the times: The political culture of gaming in the Netherlands. In J. McMillen (Ed.), *Gambling Cultures: Studies in history and interpretation* (pp. 199–222). New York: Routledge.

Kingma, S. (2004). Gambling and the risk society: The liberalisation and legitimation crisis of gambling in the Netherlands. *International Journal of Gambling Studies, 4*(1), 47–67.

Kitchen, H., & Powells, S. (1991). Lottery expenditures in Canada: A regional analysis of determinants and incidence. *Applied Economics, 23*(12), 1845–52.

Kitts, J.A. (2006). Collective action, rival incentives, and the emergence of antisocial norms. *American Sociological Review, 71*(2), 235–59.

Klassen, T.R., & Cosgrave, J.F. (2009). Legitimation and expansion in Ontario. In J.F. Cosgrave, & T.R. Klassen (Eds.). *Casino state: Legalized gambling in Canada*. (pp. 122–39). Toronto: University of Toronto Press.

Kleindienst, L. (2005, March 25). Bid to limit slot machines to bingo-style gambling stumbles in Legislature. *Sun-Sentinel.com*. Retrieved February 2, 2010, from http://www.sun-sentinel.com/news/local/southflorida/sfl-fslots25m ar25,0,4256759.story

Kohn, M.L. (1987). Cross-national research as an analytic strategy: American Sociological Association, 1987 Presidential Address. *American Sociological Review, 52*(6), 713–31.

Kosmin, B.A., Mayer, E., & Keysar, A. (2001). *American religious identification survey 2001*. Retrieved January 28, 2006, from http://www.gc.cuny.edu/ faculty/research_studies/aris.pdf

KPMG. (2002). *Casino market assessment Moncton, New Brunswick, final report*. Prepared for City of Moncton. Retrieved April 3, 2010, from http:// www.moncton.ca/Assets/Government+English/Publications+English/ Casino+Market+Assessment.pdf

Ladouceur, R., & Sévigny, S. (2006). The impact of video lottery game speed on gamblers. *Electronic Journal of Gambling Issues, 17*(August). Retrieved January 28, 2010, from http://www.camh.net/egambling/issue17/ladouceur. html

Lasch, C. (1979). *The culture of narcissism*. New York: W.W. Norton.

Lash, S., & Urry, J. (1994). *Economies of signs & space.* London: Sage.

Lee, C., & Back, K. (2003). Pre- and post-casino impact of residents' perception. *Annals of Tourism Research, 30*(4), 868–85.

Leitner, S. (2003). Varieties of familialism: The caring functions of the family in comparative perspective. *European Societies, 5*(4), 353–75. Retrieved March 30, 2010, from doi: 10.1080/1461669032000127642

Lieberson, S. (1991). Small N's and big conclusions: An examination of the reasoning in comparative studies based on a small number of cases. *Social Forces, 70*(2), 307–20.

Light, S.A., & Rand, K.R. (2005). *Indian gaming and tribal sovereignty: The casino compromise.* Lawrence: University Press of Kansas.

Lindberg, K., Petrenko, J., Gladden, J., & Johnson, W.A. (1998). Traditional organized crime in Chicago. *International Review of Law, Computers & Technology, 12* (1), 47–73.

Lipset, S.M. (1963). The value patterns of Democracy: A case study in comparative analysis. *American Sociological Review, 28*(4), 515–31.

Livingstone, C. (2005). Desire and the consumption of danger: Electronic gaming machines and the commodification of interiority. *Addiction Research & Theory, 13*(6), 523–34. Retrieved January 17, 2005, from Informa Healthcare doi: 10.1080/16066350500338161

Loto-Québec. (n.d.). Creation of a legitimate, state-managed network. Retrieved January 22, 2010, from http://lotoquebec.com/loteriesvideo/en/about-us/our-beginnings

Loto-Québec. (2004). *Loto-Québec 2004–2007 development plan: Assuring a balance between business mission and social responsibility.* Retrieved January 17, 2010, from http://lotoquebec.com/corporatif/pdf/plan_de_developpement_en.pdf

Lotteries Commission of New Brunswick. (n.d.). Retrieved April 3, 2010, from http://www.gnb.ca/0162/gaming/gaming_policy-e.pdf

Lottery Post. (2005, January 27). Oregon Lottery adds slot games to video poker machines. Retrieved January 12, 2010, from http://www.lotterypost.com/news/106466

Louisiana. (n.d.). *Louisiana State Constitution of 1974.* Retrieved January 16, 2010, from http://senate.legis.state.la.us/Documents/Constitution/constitution.pdf

Louisiana State and Local Government. (n.d.). *Chapter 2– State Government functions, Part J – Gaming.* Retrieved January 30, 2010, from http://house.louisiana.gov/slg/PDF/Chapter%202%20Part%20J%20-%20Gaming.pdf

Louisiana State Legislature. (n.d.). *Louisiana Gaming Control Law RS27:2.* Retrieved February 6, 2011, from http://www.legis.state.la.us/lss/lss.asp?doc=84898

Maddison, S. (2008). Indigenous autonomy matters: What's wrong with the Australian government's 'intervention' in Aboriginal communities? *Australian journal of human rights, 14*(1), 41–61.

Maine Secretary of State. (n.d.). *Referendum election tabulations November 4, 2003 statewide totals and county summaries.* Retrieved January 10, 2010, from http://www.maine.gov/sos/cec/elec/2003n/gen03sum.htm & http://www.maine.gov/sos/cec/elec/2003n/intco03n.htm

Maine Secretary of State. (2007, April 26). *Secretary of State Matthew Dunlap announces Washington County racino referendum.* Retrieved January 10, 2010, from http://www.maine.gov/tools/whatsnew/index.php?topic=Portal+News&id=36941&v=Article-2006

Manitoba. (1991). *The Manitoba Lotteries Corporation Act (C.C.S.M. c. L210) Video Lottery Regulation 245/91.* Retrieved January 20, 2010, from http://web2.gov.mb.ca/laws/regs/pdf/l210-245.91.pdf

Manitoba. (1993). *Legislative Debates* (Hansard), 35th Parl., 4th Sess. (April 26, 1993). Retrieved January 10, 2010, from http://www.gov.mb.ca/legislature/hansard/4th-35th/vol_49a.html

Manitoba. (1999). *C.C.S.M. c. G7 The Gaming Control Local Option (VLT) Act.* Retrieved January 11, 2010, from Government of Manitoba, Laws of Manitoba. http://web2.gov.mb.ca/laws/statutes/ccsm/g007e.php

Manitoba Gaming Control Commission. (n.d.). History of gambling in Manitoba: 1969 to the present. Retrieved January 18, 2010, from http://www.mgcc.mb.ca/gaming_in_mb_history.html#85

Manitoba Gaming Control Commission. (1998). *Municipal VLT plebiscite review, July 1998.* Retrieved January 18, 2010, from http://www.mgcc.mb.ca/forms/municipal_vlt_plebiscite_review.pdf

Manitoba Intercultural Council. (1985). *Lotteries committee report on the Manitoba intercultural council and the Provincial gaming system,* March 16, 1985.

Manitoba Lottery Policy Review. (1995). *Working group report (Desjardin Report).* Retrieved January 11, 2010, from http://www.mgcc.mb.ca/forms/desjardins_report.pdf

Manley, P., Wysong, J.W., & Favero, P.G. (n.d.). United States, Regional, and Maryland employment growth, *University of Maryland Cooperative Extension Fact Sheet No. 403.* Retrieved January 31, 2010, from http://extension.umd.edu/publications/PDFs/FS403.pdf

Mann, M. (2004). *Fascists.* Cambridge: Cambridge University Press.

Marenko, J. (2008). The Indian Act: Historical Overview. *Judicial System & Legal Issues.* Retrieved January 31, 2010, from http://www.mapleleafweb.com/features/judicial-system-legal-issues

Marin, A. (March, 2007). Investigation into the Ontario Lottery and Gaming Corporation's protection of the public from fraud and theft: 'A Game of Trust.' *Ontario Ombudsman Report*. Retrieved February 16, 2010, from http://www.ombudsman.on.ca/media/3268/a_game_of_trust_20070326.pdf

Markovich, D. (2003). Genocide, a crime of which no Anglo-Saxon nation could be guilty. *Murdoch University Electronic Journal of Law, 10*(3). Retrieved January 29, 2010, from http://www.austlii.edu.au/cgi-bin/sinodisp/au/journals/MurUEJL/2003/27.html?query=^aborigine#Conclusion_T

Marshall, D. (2005). The gambling environment and gambler behaviour: Evidence from Richmond-Tweed, Australia. *International Journal of Gambling Studies, 5*(1), 63–83.

Martin, P. (2003). Slots on the streets question Norway's 'no casino' stance. *Coinslot European News*. Retrieved February 24, 2008, from www.ateonline.co.uk/library/CR10_p10_EuroNews.pdf

Maryland Budget and Tax Policy Institute. (2008). *The regular person's guide to the Maryland slot machine referendum*. Retrieved March 21, 2010, from http://www.marylandpolicy.org/documents/TheRegularPersonsGuidetoSlots908Final.pdf

Maryland Department of Legislative Services. (2004). *Legislators' guide to video lottery terminal gambling*. Prepared by the Office of Policy Analysis. Retrieved February 5, 2010, from http://mlis.state.md.us/other/Fiscal_Briefings_and_Reports/00_Leg%20Guide%20to%20VLT%20Gambling.pdf

Maryland Department of Legislative Services. (2007). *Senate Bill 98, fiscal and policy note, gaming - slot machines - ownership and operation by eligible nonprofit organizations*. Retrieved February 5, 2010, from http://mlis.state.md.us/2007rs/bills/sb/sb0098f.pdf

Maryland State Board of Elections. (n.d.). *Question 02 - Authorizing Video Lottery Terminals (Slot Machines) to Fund Education*. Retrieved March 21, 2010, from http://www.elections.state.md.us/elections/2008/questions/general/Statewide_Ballot_Question_Results.html

Mason, J.L., & Nelson, M. (2001) *Governing gambling*. New York: The Century Foundation Press.

Mason, W.D. (2000). *Indian gaming: Tribal sovereignty and American politics*. Norman: University of Oklahoma Press.

Maxwell, S.J., Egbarts, C.J., & Stewart, T.T. (1999). Missouri. In A.N. Cabot, W.N. Thompson, A. Tottenham, & C.G. Braunlich (Eds.). *International Casino Law* (pp. 92–7). Las Vegas: Institute for the Study of Gambling and Commercial Gaming.

McCarthy, B. (2009, 10 February). House kills lottery. *WyomingNews.Com*. Retrieved March 29, 2010, from http://www.wyomingnews.com/articles/2009/02/10/news/20local_02-10-09.txt

McCarthy, J.D., & Zald, M.N. (1977). Resource mobilization and social movements: A partial theory. *American Journal of Sociology, (82)*6, 1212–41.

McCulloch, A.M. (1994). The politics of Indian gaming: Tribe/State relations and American federalism. *Publius*, 24(3), 99–112.

McIntosh, C., & Hayward, D. (2000). The Neo-liberal revolution and the regional state in Canada and Australia. *Paper presented at the International Political Science Association Conference, Québec, Canada,* August, 2000. Retrieved December 18, 2009, from http://www.sisr.net/publications/0008mcintosh.pdf

McKenna, P. (2007). The politics of gaming in the garden province. *Journal of Canadian Studies, 41*(1), 51–73.

McKenna, P. (2008). *Terminal damage: The politics of VLTs in Atlantic Canada.* Blackpoint: Fernwood.

McMillen, J. (1988a). The future: Golden goose or Trojan horse – Symposium Summation. In C. S. Campbell, & J. Lowman (Eds.), *Gambling in Canada: Golden goose or Trojan horse? Proceedings of the First National Symposium on Lotteries and Gambling* (pp. 371–409). Burnaby: Simon Fraser University.

McMillen, J. (1988b). Gambling on casinos: A political economy of Australian developments. *Journal of Gambling Behavior, 4*(3), 152–70. Retrieved February 20, 2010, from Springerlink doi: 10.1007/BF01018329

McMillen, J. (1990). Casino policies: Have Australians had a fair deal? *Journal of Gambling Studies, 6*(1), 3–29. Retrieved February 20, 2010, from Springerlink doi: 10.1007/BF01015746

McMillen, J. (1993). *Risky business: The political economy of Australian casino development.* Unpublished PhD thesis, University of Queensland.

McMillen, J. (1996a). Understanding gambling: History, concepts and theories. In J. McMillen (Ed.), *Gambling cultures: Studies in history and interpretation* (pp. 6–42). New York: Routledge.

McMillen, J. (1996b). From glamour to grind: The globalisation of casinos. In J. McMillen (Ed.), *Gambling cultures: Studies in history and interpretation* (pp. 263–87). New York: Routledge.

McMillen, J. (1997). Social priorities in gaming policy. Case studies from two Australian states. In W. Eadington, & J. Cornelius (Eds.), *Public policy, the social sciences and gambling* (pp. 103–26). Institute for the Study of Gambling and Commercial Gaming, University of Nevada.

McMillen, J. (2009). Gambling policy and regulation in Australia. In J.F. Cosgrave, & T.R. Klassen (Eds.), *Casino state: Legalized gambling in Canada* (pp. 91–120). Toronto: University of Toronto Press.

McMillen, J., & Eadington, B. (1986). The evolution of gambling laws in Australia. *8 N.Y.L. School Journal of International Comparative Law* (1986–1987). 167–192.

McMillen, J., & Togni, S. (2000). Study of gambling in the Northern Territory 1996–97. *Report prepared for the NT Racing and Gaming Authority by the Australian Institute for Gambling Research.* Sydney: New South Wales. Retrieved February 5, 2010, from http://www.nt.gov.au/justice/licenreg/documents/reports/NTGRMcMillenReport2000.pdf

McNaught, A., & Poelking, S. (1996). *Video lottery terminals: Current issue paper 178,* Legislative Research Service – Ontario Legislative Library, Toronto, Ontario

McQueen, P. (2004, September). North America sees dramatic growth. *International gaming and wagering business, Lottery Beat.* Retrieved January 10, 2010, from http://www.igwb.com/Archives_Davinci?article=1080

Meier, G.M. (1971). The Bretton Woods agreement – twenty-five years after. *Stanford Law Review, 2,* 235–75. Retrieved December 10, 2009, from http://heinonline.org.

Metcalfe, A. (1985). The day the workers went on strike because the sun did shine. *Social Analysis, 17,* 3–16.

Miers, D. (1996). Objectives and systems in the regulation of commercial gambling. In J. McMillen (Ed.), *Gambling cultures: Studies in history and interpretation* (pp. 288–311). New York: Routledge.

Mikesell, J.L., & Zorn, C.K. (1986). State lotteries as fiscal savior or fiscal fraud: A look at the evidence. *Public Administrative Review, 46*(4), 311–20.

Mikesell, J.L., & Zorn, C.K. (1988). State lotteries for public revenue. *Public Budgeting and Finance, 8*(1), 38–47.

Miller, D.E., & Pierce, P.A. (1997) Lotteries for education: Windfall or hoax? *State and Local Government Review, 29*(1), 34–42.

Missouri Gaming Commission. (n.d.). *The history of riverboat gaming in Missouri.* Retrieved January 22, 2010, from http://www.mgc.dps.mo.gov/history_rb.htm

Montana Department of Justice. (n.d.). *History of gambling in Montana.* Retrieved February 20, 2010, from http://doj.mt.gov/gaming/historygambling.asp

Montana Department of Justice, Gambling Control Division. (2002). *Biennial report fiscal years 2001 and 2002 and report of the 2001–2002 Gaming Advisory Council December 2002.* Retrieved January 20, 2010, from http://www.doj.mt.gov/gaming/statisticsreports/biennialreport/fy01fy02.pdf

Montana Initiative and Referendum Issues. (n.d.). Retrieved February 10, 2010, from http://sos.mt.gov/Elections/forms/history/initandref2006tbl.pdf

Moody, G. (1995). The roots, significance, value and legalisation of gambling. *Journal of Gambling Studies, 11*(1), 35–59.

Mooney, C.Z. (2000). The decline of federalism and the rise of morality-policy conflict in the United States. *Publius, 30*(1–2), 171–88.

Moore, B., Jr. (1966). *Social origins of dictatorship and democracy: Lord and peasant in the making of the modern world.* Boston: Beacon Press.

Moore, B., Jr. (1985). Reflections on comparative history [Review of the book *Force, fate and freedom: On historical sociology*]. *Contemporary Sociology, 14*(1), 14–15.

Moran, P.W. (1997). Great expectations: The legitimization of gambling in America, 1964–1995. *Journal of Popular Culture, 31*(1), 49–65.

Morrison, S. (2002). Approaching organized crime: Where are we now and where are we going. *Report No. 231, Australian Institute of Criminology: trends and issues in crime and criminal justice.* Retrieved February 15, 2010, from http://www.aic.gov.au/documents/6/B/2/%7B6B21C915-591C-4478-AEB6-ED58E6241D86%7Dti231.pdf

Morton, S. (2003). *At odds: Gambling and Canadians 1919–1969.* Toronto: University of Toronto Press.

Nathan, R. (1999) Colorado. In A.N. Cabot, W.N. Thompson, A. Tottenham, & C.G. Braunlich (Eds.). *International Casino Law* (pp. 17–25). Las Vegas: Institute for the Study of Gambling and Commercial Gaming.

National Archives of Australia. (n.d.). *Commonwealth of Australia Constitution Act 1900 (UK).* Retrieved February 2, 2010, from http://www.foundingdocs.gov.au/resources/transcripts/cth1_doc_1900.pdf

National Indian Gaming Commission. (n.d.). *Budget justifications and performance information fiscal year 2010, the United States Department of the Interior.* Retrieved February 4, 2010, from http://www.nigc.gov/LinkClick.aspx?fileticket=2bPGwOL1ZsI%3D&tabid=917

Nealon, J.T. (2006). Take me out to the slot machines: Reflections on gambling and contemporary American culture. *The South Atlantic Quarterly, 105*(2), 465–74.

Nelson, M., & Mason, M. (2003). The politics of gambling in the South. *Political Science Quarterly, 118*(4), 645–69.

Nelson, S., & Rubenstein, A. (2004). Reading around the lines: Do trends in gambling approval and participation reflect the times? *The Wager, 9*(32). Retrieved February 5, 2010, from http://www.basisonline.org/2004/08/the-wager-vol-1.html

Neri, F. (1998). The economic performance of the states and territories of Australia: 1861–1992, *Economic Record, June, 74*(225), 105–20.

Nethery, A. (n.d.). A modern-day concentration camp: Using history to make sense of Australian immigration detention centres. In K. Neumann, & G. Tavan (Eds.), *Does history matter? Making and debating citizenship, immigration and refugee policy in Australia and New Zealand.* Retrieved January 31, 2010, from http://epress.anu.edu.au/anzsog/immigration/pdf/whole_book.pdf

Nevada Legislature. (n.d.). *Table of Titles and Chapters: Nevada Revised Statutes, Counties Government, NRSS 244.345, Dancing halls, escort services, entertainment by referral services and gambling games or devices; limitation on licensing of houses of prostitution.* Retrieved January 28, 2010, from http://www.leg.state.nv.us/nrs/NRS-244.html#NRS244Sec345

The Nevada Observer. (n.d.). *Organized crime in interstate commerce: Final report of the Special Committee to Investigate Organized Crime in Interstate Commerce.* United States Government Printing Office, Washington, 1951. Retrieved February 7, 2011, from http://www.nevadaobserver.com/Reading%20 Room%20Documents/Kefauver%20Final%20Report.htm

New Advent Catholic Encyclopaedia. (n.d.). Retrieved February 15, 2010, from http://www.newadvent.org/cathen/02113b.htm

New Brunswick. (n.d.). *Video Lottery Program Review.* Retrieved February, 2010, from http://www.gnb.ca/0162/reports/vlt/index.htm

New Brunswick. (1990). *New Brunswick Regulation 90–142, Video Lottery Scheme Regulation – Lotteries Act.* Retrieved February, 2010, from http://www.gnb. ca/0162/reports/vlt/index.htm

New Brunswick. (2001). *New Brunswick Regulation 2001–29, Video Lottery Scheme Referendum Act.* Retrieved February, 2010, from http://www.gnb. ca/0062/acts/acts/v-02-2.htm

New Brunswick. (2003). *2001 Provincial Referendum Results.* Office of the Chief Electoral Officer. Retrieved February 5, 2010, from http://www.gnb.ca/ elections/01mun/01refresult-e.asp

New Brunswick. (2008). *Gaming Control Act – Chapter G.-15 Section 2.* Retrieved April 3, 2010, from http://www.gnb.ca/0062/acts/acts/g-01-5.htm

New Brunswick Department of Finance. (2007). *Responsible management, responsible play in a responsible environment: A responsible approach to gaming in New Brunswick.* Retrieved from http://www.gnb.ca/0162/gaming/gam- ing_policy-e.pdf

New Hampshire Lottery Commission. (n.d.). *History of the New Hampshire lot- tery.* Retrieved February 5, 2010, from http://www.nhlottery.com/AboutUs/ History.aspx

New Jersey Lottery Commission. (n.d.). *History of the New Jersey lottery.* Retrieved January 22, 2010, from http://www.state.nj.us/lottery/general/6-2-2_history.htm

New South Wales Lotteries. (n.d.). *About NSW lotteries: Corporate history.* Retrieved February 5, 2010, from http://www.nswlotteries.com.au/about/ history.html

New York State Senate Standing Committee on Racing Gaming and Wagering. (2005). *Annual report.* Retrieved February 5, 2010, from www. racing.state.ny.us/pdf/2005_Annual_Report.pdf

New York Times. (1984, February 5). *Around the Nation; Montana court rules poker machines illegal.* Retrieved April 10, 2010, from ABI Inform Trade and Industry (Proquest) Document ID: 950788551.

New Zealand Department of Internal Affairs. (n.d.) *Gambling expenditure statistics table (1983–2007)*. Retrieved January 15, 2010, from http://www.dia.govt.nz/Pubforms.nsf/URL/Expendstats07.pdf/$file/Expendstats07.pdf

New Zealand Department of Internal Affairs. (2005). *Society, site and gaming machine numbers at December 2005*. Retrieved January 15, 2010, from http://www.dia.govt.nz/Pubforms.nsf/URL/StatsDec2005.pdf/$file/StatsDec2005.pdf

Newfoundland and Labrador. (1991). *Statutes of Newfoundland 1991, Chapter 53, An act respecting the regulation of lotteries and amusement devices in the Province*. Retrieved January 15, 2010, from http://www.assembly.nl.ca/Legislation/sr/statutes/l5391.htm

Newfoundland and Labrador Auditor General. (2004). *Report of the Auditor General to the House of Assembly on reviews of departments and Crown Agencies for the year ended 31 March 2004*. Retrieved February 5, 2010, from http://www.ag.gov.nl.ca/ag/annualReports/2004AnnualReport/AR2004.htm

Newfoundland and Labrador Legislative Assembly. (2004). *Legislative Debates (Hansard), 45th Assembly, 1st Session. (December 6, 2004)*. Retrieved January 22, 2010, from http://www.assembly.nl.ca/business/hansard/ga45session1/04-12-06.htm

Nibert, D. (2000). *Hitting the lottery jackpot: State governments and the taxing of dreams*. New York: Monthly Review Press.

Nikiforuk, A. (2006). Alberta's Gamble with Gambling: The crack cocaine of gambling hooks a senior mandarin – and the provincial treasury. *The Walrus, November 2006*. Retrieved January 11, 2010, from http://www.walrusmagazine.ca/articles/2006.11-society-alberta-lottery/

Norrie, K., & Wilson, L.S. (2000). On re-balancing Canadian fiscal federalism. In H. Lazar (Ed.), *Toward a new mission statement for Canadian fiscal federalism* (pp. 79–98). Institute of Intergovernmental Relations, Montréal & Kingston: McGill-Queen's University Press.

Norsk Tipping. (2006). *Årsrapport (Annual Report) 2006*. Retrieved January 15, 2010, from Norsk Tipping Annual Reports https://www.norsk-tipping.no/selskapet/_binary?download=true&id=397

North American Association of State and Provincial Lotteries [NASPL]. (2006). *Member lotteries, sales and profits*. Retrieved February 10 2010, from http://www.naspl.org/index.cfm?fuseaction=content&PageID=3&PageCategory=3

Northern Territory. (n.d.). *Department of Justice community benefit fund*. Retrieved February 5, 2010, from http://www.nt.gov.au/justice/policycoord/cbf/index.shtml

Northern Territory. (1995 [2005]). *Gaming Machine Act 1995*. Retrieved February 4, 2010, from http://www.austlii.edu.au/au/legis/nt/consol_act/gma112/

Northern Territory Treasury Department of Racing, Gaming & Licensing. (2005). *Community gaming machines: Annual performance trend, gross profit and gaming machine numbers 2004–05.* Retrieved May 24, 2006, from http://www. nt.gov.au/ntt/licensing/statistics/statistics.shtml

Novarro, N.K. (2002). Does earmarking matter? The case of state lottery profits and educational spending. *Stanford Institute for Economic Policy Research Discussion Paper No. 02 – 19.* Retrieved February 5, 2010, from http://www. siepr.stanford.edu/papers/pdf/02-19.pdf

Nova Scotia. (1993). *The interim report of the Standing Committee on Community Services: Video Gambling and Gambling policies in Nova Scotia (1993).* Retrieved February 5, 2010, from https://dspace.ucalgary.ca/bitstream/1880/252/2/ acq_sm.pdf

Nova Scotia. (1994). *Report of the Standing Committee on Community Services: Gaming in Nova Scotia (February 2004).* Retrieved February 5, 2010, https:// dspace.ucalgary.ca/bitstream/1880/519/1/add.pdf

Nova Scotia Gaming Control Commission. (1996). *A year in review: Gaming in Nova Scotia: The first annual report, Nova Scotia Gaming Control Commission, 1995–1996, 4,* 14 (fn.19).

Nova Scotia Lottery Commission. (1993). *Gaming in Nova Scotia: An initial report and recommendations to the government of Nova Scotia from the Nova Scotia Lottery Commission.* Halifax, Nova Scotia: The Government of Nova Scotia. Retrieved January 15, 2010, from https://dspace.ucalgary.ca/bitstream/1880/464/1/aeu.pdf

Nova Scotia Royal Gazette 2002, Appendix A. (n.d.). *Amendments made to the Casino Regulations made by the Governor in Council pursuant to Section 127, of Chapter 4 of the Acts of 1994–1995, The Gaming Control Act.* Retrieved April 3, 2010, from http://www.gov.ns.ca/just/regulations/rg2/2002/de1302.pdf

Nuwer, D.S. (n.d.). Gambling in Mississippi: Its early history. *Mississippi History Now: An Online Publication of the Mississippi Historical Society.* Retrieved February 5, 2010, from http://mshistory.k12.ms.us/index.php?id=80

Oberschall, A. (1973). *Social conflict and social movements.* Englewood Cliffs: Prentice-Hall.

O'Connor, J.S., Orloff, S., & Shaver, S. (1999). *States, markets, families: Gender, liberalism and social policy in Australia, Canada, Great Britain, and the United States.* Cambridge: Cambridge University Press.

OECD. *See* Organisation for Economic Co-operation and Development.

O'Hara, J. (1988). *A mug's game: A history of gaming and betting in Australia.* Sydney: New South Wales University Press.

Oklahoma State Senate Legislative Brief. (2004). *Gaming.* Retrieved February 5, 2010, from http://www.oksenate.gov/publications/legisla tive_briefs/legis_brief_2004/gaming.html

Oliver, P. (1993). Formal Models of Collective Action. *Annual Review of Sociology, 19,* 271–300.

Olson, M. (1965). *The logic of collective action: Public goods and the theory of groups.* Cambridge: Harvard University Press.

Olson, L.R, Guth, K.V., & Guth, J.L. (2003). The lotto and the Lord: Religious influences on the adoption of a lottery in South Carolina. *Sociology of Religion, 64*(1), 87–110.

Omnifacts Research. (2005). *Public attitudes on gaming in Nova Scotia.* Retrieved February 3, 2010, from http://www.gov.ns.ca/govt/gamingstrategy/Public_Attitudes.pdf

Ontario. (1992). *Gaming Control Act, 1992 S.O. 1992, Chapter 24.* Retrieved January 22, 2010, from http://www.search.e-laws.gov.on.ca/en/isysquery/5757633e-35ed-4b82-a3b4-96c43ca6d49e/1/frame/?search=browseStatutes&context=

Ontario. (1993). *Ontario Casino Corporation Act, 1993.* Retrieved April 3, 2010, from http://www.e-laws.gov.on.ca/html/repealedstatutes/english/elaws_rep_statutes_93o25_e.htm

Ontario Legislative Assembly. (1992). *Legislative Debates (Hansard),* 35th Parl., 2nd Session (May 11, 1992). Retrieved February 8, 2010, from http://hansard index.ontla.on.ca/hansardeissue/35-2/l020.htm

Ontario Legislative Assembly. (1996). *Bill 75, Alcohol, Gaming and Charity Funding Public Interest Act, 1996.* Retrieved February 18, 2008, from Legislative Assembly of Ontario, Bills and Lawmaking, Current Parliament 36:1, Retrieved February 5, 2010, from http://www.ontla.on.ca/web/bills/bills_detail.do?locale=en&BillID=1395&BillStagePrintId=&btn Submit=go

Ontario Legislative Assembly. (1996, October 10). *Legislative Debates (Hansard).* 36th Parl., 1st Session (Oct 10, 1996). *Video Lottery Terminals.* Retrieved February 8, 2010, from http://www.ontla.on.ca/web/house-proceedings/house_detail.do?Date=1996-10-10&Parl=36&Sess=1&locale=en

Ontario Legislative Assembly. (1996, November 5). *Legislative Debates (Hansard).* 36th Parl., 1st Session (Nov 5, 1996). *Video Lottery Terminals.* Retrieved February 8, 2010, from http://www.ontla.on.ca/web/house-proceedings/house_detail.do?locale=en&Date=1996-11-05&Parl=36&Sess=1&detailPage=/house-proceedings/transcripts/files_html/1996-11-05_L120.htm#P89_26786

Oregon Lottery. (n.d.). *Video lottery in Oregon – the history.* Retrieved August 30, 2007, from http://www.oregonlottery.org/video/info.html

Oregon State. (2005). *Chapter 461 — Oregon State Lottery, Section 461.215 Video lottery games.* Retrieved January 10, 2010, from http://www.leg.state.or.us/ors/461.html

Organisation for Economic Co-operation and Development (OECD). (1991a, July). Growth of real GNP/GDP in the OECD area. *OECD Economic Outlook 49,* p. 191. Paris: Author.

OECD. (1991b, July). Standardised unemployment rates. *OECD Economic Outlook 49*, p. 208. Paris: Author.

OECD. (1999a, June). Growth of real GNP/GDP in the OECD area. *OECD Economic Outlook 65*, p. 227. Paris: Author.

OECD. (1999b, June). Standardised unemployment rates. *OECD Economic Outlook 65*, p. 248. Paris: Author.

OECD. (2002a, June). Growth of real GNP/GDP in the OECD area. *OECD Economic Outlook 71*, p. 207. Paris: Author.

OECD. (2002b, June). Standardised unemployment rates. *OECD Economic Outlook 71*, p. 221. Paris: Author.

OECD. (2006a, December). Growth of real GNP/GDP in the OECD area. *OECD Economic Outlook 80*, p. 167. Paris: Author.

OECD. (2006b, December). Standardised unemployment rates. *OECD Economic Outlook 80*, p. 180. Paris: Author.

Ormaechea, M. (1995, July 28). Gentleman's agreement. *NB Now, CBC Television News for New Brunswick*.

Osborne, J.A. (1989). *The legal status of lottery schemes in Canada: Changing the rules of the game*. Unpublished LLM Thesis, Faculty of Law, University of British Columbia.

Oster, E. (2004). Are all lotteries regressive? Evidence from the powerball. *National Tax Journal, 57*(2), 179–87. Retrieved October 11, 2006, from ABI Inform Trade and Industry (Proquest) Document ID: 657051531.

Paige, J.M. (1999). Conjuncture, comparison, and conditional theory in macro-social inquiry. *American Journal of Sociology, 105*(3), 781–800.

Painter, M. (1991). Policy diversity and policy learning in a federation: The case of Australian state betting laws. *Publius: The Journal of Federalism, 21*, 143–57.

Panetta, A. (2002, January 24). Cops probe PQ minister's claim he was offered kickback to oppose gambling. *Canadian Press Newswire*. Toronto. Retrieved July 17, 2007, from ABI Inform Trade and Industry (Proquest) Document ID: 376199011

Parkin, A. (2005). South Australia, July to December 2004. *Australian Journal of Politics and History, 51*(2), 303–9.

Parliamentary Joint Committee on the Australian Crime Commission. (2009). Inquiry into the legislative arrangements to outlaw serious and organised crime groups. Retrieved February 15, 2010, from http://www.aph.gov.au/Senate/committee/acc_ctte/laoscg/report/report.pdf

Parvin, R.D., & Koven, S.G. (1995). Limits on economic development policy: State supported gambling in Iowa, *Review on Policy Research*,

14(3–4), 431–52. Retrieved February 18, 2008, from Blackwell Synergy. doi:10.1111/j.1541-1338.1995.tb00720.x

Paul, D.N. (2006). *We were not the savages*. Blackpoint: Fernwood.

Peppard, D.M., Jr. (1987). Government as bookie: Explaining the rise of lotteries for revenue. *Review of Radical Political Economics, 19*(3), 56–68.

Perkins, S. (2004). *Charitable and nonprofit gambling in Washington State: A research project for the Washington State Gambling Commission*. Practical Solutions: Author. Retrieved August 3, 2007, from http://www.wsgc.wa.gov/docs/npg_report/complete.pdf

Peters, M. (2004, October 15). Gaming firm gets license. *Portland Press Herald*. Retrieved February 18, 2010, from http://news.mainetoday.com/indepth/gambling/041015racino.shtml

Peterson, V.W. (1949). Gambling – should it be legalized? *Journal of Criminal Law, Criminology and Police Science, 40*(3), 259–329.

Phillips, T. (1996). Symbolic boundaries and national identity in Australia. *British Journal of Sociology, 47*(1), 113–34.

Phillips, T., & Smith, P. (2000). What is 'Australian?' Knowledge and attitudes among a gallery of contemporary Australians, *Australian Journal of Political Science, 35*(2), 203–44. Retrieved February 18, 2008, from Routledge http://www.ingentaconnect.com/content/routledg/cajp/2000/00000035/00000002/art00002

Pierce, P.A., & Miller, D.E. (1999). Variations in the diffusion of lottery adoptions: How revenue dedication changes morality politics. *Policy Studies Journal, 27*(4), 696–706.

Pinard, M., & Hamilton, R. (1986). Motivational dimensions in the Québec independence movement: A test of a new model. *Research in Social Movements, Conflicts and Change, 9,* 225–80.

Pinard, M. (1983a). From deprivation to mobilization: The role of some internal motives reexamined. *Paper presented at the Annual Meetings, American Sociological Association,* September, 1983.

Pinard, M. (1983b). From deprivation to mobilization: II. Incentives, ideals, and a general motivation model. *Paper presented at the Annual Meetings, American Sociological Association,* September, 1983.

Pinto, S., & Wilson, P. (1990). Gambling in Australia. *Report No. 24, Australian Institute of Criminology: Trends and issues in crime and criminal justice.* Retrieved February 15, 2010, from http://www.aic.gov.au/documents/A/A/2/%7BAA236B7C-0159-4A84-8F90-C74158D97540%7Dti24.pdf

Pirog-Good, M., & Mikesell, J.L. (1995). Longitudinal evidence of the changing socio-economic profile of a state lottery market. *Policy Studies Journal, 23*(3), 451–65.

Plotz, D. (1999, October 15). Flushed. Why South Carolina killed its gambling industry. *Slate Magazine.* Retrieved October 5, 2010, from http://www.slate.com/id/36673/

Porter, D.H., Curtis, G.F., Robinette, J.J., Claxton, B., & Cronkite, F.C. (1936) Survey of Canadian Legislation, *University of Toronto Law Journal, 1*(2), 358–77. Retrieved June 6, 2007, from http://heinonline.org

Prah, P.M. (2004, May 18). States turn to gambling to fix budget woes. Retrieved January 11, 2010, from *Stateline.org* http://www.stateline.org/live/ViewPage.action?siteNodeId=136&languageId=1&contentId=15650

Preston, F.W., Bernhard, B.J., Hunter, R.E., & Bybee, S.L. (1998). Gambling as stigmatized behavior: Regional relabeling and the law. *Annals of the American Academy of Political & Social Science, 556,* 186–96.

Price, D.I., & Novak, E.S. (1999). The tax incidence of three Texas lottery games: Regressivity, race and education. *National Tax Journal, 52*(4), 741–51 Retrieved October 11, 2009, from ABI Inform/Global Data Base

Prince Edward Island. (n.d.). *Lotteries commission act, video lottery scheme regulation.* Retrieved June 12, 2007, from http://www.canlii.org/pe/laws/regu/1991r.361/20050801/whole.html

Pringle, J.D. (1959). *Australian Accent.* London: Chatto and Windus.

Productivity Commission. (1999). *Australia's gambling industries. Report No. 10.* Canberra: Ausinfo.

Pryor, F.L. (2008). Macro-determinants of gambling in industrialized nations. *Kylos, 61*(1), 101–13. Retrieved December 18, 2009, from Wiley Interscience. doi: 10.1111/j.1467-6435.2008.00394.x

Pulliam, C. (2003). *North Carolina lottery for education: What are the odds our schools will win?* Retrieved November 9, 2006, from http://www.advocatesfored.org/publications/Lottery-%20Exec%20Summary.pdf

Putnam, R.D. (2000). *Bowling alone: The collapse and revival of American community.* New York: Simon and Schuster.

Québec – A. (n.d). *An Act respecting lotteries, publicity contests and amusement machines (R.S.Q., Chapter L-6).* Retrieved January 18, 2010, from http://www.canlii.org/en/qc/laws/stat/rsq-c-l-6/latest/rsq-c-l-6.html

Québec – B. (n.d.). *An Act respecting the Régie des alcools, des courses et des jeux (R.S.Q., Chapter R-6.1).* Retrieved January 12, 2010, from http://www.canlii.org/en/qc/laws/stat/rsq-c-r-6.1/latest/rsq-c-r-6.1.html

Québec – C. (n.d.). *An Act respecting the Société des loteries du Québec (R.S.Q., c. S-13.1, s. 13).* Retrieved January12, 2010, from http://www.canlii.org/en/qc/laws/stat/rsq-c-s-13.1/latest/rsq-c-s-13.1.html

Québec – D. (n.d.). *By-law respecting video lottery system (c. S-13.1, r.6), An Act respecting the Société des loteries du Québec (R.S.Q., c. S-13.1, s. 13).* Retrieved January 12, 2010, from http://www2.publicationsduquebec.gouv.qc.ca/

dynamicSearch/telecharge.php?type=2&file=%2F%2FS_13_1%2FS13_1R 6_A.htm

Queensland Office of Gaming Regulation. (1999). *Review of gaming in Queensland*. Retrieved May 14, 2008, from http://www.qogr.qld.gov.au/publi cations/reports/reports-reviews/full_report.pdf

Ragin, C.C. (1987). *The comparative method: Moving beyond qualitative and quanti- tative strategies*. Berkeley: University of California Press.

Ragin, C.C. (1994). *Constructing social research: The unity and diversity of method*. Thousand Oaks: Pine Forge Press.

Raha-automaattiyhdistys. (n.d.). *Payazzo*. Retrieved April 6, 2010, from http:// www.ray.fi/inenglish/pelitoiminta/peliautomaatit/pajatsopelit.php

Raha-automaattiyhdistys. (2006). *Annual Report 2006*. Retrieved April 5, 2010, from http://www.ray.fi/inenglish/raytietoa/ray/rayvuosikertomus.php?ll=3

Read, F. (1935). Recent Manitoba Legislation. *Fortnightly Law Journal, 5*, 259.

Reid, S.A. (1985). The Churches' campaign against casinos and poker machines in Victoria. In G. Caldwell, B. Haig, M. Dickerson, & L. Sylvan (Eds.). *Gambling in Australia* (pp. 28–44). Sydney: Croom Helm.

Reiner, R., Livingstone, S., & Allen, J. (2001). Casino culture: Media and crime in a winner-loser society. In K. Stenson, & R.R. Sullivan (Eds.), *Crime, risk and justice: The politics of crime control in liberal democracies* (pp. 174–94). Devon: Willan.

Reinhardt, S., & Steel, L. (2006). A brief history of Australia's tax system. Paper presented to the 22nd APEC Finance Minster's Working Group. Retrieved February 11, 2010, from http://www.treasury.gov.au/documents/ 1156/PDF/01_Brief_History.pdf

Reith, G. (1999). *The age of chance*. London: Routledge.

Revheim, T., & Buvik, K. (2009). Opportunity structure for gambling and problem gambling among employees in the transport industry. *International Journal of Mental Health Addiction*. Retrieved March 29, 2010, from Springerlink. doi: 10.1007/s11469-008-9179-8

Rhode Island Lottery. (2006). Comprehensive annual financial report for the fiscal year ended June 30, 2006. Retrieved August 30, 2009, from http:// www.rilot.com/docs/financial/CAFR_FYE_June06.pdf

Ritzer, G. (1995). *Expressing America: A critique of the global credit card society*. Thousand Oaks: Pine Forge Press.

Ritzer, G. (2004). *The McDonaldization of society: Revised new century edition*. Thousand Oaks: Pine Forge Press.

Roberts, A. (1969). Reflections on gambling and organized crime. *Crimino- logica, 7*(1), 26–31.

Robinson, C.B. (1936). Recent criminal cases, *Journal of the American Institute of Criminal Law and Criminology 1936–1937, XXVII May–June 1936 to Mar–Apr*

1937, 909–20. Chicago: Northwestern University Press. Retrieved April 2, 2010, from http://heinonline.org

Robinson, R.G. (1983). The history of the law of gaming in Canada. Retrieved April 10, 2010, from https://dspace.ucalgary.ca/bitstream/1880/1477/1/ahf.pdf

Rochester Downtown. (2005, September). Gaming in Rochester and New York State: Timeline & news briefs. Retrieved February 10, 2010, from http://www.rochesterdowntown.com/news/rddc_casino/ROCHESTER/ROCH11.pdf

Rose, I.N. (n.d.). Status of Enabling Gambling Laws. Gambling and the Law – Archive. Retrieved April 10, 2010, from http://www.gamemasteronline.com/Archive/Gambling-Law/StatusofGamingEnablingLaws.shtml

Rose, I.N. (2002, February 13). *Status of gambling laws – Part 4: New Jersey – Rhode Island*. Retrieved April 9, 2010, from http://rose.casinocitytimes.com/articles/982.html

Rose, I.N. (2008). The explosive but sporadic growth of gamling [sic] in Asia. *International Masters of Gaming Law: Members Articles*. Retrieved March 30, 2010, from http://www.gaminglawmasters.com/articles/rose2008-asia.php

Rosecrance, J. (1988). *Gambling without guilt: The legitimization of an American pastime*. Pacific Grove: Brooks/Cole Publishing Company.

Rosenbaum, M.S., & Spears, D.L. (2006). Legalization of gambling in Hawaii. *Journal of Travel & Tourism Marketing, 20*(3), 145–51. Retrieved April 10, 2010, from http://dx.doi.org/10.1300/J073v20n03_10

Royal Canadian Mounted Police. (2008). *2007/2008 The year in review: Commanding Officer's message*. Retrieved April 3, 2010, from http://www.rcmp-grc.gc.ca/nb/publications/annualreport-rapportannuel_07_08-eng.htm

Rubenstein, R., & Scafidi, B. (2002). Who pays and who benefits: Examining the distributional consequences of the Georgia Lottery for Education. *National Tax Journal, 55*(2), 223–38. Retrieved October 11, 2009, from ABI Inform Trade and Industry (Proquest) Document ID: 147532121

Rychlak, R.J. (1995). The introduction of casino gambling: Public policy and the law. *Mississippi Law Journal, 64*(1994–5), 291–361.

Sack, K. (2000, May 10). Former Louisiana Governor guilty of extortion on casinos. *New York Times Online Archives*. Retrieved April 8, 2010, from http://query.nytimes.com/gst/fullpage.html?res=9502E1DC1E38F933A25756C0A96 69C8B63&sec=&spon=&pagewanted=1

Sallaz, J. (2006). The making of the global gambling industry: An application and extension of field theory. *Theory and Society, 35*(3), 265–97. Retrieved November 12, 2009, from http://www.springerlink.com/content/v83029h02tmw3387/doi: 10.1007/s11186-006-9002-0

Saskatchewan Indian Cultural Centre. (n.d.). *History of the Indian Act (Part One)*. Retrieved February 1, 2010, from http://www.sicc.sk.ca/saskindian/a78mar04.htm

Saskatchewan Legislative Assembly. (1994). *Legislative Debates* (Hansard), April 5, 1994, 11–14. Retrieved April 5, 2010, from http://www.legassem bly.sk.ca/Hansard/22L4S/940405.PDF

Sassen, S. (1999). Global financial centers. *Foreign Affairs, 78*(1), 75–87. Retrieved January 18, 2010, from ABI Inform Trade and Industry (Proquest) Document ID: 37683614

Satterthwaite, S. (2005). Faster horses, older whiskey, and more money: An analysis of religious influence on referenda voting. *Journal for the scientific study of religion, 44*(1), 105–12.

Schneider, G. (2004, December 12). Video gambling is thriving in the open, outside the law. *Courier Journal.* Retrieved January 12, 2009, from http://www.courier-journal.com/localnews/2004/12/12ky/A1-gamb1212-16553.html

Schull, N.D. (2005). Digital gambling: The coincidence of desire and design. *The Annals of the American Academy of Political and Social Science, 597,* 65–81.

Schwartz, D.G. (2006). *Roll the bones: The history of gambling.* New York: Gotham.

Scott, F., & Garen, J. (1994). Probability of purchase, amount of purchase, and the demographic incidence of the lottery tax. *Journal of Public Economics, 54*(1), 121–44.

Selby, W. (1996). Social evil or social good? Lotteries and State regulation in Australia and the United States. In J. McMillen (Ed.), *Gambling cultures: Studies in history and interpretation* (pp. 263–87). New York: Routledge.

Sezioni Appparecchi per Pubbliche Attrazioni Ricreative (SAPAR). (n.d.). Retrieved April 5, 2010, from http://www.euromat.org/uploads/documents/9-74-emt-0705-rb-country_report_2006_italy.pdf

Shepard, T.B., III, & Netz, C.L. (1999) Mississippi. In A.N. Cabot, W.N. Thompson, A. Tottenham, & C.G. Braunlich (Eds.), *International Casino Law.* (pp. 72–91). Las Vegas: Institute for the Study of Gambling and Commercial Gaming.

Skocpol, T. (1979). *States and social revolutions: A comparative analysis of France, Russia, and China.* New York: Cambridge University Press.

Skocpol, T. (1984). Emerging agendas and recent strategies in historical sociology. In T. Skocpol (Ed.), *Vision and Method in Historical Sociology.* New York: Cambridge University Press.

Skolnick, J.H. (1978). *House of cards: The legalization of casino gambling.* Boston: Little, Brown and Company

Smith G.J., & Hinch, T.D. (1996). Canadian casinos as tourist attractions: Chasing the pot of gold. *Journal of Travel Research, 34,* 37–45. Retrieved April 1, 2010, from http://jtr.sagepub.com/cgi/content/abstract/34/3/37

Smith, G.J., & Rubenstein, D. (2009). Accountability and social responsibility in Ontario's legal gambling regime. *Final Report to Ontario Problem Gambling Research Centre (OPGRC).* Retrieved June 21, 2010, from http://

www.responsiblegambling.org/articles/2555%20smith%20and%20ruben
stein%20final%20report%20FINAL.pdf

Smith, G.J., & Wynne, H.J. (2004). *VLT gambling in Alberta: A preliminary analy-sis*. Retrieved February 25, 2010, from https://dspace.ucalgary.ca/bitstream/
1880/1632/1/VLT_Gambling_Alberta.pdf

Smith, J.P. (2000). Gambling taxation: Public equity in the gambling business.
The Australian Economic Review, 33(2), 120–44.

Société de la loterie de la Suisse Romande. (2003). *Rapport d'activité (2003)*

Société des casinos du Québec. (n.d.) *History*. Retrieved April 3, 2010, from
http://www.casinosduquebec.com/montreal/en/casinos-du-quebec

South Australia. (2002). *Gaming machine act 1992 reprint 8*. Retrieved April 9,
2010, from http://www.legislation.sa.gov.au/LZ/C/A/GAMING%20
MACHINES%20ACT%201992/2001.09.30/1992.49.PDF

South Australia Independent Gambling Authority. (n.d.). *Inquiry into gaming
machine entitlements*. Retrieved April 10, 2010, from http://www.iga.sa.gov.
au/pdf/guidelines/IGA-GM-Entitlements-Rept.pdf

South Australian Lotteries. (n.d.). *About us. The whole story*. Retrieved January 14,
2010, from http://www.salotteries.com.au/Content.aspx?p=113

South Dakota. (1998). *An act to study the effects of gaming in South Dakota*.
Seventy-third Session Legislative Assembly. Retrieved February 15, 2010,
from http://legis.state.sd.us/sessions/1998/bills/SB147S.pdf

South Dakota Lottery. (n.d.). *History*. Retrieved January 22, 2010, from http://
lottery.sd.gov/about/

South Dakota Secretary of State. (1994). *South Dakota 1994 general election returns
for ballot questions*. Retrieved January 11, 2010, from http://www.sdsos.gov/
electionsvoteregistration/pastelections_electioninfo94_GEreturnsballot
questions.shtm

South Dakota Secretary of State. (2006). *South Dakota 2006 ballot questions*.
Retrieved August 21, 2009, from http://www.sdsos.gov/electionsvoteregi
stration/electvoterpdfs/2006SouthDakotaBallotQuestionPamphlet.pdf

Stanley, O. (2002). The potential use of tax incentives for indigenous busi-
nesses on indigenous land. CAEPR Working Paper No. 17/2002. *Centre for
Aboriginal Economic Policy Research. Australian National University*. Retrieved
February 2, 2010, from http://www.anu.edu.au/caepr/Publications/WP/
CAEPRWP17.pdf

Starkey, L.M., Jr. (1964). *Money, mania and morals: The churches and gambling*.
Nashville: Abington Press.

State ex rel. Mountaineer Park v. Polan, 438 S. E. 2d 308. (W.Va. 1993).
Retrieved February 27, 2010, from http://www.state.wv.us/wvsca/docs/
fall93/21767.htm

State Library of Victoria. (n.d.). *Batman's treaty*. Retrieved February 1, 2010, from http://www.slv.vic.gov.au/ergo/batmans_treaty

State of Alaska. (2003). Calendar year 2003 annual report of gaming operations. *Department of Revenue, Tax Division, Gaming Group*. Retrieved January 12, 2010, from http://www.tax.alaska.gov/programs/documentviewer/viewer.aspx?194r

State of Arkansas. (n.d.). Proposed Amendment 55: Allow wagering in Garland County. *Initiatives and Amendments 1938–2006*. Retrieved February 3, 2010, from http://www.sos.arkansas.gov/elections/elections_pdfs/initiatives_amendments_1938-2006.pdf

State of Hawaii. (2008). *2008 annual visitor research report*. Report from the Department of Business, Economic Development & Tourism. Retrieved January 7, 2010, from http://hawaii.gov/dbedt/info/visitor-stats/visitor-research/2008-annual-visitor.pdf

Statistics Canada – A. (n.d.). *Provincial and territorial economic accounts: Data tables catalogue no. 13-018-x*. Retrieved January 15, 2010, from Dalhousie University, Killam Library Data Services.

Statistics Canada – B. (n.d.). *Trips by Canadians in Canada, by province and territory*. Retrieved February 11, 2010, from http://www40.statcan.gc.ca/l01/cst01/arts26a-eng.htm

Statistics Canada – C. (n.d.). *Travellers to Canada by United States state of origin, top 15 states of origin*. Retrieved February 11, 2010, from http://www40.statcan.gc.ca/l01/cst01/arts40i-eng.htm

Statistics Canada. (2003). *Religions in Canada catalogue no. 96f0030XIE2001015*. Retrieved January 22, 2006, from http://www12.statcan.ca/english/census01/Products/Analytic/companion/rel/pdf/96F0030XIE2001015.pdf

Stedman Weidenbener, L. (2004, December 13). Two states, two decisions: Legalize games, ban them: Oregon's video machines legal, profitable; South Carolina ends 14 'unregulated' years. *Courier-Journal*. Retrieved November 31, 2009, from http://www.courier-journal.com/localnews/2004/12/13ky/A1-states1213-11811.html

Strange, S. (1986). *Casino capitalism*. Oxford: Blackwell.

Street, L. (1991). *Inquiry into the establishment and operation of legal casinos in NSW: Report to the New South Wales government*. Retrieved February 15, 2010, from http://www.casinocontrol.nsw.gov.au/resource/reports/StreetReport.pdf

Stutz, H. (2005, January 27). State lottery faces usual obstacles: Proposals have failed in previous Legislatures; gaming leaders remain opposed. *Las-Vegas Review Journal*. Retrieved November 9, 2010, from http://nl.newsbank.com/nojavascript.html

Supreme Court of Canada Judgment. (1994). *R v. Kent, [1994] 3 S.C.R. 133, 1994*. Retrieved January 31, 2010, from http://scc.lexum.umontreal.ca/en/1994/1994rcs3-133/1994rcs3-133.html

Supreme Court of Canada Judgment. (1996). *R v. Pamajewon, [1996] 2 S.C.R. 821, 199*. Retrieved January 31, 2010, from http://csc.lexum.umontreal.ca/en/1996/1996scr2-821/1996scr2-821.html

Supreme Court of Canada Judgment. (2003). *Siemens v. Manitoba (Attorney General), 2003 SCC 3, [2003] 1 S.C.R. 6*. Retrieved January 11, 2010, from http://scc.lexum.umontreal.ca/en/2003/2003scc3/2003scc3.html

Supreme Court of Louisiana. (2001). *Latour et al. vs. the State of Louisiana 00-CA-1176, 2001*. Retrieved January 30, 2010, from http://www.lasc.org/opinions/2001/00ca1176.opn.pdf

Supreme Court of Pennsylvania. (2005, J-19). *Pennsylvanians against Gambling Expansion Fund, Inc. et al. v. Commonwealth of Pennsylvania et al. No. 229 MM 2004*, Argued March 9, 2005. Retrieved February 18, 2010, from http://www.aopc.org/OpPosting/Supreme/out/J-19-2005mo.pdf

Supreme Court of Prince Edward Island. (2005). *M & M Amusement v. Government of Prince Edward Island 2005 PESCTD 50*. Retrieved February 18, 2010, from http://www.gov.pe.ca/courts/supreme/reasons/4641.pdf

Supreme Court of the United States Judgment 02-695. (2003). *State of Iowa v. Racing Association of Central IOWA, IOWA Greyhound Association, Dubuque Racing Association, LTD. and IOWA West Racing Association*. Retrieved March 31, 2010, from http://www.state.ia.us/government/ag/latest_news/releases/apr_2003/13086%20pdf%20davis.pdf

Supreme Court of the United States Judgment 30 U.S. 1. (1831). *The Cherokee Nation v. Georgia*. Retrieved January 31, 2010, from http://caselaw.lp.findlaw.com/scripts/getcase.pl?court=US&vol=30&invol=1

Supreme Court of the United States Judgment 480 U.S. 202 (1987). *California v. Cabazon Band of Mission Indians*. Retrieved January 29, 2010, from http://laws.findlaw.com/us/480/202.html

Svallfors, S. (2003). Welfare regimes and welfare opinions: A comparison of eight western countries. *Social Indicators Research, 64*(3), 495–520.

Swiss Institute of Comparative Law. (2006). *Study of gambling services in the internal market of the European Union: Final report. 14 June 2006*. Retrieved March 12, 2010, from European Commission (Europa) http://ec.europa.eu/internal_market/services/gambling_en.htm

Tamony, P. (1968). The one-armed bandit. *Western Folklore, 27*(2), 117–24. Retrieved March 12, 2010, from JSTOR. doi: 10.2307/1498153

Tanioka, I. (2000). *Pachinko and the Japanese society*. Japan: Institute of Amusement Industries.

Tannewald, R. (1998). Come the devolution, will the states be able to respond? *New England Economic Review, May/June*, 53–73.

Tasmania. (1993). *Gaming control act.* Retrieved January 30, 2010, from http://www.austlii.edu.au/au/legis/tas/consol_act/gca1993156/

Tasmania. (2002). Select committee of the legislative council impacts of gaming machines. Retrieved April 10, 2010, from http://www.parliament.tas.gov.au/ctee/REPORTS/gamingreport.pdf

Tasmania Parliamentary Library. (n.d.). *Referendums in Tasmania.* Retrieved January 30, 2010, from http://www.parliament.tas.gov.au/tpl/InfoSheets/referendums.htm

Texas Legislative Council. (2004). *Facts at a glance: Video lottery terminals in licensed racetracks in other states.* Austin, TX. Retrieved January 30, 2010, from http://www.tlc.state.tx.us/pubspol/videolottracetrac.pdf

Thelen, K. (1999). Historical institutionalism in comparative politics. *Annual Review of Political Science, 2*(1), 369–404. Retrieved January 30, 2010, from http://arjournals.annualreviews.org doi: AN 5366751

Thompson, W.N. (1984). Casino legalizations: A stalled Movement. *State Government, 57*(2), 60–5.

Thompson, W.N. (1994). *Legalized gambling: A reference handbook.* Santa Barbara: ABC-CLIO.

Thompson, W.N. (1998a). Casinos de juegos del mundo: A survey of world gambling. *Annals of the American Academy of Political and Social Science, 56,* 11–21.

Thompson, W.N. (1998b). Monaco. In A.N. Cabot et al. (Eds.), *International Casino Law* (pp. 371–80). Las Vegas: Institute for the Study of Gambling and Commercial Gaming.

Thrift, N. (1992). Muddling through: World orders and globalization. *The Professional Geographer, 44*(1), 3–7.

Thrower, R.W. (1971). Introduction. Symposium: Organized Crime. *Journal of Public Law, 33,* 33–40.

Tilly, C. (1978). *From mobilization to revolution.* Reading: Addison-Wesley Pub. Co.

Tilly, C. (1984). *Big structures, large processes, huge comparisons.* New York: Russell Sage Foundation.

Time (1953, March 2). *Idaho: Out, damned slot.* Retrieved March 30, 2010, from http://www.time.com/time/magazine/article/0,9171,822638,00.html

Ulbrich, H.H. (1998). *Gambling in South Carolina: A special edition.* Retrieved January 31, 2010, from http://www.strom.clemson.edu/insight/gambling.pdf

United States Census Bureau – A. (n.d.). *Population estimates: State estimates by demographic characteristics.* Retrieved January 15, 2010, from http://www.census.gov/popest/states/asrh/tables/SC-EST2005-01Res.xls

United States Census Bureau – B. (n.d.). *Arts, recreation, & travel: Travel and tourism*. Retrieved February 11, 2010, from http://www.census.gov/compendia/statab/cats/arts_recreation_travel/travel_and_tourism.html

United States Census Bureau. (2001a). *Statistical abstract of the United States No. 66 religious preference, church membership, and attendance: 1980 to 2000*. Retrieved January 15, 2010, from https://www.census.gov/prod/2002pubs/01statab/pop.pdf

United States Census Bureau. (2001b). *Statistical abstract of the United States No. 67 self-described religious identification of adult population: 1990 and 2001*. Retrieved January 15, 2010, from http://www.census.gov/prod/2004pubs/04statab/pop.pdf.

United States Commission on the Review of the National Policy toward Gambling. (1976). *Gambling in America: Final report*.

United States Department of Commerce, Office of Travel and Tourism Industries – A. (n.d.). *Top ten international markets: 2008 visitation and spending*. Retrieved February 11, 2010, from http://tinet.ita.doc.gov/outreachpages/download_data_table/2008_Top_10_Markets.pdf

United States National Gambling Impact Study Commission. (1999). *Final report*. Retrieved March 12, 2010, from http://govinfo.library.unt.edu/ngisc/reports/fullrpt.html

United States of America v. Calabrese at al. (2006, August). *United States District Court, North District of Illinois, Eastern Division. No. 2 CR 1050*. Retrieved January 12, 2009, from http://www.usdoj.gov/usao/iln/indict/2007/us_v_calabrese_etal_third.pdf

United States Senate Special Committee to Investigate Organized Crime in Interstate Commerce (Kefauver Inquiry 1951). Retrieved January 15, 2010, from http://www.bpl.org/online/govdocs/kefauver_committee.htm

Urban, R.J. (1958). Gambling today via the free replay pinball machine. *Marquette Law Review, 42*(1), 98–115.

van Elteren, M. (1996) GATT and beyond: World trade, the arts and American popular culture in Western Europe, *The Journal of American Culture, 19*(3), 59–73 Retrieved February 18, 2010, from Blackwell Synergy doi: 10.1111/j.1542-734X.1996.1903_59.x

Van Speelautomaten. (2007) *The Netherlands Country Report 2007*. Retrieved January 15, 2010, from http://www.euromat.org/uploads/documents/10-76-emt-0705-rb-country_report_2006_the_netherlands.pdf

Vercher, E., & Thompson, W.N. (1999). France. In A.N. Cabot et al. (Eds.), *International Casino Law* (pp. 358–70). Las Vegas: Institute for the Study of Gambling and Commercial Gaming.

Violante, V. (2009, 26 November). Casino's bid to rake in 200 pokies. *Canberra Times*. Retrieved February 21, 2010, from http://www.canberratimes.com.

au/news/local/news/general/casinos-bid-to-rake-in-200-pokies/1688328.
aspx?storypage=2

Volberg, R. (1997). *Gambling and problem gambling in Oregon*. Report to the Oregon Addiction Treatment Foundation. Retrieved February 18, 2010, from http://www.gamblingaddiction.org/oregonreport/OregonReport-02.htm

von Herrmann, D. (1999). The decision to legalize gambling: A model of why States do what they do. *International Journal of Public Administration, 22*(11,12), 1659–80.

von Herrmann, D. (2002). *The big gamble: The politics of lottery and casino expansion*. Westport: Praeger.

The Wager. (1999, January 26). *The changing geography of casino gambling*. Retrieved January 30, 2010, from http://www.basisonline.org/1999/01/index.html

Wallerstein, I. (1974). *The modern world-system*. New York: Academic Press.

Wangersky, R. (2006). What gambling report doesn't say. *Corner Brook, the Western Star*. Retrieved January 17, 2010, from Responsible Gaming Organization http://www.responsiblegambling.org/staffsearch/e-library_news_results_details.cfm?intID=8864

Washington Secretary of State. (n.d.). *Initiatives to the People - 1914 through 2006*. Retrieved August 12, 2009, from http://www.secstate.wa.gov/elec tions/initiatives/statistics_initiatives.aspx

Webb, A. (2003, January 31) Horse racing industry says gaming saved the Races, *New Mexico Business Weekly*. Retrieved August 31, 2009, from http://albuquerque.bizjournals.com/albuquerque/stories/2003/02/03/story3.html

Weber, M. ([1930] 1976). *The Protestant ethic and the spirit of capitalism*. London: G. Allen and Unwin.

Weber, M. (1968). *Economy and society: An outline of interpretive sociology*. G. Roth, & C. Wittich (Eds.). New York: Bedminister Press.

Weitzer R. (2009). Legalizing prostitution: Morality politics in Western Australia. *British Journal of Criminology, 49,* 88–105. Retrieved March 15, 2010, from doi: 10.1093/bjc/azn027

Western Australia Gaming and Wagering Commission Act. (1987[2007]). Retrieved February 18, 2010, from *Western Australia Legislation* http://www. austlii.edu.au/au/legis/wa/consol_act/gawca1987277/

Western Australia Parliament. (2006, November 1). *Australia betting and racing legislation amendment bill 2006 second reading*. Retrieved December 13, 2009, from http://www.parliament.wa.gov.au/hansard/hans35.nsf/(ATT)/9B A17249C9234CCC4825721B002D1343/$file/C37+S1+20061101+p7989f-8005a.pdf

West Virginia Legislature. (n.d.). *West Virginia Code Chapter 29. Miscellaneous Boards and Officers. Article 221. Racetrack Video Lottery*. Retrieved February 6, 2011, from http://www.legis.state.wv.us/WVCODE/ChapterEntire. cfm?chap=29&art=22A

Whitmire, T. (2006). Electronic tables may change the face of casino poker games. *Courier Press.com*. Retrieved January 7, 2010, from http://www. responsiblegambling.org/staffsearch/e-library_news_results_details. cfm?intID=9280

Widmer, E.D., Treas, J., & Newcomb, R. (1998). Attitudes toward nonmarital sex in 24 countries. *The Journal of Sex Trade Research, 35*(4), 349–58.

Wigginton, M.H. (1998). *Report of the Chief Electoral Officer of Prince Edward Island.* Retrieved January 25, 2010, from http://www.electionspei.ca/provincial/ historical/ceoreports/plebiscite/plebiscite-charlottetown-vlt-1997.pdf

Wilcox, M. (1983). *Report of board of inquiry into poker machines.* Melbourne: Government Printer.

Wood, J. (1997). Royal Commission into the New South Wales police service, Sydney Australia. *Presented at the 8th International Anti-Corruption Conference.* Retrieved February 15, 2010, from http://www.8iacc.org/papers/ jwood.html

World Health Organization. (2004). *Global status report on alcohol 2004.* Geneva: World Health Organization Department of Mental Health and Substance Abuse. Retrieved January 28, 2010, from http://www.who.int/substance_ abuse/publications/global_status_report_2004_overview.pdf

Wykes, A. (1964). *The complete illustrated guide to gambling.* Garden City: Doubleday & Company Inc.

Yale Law Journal. (1951). Federal regulation of gambling. *Yale Law Journal, 60*(8), 1396–1416. Retrieved August 10, 2009, from http://heinonline.org

Zimmerman, J.F. (2004). *Interstate economic relations.* Albany: State University of New York Press.

Zin, D. (2004). A brief history of the Michigan State casino tax. *State Notes – Topics of Legislative Interest July/August2004.* Retrieved February 4, 2010, from http://www.senate.michigan.gov/sfa/Publications/Notes/2004Notes/ NotesJulAug04dz.PDF

Zukin, S. (1991). *Landscapes of power: From Detroit to Disneyworld.* Berkeley: University of California Press.

Zukin, S. (1998). Urban lifestyles: Diversity and standardisation in spaces of consumption. *Urban Studies, 35*(5–6), 825–39.

Index

Aboriginal casinos, 9, 49–52, 54, 62, 71, 83–5, 90–1, 94, 98–9, 101, 105, 137, 173, 206n27

Aboriginal gaming: Australia, 9, 49, 96, 98–9, 105, 209n61; Canada, 9, 49, 83–5, 96, 98–100, 105, 209n59, 217n68; United States, 9, 50, 90, 94–100, 105, 137, 173, 206, 209n56

Aboriginal history, 9, 96–100, 209nn56–9; genocide, 96, 98–9, 209n57; *Royal Proclamation Act,* 97; treaties, 97–8, 209n58

ABSCAM, 83, 207n40

Advertising, 129, 158, 211n20

Aestheticization: casinos, 201n24, 213n31; gaming machines, 31, 109, 142–5, 177, 213n35; lotteries, 109

Alabama, 51, 130, 133, 166

Alaska, 52, 131, 133, 136, 167, 212n23

Alberta, 49, 63, 81, 124, 126, 155–6, 160, 163, 215–16nn50, 52, 54; *Slot Machine Act,* 215n50

Alcohol, 26, 30, 112, 116–18, 129, 140, 148–9, 158–9, 163–5, 171–3, 175, 209n61, 211n9, 212n28, 215n49, 218n78

American Religious Identification Survey, 62

Amusement with prize machines (AWPs), 31–3, 35–6, 168; fruit machines, 31, 214n40

Approved amusement devices (AADs), 149, 214n39

Aristocrat (gaming machine manufacturer), 109

Arizona, 52, 131–3, 138, 167

Arkansas, 51, 130, 133, 166, 203n8

Assiniboia Downs, 217n68

Atlantic Canada, 61, 84, 126, 158–9, 164, 205n24

Atlantic City, 49, 59, 90, 207n40, 208n48

Atlantic Lottery Corporation (ALC), 158–9

Australia: culture, xi, 72, 80, 111–18, 120, 123, 177–8, 180, 183, 188, 194; economy, xii, 50, 52, 57–60, 87, 102, 104; gambling, xi, 10, 20–1, 57, 63, 67, 69–70, 81, 103, 105, 110–12, 157, 194, 202nn5, 11; political system, 22–3, 39, 69–71, 95–6, 100–1, 103, 105, 189–91. *See also* casinos; GMOCs; lotteries

Australian Capital Territory, 48, 76, 79, 81, 117, 121–2, 147–9, 151, 189, 193–4, 205n24